THIS DATE IN

DETROIT

TIGERS

HISTORY

THIS DATE IN

DETROIT

TIGERS

HISTORY

John C. Hawkins

A day by day listing of the
events in the history of the
Detroit Tigers baseball team.

A SCARBOROUGH BOOK

STEIN AND DAY/*Publishers*/New York

First published in 1981
Copyright © 1981 by John C. Hawkins
All rights reserved
Designed by Louis A. Ditizio
Printed in the United States of America
STEIN AND DAY/ *Publishers*
Scarborough House
Briarcliff Manor, N.Y. 10510

Library of Congress Cataloging in Publication Data

Hawkins, John C.
   This date in Detroit Tigers history.

   1. Detroit.   Baseball club (American League)
—History.   I.   Title.
GV875.D6H38   796.357′64′0977434   80-5435
ISBN 0-8128-6067-5 (pbk.)

This book is lovingly dedicated to my mother,
Lottie Norton Hawkins.
Her quiet courage, enduring faith,
and warm love set a shining example
for all of us to follow.

ACKNOWLEDGMENTS

The author owes a great deal to the many people who helped see this project through to completion. To all of them, I offer a heartfelt thank you. There are a few who must be mentioned:

—The Detroit Tigers organization, especially Jim Campbell, Dan Ewald, Fred Smith, Ernie Harwell, Hal Middlesworth, and Bob Miller. A first-rate, first-class group;

—The Society for American Baseball Research, of which I am a member, and the friends I've made who have contributed to my work, including Brian Beebe, James A. Smith, Jr., and Gene Elston;

—The National Baseball Hall of Fame, especially public relations director Bill Guilfoile, a good friend;

—Larry Amman of Washington, D.C., the most zealous Tiger fan of all;

—Gary Smith, Tom Barry, and Don Verrico, three friends whose support and encouragement meant a great deal;

—Stein and Day/Publishers, for giving me this assignment, and Art Ballant, my editor, for his support and confidence in my work;

—Sue Earley, my Magnolia belle, who tackled the herculean task of typing this book and assisting in its production. She's not just a sweetheart of a secretary, but a truly great friend whom I'm very lucky to know;

—My family, including my brothers Bill and Frank, my mother and my father, Frank, who fostered a lifelong love of reading and writing;

—And last, but by no means least, my lovely wife, Dottie, and my darling daughter, Mary Julia, who patiently endured a lot of lonely evenings and Sunday afternoons. They make the sun shine, the birds sing and the flowers bloom 365 days a year.

CONTENTS

INTRODUCTION

Contrary to what the reader might think, this book is *not* a baseball book—it is a love story. It reflects the love a city and its fans have for their team. And that is really what baseball is all about, what makes it so special in American life.

This book focuses on the Detroit Tigers—strictly the American League version. Detroit had a team in the National League from 1881 to 1888 that won the league pennant in 1887. But the franchise died and a baseball team didn't return until the Tigers came in as a charter American League team.

This team has played more games than any other team in American League history. Thus, it can rightfully call itself the oldest team in the league, the senior franchise with a proud heritage and promising future.

Detroit is known as a *working* town—unpretentious, loyal, almost an overgrown small town. No team in baseball enjoys a greater devotion from its fans than the Tigers. In good times and bad, whether their team loses or wins, the fans live and die for their Tigers.

In compiling this history, the author knows he must have made an error or two, or overlooked some significant event that holds a meaning for a Tiger fan somewhere. But he also knows he has made a very honest effort to share the fond memories Tiger fans have of their heroes and the hope they hold in their hearts for the next pennant to fly over Tiger Stadium.

THIS DATE IN

DETROIT

TIGERS

HISTORY

1. CALENDAR SECTION

JANUARY

January 1

1882 — Andy Bruckmiller — B* (P 1905)

1893 — Frank Fuller — B (2B 1915-16)

1911 — Hank Greenberg — B (1B-OF 1930, 1933-41, 1945-46)

1924 — Earl Torgeson — B (1B 1955-57)

1933 — Gene Host — B (P 1956)

1953 — Lynn Jones — B (OF 1979-80)

1961 — Briggs Stadium is renamed Tiger Stadium, removing the last vestiges of the previous ownership. The changeover costs the team more than $20,000 for new concession items, a new electric stadium sign, and stationery.

January 2

1892 — George Boehler — B (P 1912-16)

1907 — Red Kress — B (SS-3B-2B 1939-40)

January 3

1891 — Charlie Harding — B (P 1913)
Bill McTigue — B (P 1916)

1941 — John Sullivan — B (C 1963-65)

1946 — First baseman Rudy York is traded to Boston for shortstop Eddie Lake. York lasts only a full season with the Red Sox before being shipped to the White Sox; Lake provides the Bengals with a solid shortstop for two seasons before suffering a broken finger and becoming a utility player.

January 4

1890 — Oscar Vitt — B (3B-2B-OF-SS 1912-18)

1930 — Don McMahon — B (P 1968-69)

1944 — Tito Fuentes — B (2B 1977)

1949 — Dennis Saunders — B (P 1970)

January 5

1948 — Bill Laxton — B (P 1976)

*B = player's birthdate

3

January 6

1886 — Billy Purtell — B (3B–SS–2B 1914)

1926 — Ralph Branca — B (P 1953–54)

1934 — Lenny Green — B (OF 1967–68)

1952 — Bob Adams — B (1B–C 1977)

January 7

1897 — Topper Rigney — B (SS–3B 1922–25)

1900 — Johnny Grabowski — B (C 1931)

1931 — Ray Semproch — B (P 1960)

1940 — Jim Hannan — B (P 1971)

1976 — Bengals ink former league batting champion Alex Johnson as a free agent. Johnson ends his career in Detroit batting .268 as an outfielder and designated hitter during the '76 season.

January 8

1935 — Reno Bertoia — B (3B–2B–SS 1953–58, 1961–62)

1936 — Chuck Cottier — B (SS–2B 1961)

January 9

1900 — Frank Burns — B (P 1929)

1936 — Julio Navarro — B (P 1964–66)

1953 — Phil Mankowski — B (3B–2B–DH 1976–79)

January 10

1888 — Del Pratt — B (2B–1B–3B 1923–24)

1928 — Jack Dittmer — B (3B–2B 1957)

1946 — George Korince — B (P 1966–67)

January 11

1899 — Alvin (General) Crowder — B (P 1934–36)

1910 — Lynwood (Schoolboy) Rowe — B (P 1933–42)

1922 — Neil Berry — B (SS–2B–3B 1948–52)

1929 — Don Mossi — B (P 1958–63)

1971 — Relief pitcher John Hiller suffers a heart attack at his home in Duluth, Minnesota. He begins a long recuperation that will result in one of baseball's greatest comebacks.

1976 — Tigers sign their number one draft pick, Steve Kemp.

January 12

1893 — Lefty Lorenzen — B (P 1913)

1903 — Tiger pitcher Win Mercer, recently named manager for the 1903 season, commits suicide at age 28 in a San Francisco hotel by inhaling gas. A suicide letter refers to the evils of women and gambling.

1924 — Outfielder Bobby Veach is sold to the Boston Red Sox. He enjoys a .295 season with them in 1924, and finishes his career the following season with the Senators and Yankees.

1945 — Bob Reed — B (P 1969–70)

1972 — Owner John Fetzer announces that the team has signed a 40-year lease for a planned $126 million domed stadium downtown along the Detroit River. The new facility will hold 52,000 for baseball, and 60,000 for football. Annual rental is set at a minimum of $450,000. (A failed bond issue, a lawsuit, and the subsequent plan for the Pontiac Silverdome scuttle this plan and any future hopes for a new downtown baseball stadium.)

January 13

1948 — Les Cain — B (P 1968, 1970–72)

1949 — Jim Foor — B (P 1971–72)

January 14

1923 — Ken Johnson — B (P 1952)

1940 — Commissioner Landis declares 91 Tiger minor leaguers free agents because he feels the team has been illegally covering up players in the farm system. Among the players freed are Roy Cullenbine, Dizzy Trout, Johnny Sain, and Benny McCoy.

1942 — Dave Campbell — B (2B–3B–1B 1967–69)

January 15

1885 — Grover Lowdermilk — B (P 1915–16)

1920 — Steve Gromek — B (P 1953–57)

1943 — Mike Marshall — B (P 1967)

1949 — Luis Alvarado — B (3B 1977)

January 16

1888 — Brad Kocher — B (C 1912)

1908 — Johnny Watson — B (SS 1930)

January 17

1893 — Bill Morrisette — B (P 1920)

1915 — Mayo Smith — B (MGR 1967–70) .

1919 — The Tigers obtain catcher Eddie Ainsmith, outfielder Chick Shorten, and pitcher Elmer Love from the Red Sox for third baseman Oscar Vitt. All three new players enjoy a good season for the Bengals while Vitt contributes little to Boston.

1933 — J. W. Porter — B (C–OF–1B 1955–57)

1935 — Dick Brown — B (C 1961–62)

1952 — Owner Walter O. Briggs, Sr. dies. Team stock goes into an estate and his son, Walter O., Jr. (Spike), becomes president.

January 18

1895 — Danny Clark — B (2B–OF–3B 1922)

1903 — Nolan Richardson — B (3B–SS 1929, 1931–32)

1947 — The Tigers sell aging star Hank Greenberg to the Pittsburgh Pirates for $35,000. At age 36, Greenberg is slowing up in the field. He plays the 1947 season at Pittsburgh and then retires to become a front-office executive with Cleveland and the White Sox.

1950 — Marv Lane — B (OF 1971–74, 1976)

January 19

1895 — Danny Boone — B (P 1921)

1906 — Rip Radcliff — B (OF–1B 1941–43)

January 20

1888 — Bill James — B (P 1915–19)

1913 — Jimmy Outlaw — B (OF–3B 1943–49)

1945 — Dave Boswell — B (P 1971)

January 21

1892 — Bernie Boland — B (P 1915–20)

1900 — Willie Ludolph — B (P 1924)

1937 — Bill Graham — B (P 1966)

1947 — Bob Reynolds — B (P 1975)

January 22

1877 — Tom Jones — B (1B–3B 1909–10)

1881 — Ira Thomas — B (C 1908)

1906 — Ivey Shiver — B (OF 1931)

1908 — Prince Oana — B (P 1943, 1945)

1925 — Johnny Bucha — B (C 1953)

1951 — Leon Roberts — B (OF–DH 1974–75)

January 23

1873 — Red Donahue — B (P 1906)

1896 — Billy Mullen — B (3B 1926)

1898 — John Mohardt — B (OF 1922)

1951 — Charlie Spikes — B (OF 1978)

January 24

1895 — Joe Cobb — B (PH 1918)

1905 — Rufus Smith — B (P 1927)

January 25

1917 — Carl McNabb — B (PH 1945)

1951 — Vern Ruhle — B (P 1974–77)

January 26

1884 — Tubby Spencer — B (C–1B 1916–18)

1906 — Charley Gelbert — B (SS 1937)

1927 — Bob Nieman — B (OF 1953–54)

1943 — Cesar Gutierrez — B (SS–3B–2B 1969–71)

January 27

1882 — Elijah Jones — B (P 1907, 1909)

1927 — Commissioner Landis exonerates Ty Cobb and Cleveland's Tris Speaker of charges that they conspired to fix a game on September 25, 1919. The accusation, made by former Tiger pitcher Hubert (Dutch) Leonard, claims that Indian pitcher (Smokey) Joe Wood also was involved in the bookmaking scheme. Cobb fights the charge vigorously, threatening to reveal embarrassing information about team accounting and turnstile counting practices.

1935 — Steve Demeter — B (3B 1959)

January 28

1869 — Ducky Holmes — B (OF 1901–02)

1887 — Jack Coffey — B (2B–3B 1918)

1900 — Emil Yde — B (P 1929)

1958 — The Tigers obtain infielder Ozzie Virgil and first baseman Gail Harris from the San Francisco Giants for third baseman Jim Finigan and $25,000. The trade makes Virgil the first Black ever to play for Detroit. The deal pays dividends for the Tigers as Harris starts at first base and Virgil proves a competent utility player. Finigan is a bust for the Giants, but the money helps keep Giant owner Horace Stoneham's bar well-stocked.

1975 — The Tigers sign shortstop Gene Michael following his release by the Yankees.

January 29

1880 — Bill Burns — B (P 1912)

1885 — Hack Simmons — B (1B–3B–OF 1910)

1904 — Ray Hayworth — B (C 1926, 1929–38)

January 30

1923 — Walt Dropo — B (1B 1952–54)

1930 — Sandy Amoros — B (OF 1960)

1954 — Dave Stegman — B (OF 1978–80)

1975 — Catcher Gerry Moses is sold to the New York Mets.

1978 — After one successful season at second base, Tito Fuentes is sold to the Montreal Expos.

Second baseman Steve Dillard is obtained from Boston for minor league pitchers Michael Burns and Frank Harris.

January 31

1893 — George Burns — B (1B 1914–17)

1896 — Pinky Hargrave — B(C 1928–30)

1931 — Duke Maas — B(P 1955–57)

1932 — Hank Aguirre — B(P 1958–67)

FEBRUARY

February 1

1875 — Billy Sullivan — B(C 1916)

1921 — Dave Madison — B(P 1952–53)

1931 — Bob Smith — B(P 1959)

1943 — Ron Woods — B(OF 1969)

1977 — A raging fire destroys the Tiger Stadium press box, already slated for replacement under stadium renovation plans.

February 2

1884 — Ray Demmitt — B(OF 1914)

1920 — Zeb Eaton — B(P 1944–45)

1936 — Ty Cobb, the greatest Tiger of them all, is the first player voted into the newly-formed Baseball Hall of Fame.

February 3

1925 — Harry Byrd — B(P 1957)

1935 — Dick Tracewski — B(SS–2B–3B 1966–69)

1944 — Wayne Comer — B(OF–C 1967–68, 1972)

1947 --Joe Coleman — B(P 1971–76)

1976 — Pitcher Tom Walker is sold to the St. Louis Cardinals.

February 4

1878 — Herman (Germany) Schaefer — B(2B–3B–SS–OF 1905–09)

1890 — Eddie Ainsmith — B(C 1919–21)

1942 — Joe Sparma — B(P 1964–69)

1951 — Stan Papi — B(2B–3B–SS–1B 1980–present)

February 5

1924 — Jim Campbell — B(President and General Manager)

February 6

Nothing of significance happened on this date.

February 7

1899 — Earl Whitehill — B(P 1923–32)

February 8

1911 — Don Heffner — B(2B 1944)

1921 — Walter (Hoot) Evers — B(OF 1941, 1946–52, 1954)

February 9

1902 — Don Hankins — B(P 1927)

1925 — Vic Wertz — B(OF–1B 1947–52, 1961–63)

1949 — John Young — B(1B 1971)

1957 — Pat Underwood — B(P 1979–present)

February 10

1903 — George Quellich — B(OF 1931)

1910 — Bob Logan — B(P 1937)

1932 — Jim Stump — B(P 1957, 1959)

1933 — Jerry Davie — B(P 1959)

1948 — John Gamble — B(SS 1972–73)

February 11

1935 — George Alusik — B(OF 1958, 1961–62)

1939 — Willie Smith — B(P 1963)

1949 — Ben Oglivie — B(OF–1B–DH 1974–77)

1953 — Tom Veryzer — B(SS 1973–77)

February 12

1879 — Harry Arndt — B(OF–1B 1902)

1903 — Andy Harrington — B(PH 1925)

1942 — Pat Dobson — B(P 1967–69)

February 13

1876 — Fritz Buelow — B (C–1B 1901–04)

1893 — Ben Dyer — B (SS–3B–OF–2B–1B–P 1916–19)

1909 — George Gill — B (P 1937–39)

1911 — Hack Miller — B (C 1944–45)

1927 — Jim Brideweser — B (SS–2B–3B 1956)

1970 — Commissioner Bowie Kuhn announces he is investigating pitcher Denny McLain's "off-the-field" activities.

February 14

1952 — The Tigers obtain pitcher Dick Littlefield, catcher Matt Batts, outfielder Cliff Mapes, and first baseman Ben Taylor from the St. Louis Browns for pitcher Gene Bearden, pitcher Bob Cain, and first baseman Dick Kryhoski. The Browns get the better of the deal as Kryhoski takes over first base and Cain and Bearden join the starting rotation.

February 15

1927 — Buddy Hicks — B (SS–2B–3B 1956)

February 16

1873 — John Sullivan — B (C 1905)

1895 — Red Cox — B (P 1920)

1949 — Bob Didier — B (C 1973)

February 17

1893 — Eddie Onslow — B (1B 1912–13)
       Wally Pipp — B (1B 1913)

1901 — Eddie Phillips — B (C 1929)

1908 — Orlin Collier — B (P 1931)

1926 — Jack Crimian — B (P 1957)

1970 — *Sports Illustrated* reveals Denny McLain's 1967 involvement with mobsters in a bookmaking operation, touching off the scandal that eventually wrecks a great career.

February 18

1915 — Joe Gordon — B (MGR 1960)

1927 — Herman Wehmeier — B (P 1958)

11

1930 — Frank House — B (C 1950–51, 1954–57, 1961)

1939 — Bob Miller — B (P 1973)

1941 — Leo Marentette — B (P 1965)

1958 — The Tigers trade pitcher Hal Woodeshick and catcher-outfielder J. W. Porter to Cleveland for catcher Jim Hegan and pitcher Hank Aguirre. Aguirre goes on to a 10-year tenure with the Bengals as a reliable starting pitcher.

February 19

1923 — Russ Sullivan — B (OF 1951–53)

1939 — Jackie Moore — B (C 1965)

1944 — Chris Zachary — B (P 1972)

1970 — After a five-and-a-half hour meeting with Denny McLain, Commissioner Kuhn announces McLain's indefinite suspension for his involvement with book-making.

February 20

1894 — Harvey (Suds) Sutherland — B (P 1921)

1896 — Herold (Muddy) Ruel — B (C 1931–32)

1928 — Elroy Face — B (P 1968)

February 21

1940 — Doug Gallagher — B (P 1962)

1943 — Jack Billingham — B (P 1978–80)

1948 — Bill Slayback — B (P 1972–74)

1958 — Alan Trammell — B (SS 1977–present)

February 22

1891 — Clarence Mitchell — B (P 1911)

1898 — Tony De Fate — B (2B 1917)

1918 — Jack Sullivan — B (2B 1944)

1934 — George (Sparky) Anderson — B (MGR 1979–present)

February 23

1903 — Roy Johnson — B (OF 1929–32)

1978 — The Tigers sell pitcher Steve Grilli to the Toronto Blue Jays.

February 24

1875 — Monte Beville — B (C–1B 1904)

1882 — Bugs Raymond — B (P 1904)

1892 — Wilbur Cooper — B (P 1926)

1905 — Lynn Nelson — B (P 1940)

1930 — John (Bubba) Phillips — B (3B–OF 1955, 1963–64)

1980 — Outfielder Steve Kemp receives a salary arbitration award of $210,000 for the season. The team had offered the All-Star outfielder a salary of $150,000.

February 25

1947 — Ken Szotkiewicz — B (SS 1970)

1977 — Infielder Luis Alvarado is sold to the New York Mets.

February 26

1896 — Rip Collins — B (P 1923–27)

1934 — Don Lee — B (P 1957–58)

February 27

1896 — Cy Perkins — B (PH 1934)

1949 — John Wockenfuss — B (C–OF–DH, 1974–present)

February 28

1899 — Lil Stoner — B (P 1922, 1924–29)

1930 — Ron Samford — B (SS–2B–3B, 1955, 1957)

MARCH

March 1

1924 — Tim Thompson — B (C 1958)

March 2

1924 — Bill Taylor — B (OF 1957–58)

1932 — Chico Fernandez — B (SS–3B–1B 1960–63)

1936 — Jim Brady — B (P 1956)

March 2 (continued)

1947 — Jim Nettles — B (OF 1974)

1953 — Dave Tobik — B (P 1978–present)

March 3

1919 — Steve Souchok — B (OF–1B–3B–2B 1951–55)

1949 — The Tigers obtain outfielder Larry Doby from the Indians for outfielder Tito Francona. Doby plays only 16 games before going on to the White Sox while Francona slugs .363 for Cleveland in a utility role.

March 4

1876 — Charles (Piano Legs) Hickman — B (1B–OF 1904–05)

1919 — Les Mueller — B (P 1941, 1945)

1954 — Mark Wagner — B (SS–2B 1976–80)

March 5

1860 — Sam Thompson — B (OF 1906)

1897 — Lu Blue — B (1B–OF 1921–27)

1957 — Gerry Ujdur — B (P 1980–present)

March 6

1915 — Bob Swift — B (C 1944–53, MGR 1966)

1917 — Joe Orrell — B (P 1943–45)

1924 — Ed Mierkowicz — B (OF 1945, 1947–48)

1978 — The Tigers obtain pitcher Jack Billingham from Cincinnati for minor league pitcher George Cappuzzello and outfielder John Valle. Billingham wins 25 games in 1978 and 1979 before being shipped to Boston in 1980.

March 7

1884 — Ed Willett — B (P 1906–13)

1929 — Robert (Red) Wilson — B (C 1954–60)

March 8

1892 — Ollie O'Mara — B (SS 1912)

1893 — Ray Francis — B (P 1923)

1909 — Pete Fox — B (OF 1933–40)

1937 — Jim Small — B (OF 1955–57)

1948 — Joe Staton — B (1B 1972–73)

March 9

1882 — Lou Schiappacasse — B (OF 1902)

1893 — Lefty Williams — B (P 1913–14)

1906 — Hughie Wise — B (C 1930)

1932 — Ron Kline — B (P 1961–62)

1934 — Jim Landis — B (OF 1967)

1965 — Coach Bob Swift is named acting manager after Charlie Dressen is stricken with heart blockage.

March 10

1907 — Art Herring — B (P 1929–33)

1939 — Bill Heath — B (C 1967)

March 11

1903 — Art Ruble — B (OF 1927)

1906 — Bill Lawrence — B (OF 1932)

1911 — Al Benton — B (P 1938–42, 1945–48)

March 12

1892 — George Maisel — B (3B 1916)

1966 — Joker Marchant Stadium is dedicated in Lakeland, Florida before a crowd of 4,919. The Tigers beat the Twins, 4–2.

March 13

1879 — Mal Eason — B (P 1903)

1892 — Eric Erickson — B (P 1916, 1918–19)

1922 — Cliff Mapes — B (OF 1952)

1979 — The Tigers trade relief pitcher Ed Glynn to the Mets for reliever Mardie Cornejo. Glynn becomes a key lefty reliever for the Mets while Cornejo has not been heard from since.

March 14

1888 — Henry (Hub) Pernoll — B (1910, 1912)

1900 — Marty McManus — B (SS–3B–2B–1B 1927–31)

1947 — Mike Strahler — B (P 1973)

March 15

1871 — Doc Casey — B (3B 1901–02)

1879 — George Disch — B (P 1905)

March 16

1888 — Ralph Works — B (P 1909–12)

March 17

1883 — Oscar Stange — B (C–1B 1909–20, 1925)

March 18

1888 — Wiley Taylor — B (P 1911)

1916 — Eddie Lake — B (SS–2B–3B 1946–50)

1919 — Hal White — B (P 1941–43, 1946–52)

1925 — Fred Hatfield — B (3B–2B–SS 1952–56)

1926 — Dick Littlefield — B (P 1952)

1963 — The Tigers sell pitcher Ron Kline to the Washington Senators.

1964 — Don Mossi, a key starter for five seasons, is sold to the Chicago White Sox.

March 19

1887 — Bill Covington — B (P 1911–12)
        Billy Maharg — B (3B 1912)

1908 — Gerald (Gee) Walker — B (OF 1931–37)

1953 — Tim Corcoran — B (OF–1B–DH 1977–present)

1974 — In a three-team deal, the Tigers send pitcher Jim Perry to Cleveland and pitcher
        Ed Farmer to the Yankees. In return, the Indians send pitcher Rick Sawyer and
        outfielder Walt (No-Neck) Williams to the Yankees, who send catcher Gerry
        Moses to Detroit.

March 20

1875 — Willie Greene — B (3B 1903)

1907 — Vern Kennedy — B (P 1938–39)

1948 — Chuck Seelbach — B (P 1971–74)

1971 — The Tigers obtain pitcher Bill Zepp from Minnesota for infielder Bob Adams and a player to be named.

1979 — Second baseman Steve Dillard is sent to the Chicago Cubs for catcher Ed Putman, who is assigned to Detroit's Evansville farm club on March 24.

March 21

1904 — Frank Sigafoos — B (3B–2B–SS 1929)

1905 — Joe Samuels — B (P 1930)

1914 — Boyd Perry — B (SS–2B 1941)

1927 — Owen Friend — B (2B 1953)

1952 — Fernando Arroyo — B (P 1975, 1977–79)

1977 — Tiger ace Mark Fidrych tears the cartilage in his left knee and undergoes surgery 10 days later. This injury starts the Bird on an up-and-down cycle as he struggles to regain his former masterful pitching form.

March 22

1906 — Marv Owen — B (3B–SS–1B–2B 1931, 1933–37)

March 23

1963 — The Tigers trade first baseman Larry (Bobo) Osborne to the Washington Senators for outfielder Wayne Comer and cash.

1978 — Pitchers Roric Harrison and Rick Folkers are released.

March 24

1925 — Dick Kryhoski — B (1B 1950–51)

1937 — Dick Egan — B (P 1963–64)

1972 — Infielder Cesar Gutierrez is sold to Montreal.

March 25

1868 — Frank Dwyer — B (MGR 1902)

1901 — John E. Fetzer — B (Owner)

1938 — Alan Koch — B (P 1963–64)

1969 — The Tigers sell first baseman Don Pepper to the Expos.

March 26

1889 — Joe Burns — B(OF 1913)

1974 — Catcher Bob Didier is sold to the Red Sox.

March 27

1973 — Detroit acquires pitcher Jim Perry from Minnesota for pitcher Dan Fife and cash. Perry becomes the first player in history to exercise his trade approval rights under the new "5 and 10" rule.

1978 — Pitcher Vern Ruhle is released.

March 28

1875 — Jimmy Barrett — B(OF 1901–05)

1977 — The Tigers release outfielder Marv Lane.

March 29

1873 — Duff Cooley — B(OF 1905)

1889 — George (Squanto) Wilson — B(C 1911)

1915 — Johnny Gorsica — B(P 1940–44, 1946–47)

1921 — Ferris Fain — B(1B 1955)

1944 — Denny McLain — B(P 1963–70)

1975 — The Tigers trade first baseman Reggie Sanders to Atlanta for first baseman Jack Pierce. This trade proves a "wash" for both teams as neither player produces.

March 30

1874 — Ed Gremminger — B(3B 1904)

1923 — The Red Sox announce they will file a $15,000 claim against Detroit because pitcher Carl Holling has not reported as part of the trade sending infielder Del Pratt to the Tigers.

1971 — The Tigers trade pitcher Jerry Robertson to the New York Mets for pitchers Dean Chance and Bill Denehy.

March 31

1891 — Johnny Couch — B(P 1917)

1918 — Marv Grisson — B(P 1949)

1942 — The Tigers sell pitcher Bobo Newsom to the Senators.

1946 — Bill Denehy — B(P 1971)

APRIL

April 1

1912 — Jake Wade — B (P 1936–38)

1914 — Murray Franklin — B (SS–3B 1941–42)

1936 — Ron Perranoski — B (P 1971–72)

1937 — Outfielder Babe Herman is acquired from Cincinnati.

1944 — Rusty Staub — B (OF–DH 1976–79)

April 2

1869 — Hughie Jennings — B (MGR 1907–20, SS–2B–1B 1907, 1909, 1912, 1918)

1878 — Ed Siever — B (P 1901–02, 1906–08)

1889 — Harry Moran — B (P 1912)

1910 — Cotton Pippen — B (P 1939–40)

1919 — Earl (Lefty) Johnson — B (P 1951)

1927 — Billy Pierce — B (P 1945, 1948)

1937 — Dick Radatz — B (P 1969)

1973 — The Tigers trade pitcher Chris Zachary to Pittsburgh for catcher Charlie Sands.

1976 — Pitcher Lerrin LaGrow is sold to the St. Louis Cardinals.

April 3

1921 — Dick Conger — B (P 1940)

1968 — The Tigers sell pitcher Hank Aguirre to the Dodgers, ending his 10-year stay in Detroit.

April 4

1937 — Following a .327 season at the plate, outfielder Al Simmons is sold by the Tigers to the Washington Senators for $15,000.

1975 — The Tigers purchase pitcher Ray Bare from the St. Louis Cardinals.

April 5

Nothing of significance happened on this date.

April 6

1903 — Mickey Cochrane — B (C 1934–37, MGR 1934–38)

1937 — Phil Regan — B (P 1960–65)

1970 — Mickey Lolich opens the season for the Tigers in Washington with a 5–0 shutout of the Senators, striking out 10.

1971 — The Tigers, behind Mickey Lolich, beat Cleveland 8–2 before the largest opening day crowd in Tiger history, 54,089.

1975 — The Tigers release pitcher Luke Walker.

April 7

1886 — Ed Lafitte — B (P 1909, 1911–12)

1967 — The Tigers purchase catcher Jim Price from the Pirates. Price proves to be a valuable backup catcher over the next five seasons.

April 8

1918 — Bob Mavis — B (PR 1949)

1943 — John Hiller — B (P 1965–70, 1972–80)

1963 — The Tigers claim Denny McLain from the Chicago White Sox on first-year waivers. One of the all-time great steals in history.

1969 — The Tigers open the defense of their world crown before 53,572 at Tiger Stadium, beating Cleveland 6–2. Denny McLain hurls a three-hitter and Al Kaline paces the attack with a home run. Relief pitcher Johnny Wyatt is released.

1970 — The Tigers release shortstop Tom Tresh.

1971 — The Tigers sign pitcher Dave Boswell following his release by Minnesota.

April 9

1901 — Vic Sorrell — B (P 1928–37)

1904 — Guy Cantrell — B (P 1930)

1946 — Nate Colbert — B (1B–DH 1975)

1962 — The Senators, behind the pitching of Bennie Daniels, beat the Bengals 4–1 in the first game ever played in D.C. Stadium.

1964 — The Tigers purchase relief pitcher Larry Sherry from the Dodgers. Sherry becomes an effective part of the Tiger bullpen for the next three-and-a-half seasons.

April 10

1899 — Rudy Kneisch — B (P 1926)

1907 — Cliff Bolton — B (C 1937)

1913 — The Tigers open the season with Ty Cobb a holdout in Augusta, Georgia. Cobb seeks a salary of $15,000 and reaches agreement with the team two weeks later.

1930 — Frank Lary — B (P 1954–64)

April 11

1872 — Frank Kitson — B (P 1903–05)

1918 — Barney McCosky — B (OF 1939–42, 1946)

1945 — Mike Kilkenny — B (P 1969–72)

1961 — The Tigers lose to Cleveland 9–5 before an opening-day crowd of 41,643 in Detroit. Rookie second baseman Jake Wood hits a two-run homer in his first major league game for his first big league hit.

1968 — The Tigers gain first win of season as Gates Brown leads off the bottom of the ninth with a pinch-hit home run to beat Boston 4–3.

April 12

1888 — Al Klawitter — B (P 1913)

1889 — Billy Bailey — B (P 1918)

1909 — Eric McNair — B (SS–3B 1941–42)

1912 — Jack Wilson — B (P 1942)

1922 — Bill Wight — B (P 1952–53)

1933 — Charlie Lau — B (C 1956, 1958–59)

1940 — Woody Fryman — B (P 1972–74)

1955 — The Tigers lose to the Athletics in the American League's debut in Kansas City before a crowd of 32,843, including former president Harry Truman.

1960 — The Tigers acquire first baseman Norm Cash from the Indians in a trade for third baseman Steve Demeter. One of the greatest trades in Tiger history as Cash goes on to pound out 373 home runs in a 15-year career with Detroit. Demeter barely plays for Cleveland before returning to the minors.

1969 — Jim Northrup's double in the fifth inning spoils Mel Stottlemyre's bid for a no-hitter. Stottlemyre settles for a one-hit, 4–0 Yankee win in Detroit.

1977 — The Tigers trade local favorite Willie Horton to Texas for relief ace Steve Foucault. Both players last only a season with their new teams before moving on.

April 13

1866 — Herman Long — B (SS–2B 1903)

1875 — Kid Elberfeld — B (SS–3B 1901–03)

1884 — Red Killefer — B (2B–SS–3B–OF 1907–09)

1890 — Al Platte — B (OF 1913)

1900 — Rufe Clarke — B (P 1923–24)

1904 — Ken Jones — B (P 1924)

1906 — Roxie Lawson — B (P 1933, 1935–39)

1913 — Jake Mooty — B (P 1944)

1942 — Ike Brown — B (2B–1B–OF–3B 1969–74)

1960 — The Tigers trade reliever Barney Schultz to the Cubs for minor league infielders Wayne Connally and J. C. Hartman.

1962 — Pitcher Frank Lary pulls a leg muscle while running out a triple against the Yankees in the home opener. This injury triggers subsequent arm problems that help end his career.

1965 — Al Kaline knocks in five runs with a single and double to pace the Tigers to an 11–4 win over the Athletics in Kansas City. Hank Aguirre gets the win.

April 14

1898 — Jess Doyle — B (P 1925–27)

1961 — Frank Lary hurls a one-hitter to beat the White Sox 7–0 in Detroit. The only hit comes in the fifth when outfielder Jim Landis gets a single off the glove of shortstop Chico Fernandez. A home run by Rocky Colavito and three Kaline hits pace the Tiger attack.

1964 — The Tigers win home and season opener 7–3 over Kansas City before a crowd of 35,733. Jerry Lumpe and Bill Freehan each get three hits to lead a 12-hit Tiger offense.

April 15

1910 — Eddie Mayo — B (2B–SS–3B 1944–48)

1915 — Joe Hoover — B (SS–2B 1943–45)

1933 — Schoolboy Rowe hurls a six-hit, 3–0 shutout over the White Sox in his major league debut.

1949 — Ray Bare — B (P 1975–77)

1950 — Dick Sharon — B (OF 1973–74)

1961 — Outfielder Bill Bruton's first American League hit is a three-run homer off Bob Shaw in the fourth inning as the Tigers beat the White Sox 6–2 at home.

1966 — A Dick McAuliffe grand slam home run in the fourth inning paces the Bengals to an 8-3 win over the Senators in the home opener before 36,674 Tiger fans.

1972 — Detroit opens a strike-delayed season before a crowd of 31,510 at home with a 3-2 win over Boston. Mickey Lolich goes the distance for the win, yielding six hits.

April 16

1881 — Gene Ford — B (P 1905)

1892 — Hubert (Dutch) Leonard — B (P 1919-21, 1924-25)

1953 — Bruce Taylor — B (P 1977-78)

April 17

1875 — Charlie Jaeger — B (P 1905)

1950 — Pedro Garcia — B (2B 1977)

1955 — Al Kaline enjoys the biggest single game of his career as he collects six RBIs and four straight hits, including three home runs. Two of the home runs come in the sixth inning as the Tigers pound Kansas City 16-0 in Detroit. Pitcher Steve Gromek is the beneficiary of the outburst.

1960 — Tiger fans and Indian fans each are stunned as their respective heroes, Harvey Kuenn and Rocky Colavito, are traded for each other. Kuenn lasts only a season in Cleveland while Colavito wins over Detroit with four straight standout seasons. One of Jim Campbell's best deals.

1968 — Willie Horton slugs a two-run homer in the bottom of the tenth to beat Cleveland 4-3.

1971 — Willie Horton goes five for six, with two home runs and six RBIs, in a ten-inning 10-9 win over the Red Sox at home.

April 18

1880 — Sam Crawford — B (OF-1B 1903-17)

1968 — Al Kaline, playing in his 2,000th game, hits his 305th career home run as the Tigers beat the Indians 5-0 for their sixth straight win. Joe Sparma pitches a seven-hitter.

April 19

1892 — Chick Shorten — B (OF-C 1919-21)

1901 — Bernie DeViveiros — B (SS-3B 1927)

1927 — Edwin (Ty) Tyson becomes the first Tiger broadcaster, airing an 8-5 win over the Indians from Navin Field over station WWJ. "Good afternoon, boys and girls, this is Ty Tyson speaking to you from Navin Field . . ." was to become his trademark.

23

1935 — Johnny Wyatt — B (P 1968)

April 20

1897 — Lou Vedder — B (P 1920)

1912 — Navin Field is dedicated before a capacity crowd of 23,000 with a 6–5 Tiger win over the Indians in 11 innings.

1937 — Outfielder Gee Walker hits for the cycle against the Indians at home.

1948 — In his first major league at bat, on the first pitch, first baseman George Vico hits a home run.

1950 — Milt Wilcox, — B (P 1977–present)

1976 — Catcher Milt May breaks his ankle and is out for the remainder of the season.

April 21

1910 — The Tigers beat the Indians 5–0 before 19,867 Indian fans in the first game played at League Park. Ed Willett hurls the shutout.

1940 — Bill Faul — B (P 1962–64)

1965 — The Bengals win their home opener before 32,658 fans 1–0. Although the Tigers get only three hits, Don Demeter's RBI double in the fourth is all that is needed.

1968 — The Tigers stretch their winning streak to nine games as Earl Wilson and Denny McLain hurl complete game 4–1, 4–2 wins over the White Sox in Chicago.

1977 — Dave (The Rose) Rozema shuts out the Red Sox 8–0 for his first big league win.

1979 — A home game with Toronto is almost cancelled because the grounds crew, electricians, and concessions and service employees refuse to cross the umpires' picket line. The arbiters decide to remove the picket line so the game can go on "in the best interest of the fans." The Tigers wind up losing 5–4.

April 22

Nothing of significance happened on this date.

April 23

1886 — Harry Coveleski — B (P 1914–18)

1896 — Elam Vangilder — B (P 1928–29)

1944 — Catcher Hack Miller hits a home run in his first major league at bat in a game with the Indians.

April 24

1894 — Howard Ehmke — B (P 1916–17, 1919–22)

1933 — The Tigers sell pitcher George Uhle to the New York Giants for $25,000.

1964 — Mickey Lolich pitches his first major league shutout in a 5–0 triumph over the Twins in Minnesota. He throws a three–hitter and strikes out seven. Second baseman Jerry Lumpe tallies three hits and three RBIs. After the game, Manager Charlie Dressen treats the team to dinner at Schick's Cafe, rolling up a $385 tab.

April 25

1898 — Fred Haney — B (3B–2B–1B–SS 1922–25)

1901 — In the first American League game ever played, Detroit beats Milwaukee 14–13 before 8,000 at Bennett Park. Tiger fans are treated to an incredible ninth–inning comeback in which their team scores 10 runs. First baseman Frank Dillon slaps four doubles to head the Tiger attack.

1913 — Woody Davis — B (P 1938)

April 26

1903 — Dale Alexander — B (1B–OF 1929–32)

1919 — Virgil Trucks — B (P 1941–43, 1945–52, 1956)

April 27

1878 — George Winter — B (P 1908)

1903 — Pitcher George Mullin slugs three doubles in a game.

1914 — George Archie — B (PH 1938)

1973 — Tiger fans watch in dismay as the Royals' Steve Busby pitches a no-hit, 3–0 win over the home team.

April 28

1919 — Charlie Metro — B (OF 1943–44)

1927 — Charlie Maxwell — B (OF–1B 1955–62)

1930 — Tom Sturdivant — B (P 1963)

1934 — Star outfielder Goose Goslin grounds into four consecutive double plays against the Indians.

1964 — The Tigers trade outfielder-pitcher Willie Smith to the Los Angeles Angels for pitcher Julio Navarro.

April 29

1910 — Ralph Stroud pitches a five-hit, 5–0 shutout over the St. Louis Browns in his major league debut with the Tigers.

1935 — Tommy Bridges is the beneficiary of tremendous support in an 18–0 shutout of the St. Louis Browns.

1964 — Reliever Larry Sherry nails down a 5–4 win in 10 innings in Kansas City after the Tigers get the go-ahead run on outfielder Don Demeter's home run.

1969 — The Tigers release relief pitcher Roy Face, who is then picked up by the Expos.

April 30

1912 — Chet Laabs — B (OF 1937–39)

1922 — Charlie Robertson of the White Sox pitches a perfect game 2–0 win over the Tigers in Detroit.

1942 — The Tigers sell pitcher Schoolboy Rowe to the Dodgers on waivers.

1945 — The Tigers acquire outfielder Roy Cullenbine from the Indians in exchange for second baseman Dutch Meyer and outfielder-third baseman Don Ross.

1957 — The Tigers trade first baseman Jack Phillips to the Red Sox for outfielder Karl Olson.

1967 — The Orioles' Steve Barber and Stu Miller combine to no-hit the Tigers in Baltimore in the first game of a doubleheader, yet lose 2–1 on walks and errors.

MAY

May 1

1901 — The Tigers commit a record 12 errors in a game with the White Sox.

1916 — Bob Harris — B (P 1938–39)

1976 — Willie Horton extends his streak of consecutive games with an RBI to 10. (The streak began April 18 and ran to a total of 17 RBIs.)

1979 — Rusty Staub rejoins the team following a contract dispute that began in spring training.

The Tigers release infielder Dave Machemer to make room for Staub.

May 2

1901 — The Tigers win the first forfeit in American League history while playing the White Sox in Chicago. When rain begins to fall after the Tigers take the lead in the top of the inning, the White Sox try stalling to get the lead washed out. Umpire Tom Connolly declares the game a forfeit.

1939 — Tiger fans see Lou Gehrig's streak of 2,130 consecutive games end when he takes himself out of the lineup. Babe Dahlgren plays first base in his stead.

Gates Brown — B (OF–1B–DH 1963–75)

1949 — Steve Grilli — B (P 1975–77)

1959 — The Tigers trade starting pitcher Billy Hoeft to Boston for pitcher Dave Sisler and infielder Ted Lepcio.

May 3

1892 — Del Baker — B (C 1914–16, MGR 1933, 1938–42)

1959 — Jimmy Dykes is named manager to succeed Bill Norman who had gotten the team off to a disastrous 2 and 15 start. Under Dykes, the Tigers play .540 ball the rest of the season to finish fourth.

Dykes is treated to a tremendous display by Charlie Maxwell on his first day at the helm. Maxwell hits four consecutive home runs in a doubleheader, one in the first game, three in the second game.

1970 — Second baseman Dick McAuliffe has 11 assists in a game with the White Sox.

May 4

1933 — A leadoff ninth-inning home run by second baseman Charlie Gehringer spoils Yankee Lefty Gomez's bid for a no-hitter.

1936 — John Tsitouris — B (P 1957)

1938 — Howie Koplitz — B (P 1961–62)

1939 — Boston's Ted Williams becomes the first player in history to hit a home run over the right field double-deck roof in Detroit. Tiger hurler Bob Harris is the victim of the titanic blow.

1963 — The Tigers sell outfielder Bubba Morton to the Braves and purchase pitcher Tom Sturdivant from the Pirates.

May 5

1887 — Henri Rondeau — B (C–1B 1913)

1925 — Ty Cobb goes six for six, including three home runs, for a total of 16 bases against the St. Louis Browns. The next day, he hits two more home runs.

1965 — In an unusual play, relief pitcher Larry Sherry gets credit for a strikeout and wild pitch on the same pitch. White Sox second baseman Don Buford swings at the pitch for the third strike, but it hits the ground and bounces past Tiger catcher John Sullivan for a wild pitch to let a run score. Tigers lose to White Sox 4–1.

1967 — The Tigers sell relief pitcher Orlando Pena to the Indians.

May 6

1898 — Al Wingo — B (OF–3B 1924–28)

1921 — Dick Wakefield — B (OF 1941, 1943–44, 1946–49)

May 6 (continued)

1941 — In his last game before induction to the Army, Hank Greenberg hits two home runs as the Tigers beat the Yankees 7–4 at home.

1945 — Tiger starters Hal Newhouser and Al Benton post 3–0, 1–0, shutout victories over the St. Louis Browns.

1949 — Philadelphia's Bobby Shantz hurls nine no-hit innings of relief against the Tigers in Detroit, from the fourth inning to the twelfth. Athletics eventually win 5–3 in 13 innings.

1966 — Denny McLain shuts out the White Sox in Chicago 1–0 on one hit, a second-inning single by J. C. Martin. The Tigers score their only run when a Norm Cash sacrifice fly brings home McLain, who had bunted to get on.

1971 — The Tigers release pitcher Dave Boswell.

1980 — Outfielder Champ Summers has three hits, including two doubles, and two RBIs as he extends his hitting streak to 16 games and raises his batting average to .409. The Tigers beat the Mariners 9–5 in Seattle as Dan Petry gets his first win since being recalled from the minors.

May 7

1892 — Aloysius Travers — B (P 1912)

1906 — Pitcher Wild Bill Donovan singles in the fifth inning for the Tigers, then proceeds to steal second, third and home on a double steal. Donovan also collects a triple in an 8–3 win over Cleveland.

1910 — Harry Davis — B (1B 1932–33)

1962 — The Tigers sell outfielder George Alusik to Kansas City on waivers.

May 8

1880 — John Skopec — B (P 1903)

1948 — A Vic Raschi pitch fractures the wrist of third baseman George Kell in a game with the Yankees. The injury puts the Tiger star out of action until May 31, 1948.

1963 — The Tigers trade shortstop Chico Fernandez to the Milwaukee Braves for outfielder Lou Johnson and cash.

1965 — An Al Kaline home run in the 15th inning gives the Tigers a 4–3 win in Baltimore.

1968 — Centerfielder Jim Northrup makes a spectacular diving catch of a line drive by the Orioles' Brooks Robinson with the bases loaded, two out, in the eighth inning to preserve a 3–1 win in Baltimore. Northrup also has a first inning home run.

May 9

1877 — Lew Drill — B (C–1B 1904–05)

28

1916 — Philadelphia pitcher Bruno Haas makes an unforgettable major league debut by walking 16 Tigers. The Tigers set a one-game record for walks with 18.

1932 — Tom Yewcic — B (C 1957)

1972 — The Tigers trade pitcher Mike Kilkenny to Oakland for first baseman Reggie Sanders.

May 10

1868 — Ed Barrow — B (MGR 1903-04)

1913 — The Tigers lose to the Yankees 10-9 in 10 innings despite eight Yankee errors.

1947 — Tim Hosley — B (C-1B 1970-71)

1961 — The Tigers trade first baseman Dick Gernert to the Cincinnati Reds for infielder Jim Baumer.

1963 — The Tigers release first baseman Vic Wertz; he signs with the Twins on June 18.

1966 — Starting pitcher Johnny Podres is purchased from Los Angeles Dodgers.

1968 — The Tigers move into first place ahead of the Orioles as they pound the Senators 12-1. Al Kaline drives in six runs with a single, double, and homer as Denny McLain gets his fifth straight win.

May 11

1903 — Charlie Gehringer — B (2B-1B-3B 1924-42)

1907 — Rip Sewell — B (P 1932)

1941 — The Tigers release shortstop Dick Bartell, who then signs with the New York Giants.

1971 — The Tigers trade pitcher Jim Hannan to the Milwaukee Brewers for pitcher John Gelnar and infielder Jose Herrera. An imminently forgettable deal for all concerned as Gelnar and Herrera never leave the minors and Hannan pitches just a few games for the Brewers.

May 12

1897 — Joe Dugan — B (3B 1931)

1911 — Archie McKain — B (P 1939-41)

1916 — Dixie Parsons — B (C 1939, 1942-43)

Hank Borowy — B (P 1950-51)

1940 — Tom Timmerman — B (P 1969-73)

1948 — Pitcher George Susce is acquired from the Red Sox.

1957 — Lou Whitaker — B (2B-DH 1977-present)

29

May 12 (continued)

1961 — Outfielder Rocky Colavito is ejected after going into the stands behind third base at Yankee Stadium after a drunken fan who was heckling Colavito's wife and father. Following the eighth inning ejection, the Tigers win in the ninth on a home run by Tiger ace Frank Lary, whose victory boosts his pitching mastery over the Yankees to 25 wins against 8 losses.

1980 — The Tigers trade pitcher Jack Billingham to the Red Sox for minor league outfielder Sam Bowen. Bowen refuses to report and the deal is changed to a player to be named.

May 13

1877 — John Burns — B (2B 1903–04)

1883 — Jimmy Archer — B (C–2B 1907)

1884 — Alex Main — B (P 1914)

1911 — Ty Cobb hits the first grand slam of his career, off Boston's Ed Karger.

1939 — In a blockbuster deal, the Tigers send pitchers George Gill, Bob Harris, Vern Kennedy, and Roxie Lawson, third baseman Mark Christman, and outfielder Chet Laabs to the Browns for pitchers Bobo Newsom and Jim Walkup, short-stop Ralph Kress, and outfielder Roy Bell. Newsom becomes the top pitcher in the following season's drive to the top of the American League.

1945 — First baseman Rudy York strikes out four times, all on called strikes, against Boston's Dave Ferriss.

1959 — Outfielder Larry Doby is released, signs on with the White Sox.

1961 — The day after his ejection for going into the stands after a fan, Rocky Colavito drives in four runs with two home runs and two singles as the Tigers beat the Yankees 8–3 in Yankee Stadium.

1965 — Willie Horton's five RBIs from two home runs and a double lead Detroit to a 13–3 victory over the Senators in Washington.

May 14

1925 — Les Moss — B (MGR 1979)

1965 — For the second day in a row, Willie Horton gets five RBIs. Willie goes four for five with two home runs against the Red Sox in Fenway Park. The Tigers win 12–8 in 10 innings by scoring four runs off Boston reliever Dick Radatz.

1967 — Boston and Detroit combine for 28 extra-base hits in a doubleheader (Boston–16, Detroit–12).

1973 — Tiger catcher Gene Lamont is traded to Atlanta for Brave catcher Bob Didier.

May 15

1885 — Ralph (Sailor) Stroud — B (P 1910)

1912 — Ty Cobb assaults a fan who is heckling him in New York and is suspended by the league office.

1941 — The Tigers purchase outfielder-first baseman Rip Radcliff from the Browns for $25,000.

1952 — Tiger hurler Virgil Trucks throws a no-hitter against the Senators to win 1–0. A Vic Wertz home run with two outs in the ninth inning provides the winning margin. Only 2,215 Tiger fans witness the masterpiece.

1956 — The Tigers trade third baseman Fred Hatfield and outfielder Jim Delsing to the White Sox for pitcher Harry Byrd and infielders Bob Kennedy and Jim Brideweser.

1969 — Citing "personal problems," outfielder Willie Horton goes AWOL for four days. The team fines him $1,360 for leaving without permission.

1976 — Mark (The Bird) Fidrych wins his first big league start 2–1 against the Indians with a complete game, two-hitter at home.

May 16

1872 — John O'Connell — B (2B–1B 1902)

1919 — Frank (Stubby) Overmire — B (P 1943–49)

1920 — Dave Philley — B (1B–OF–3B 1957)

1928 — Billy Martin — B (SS–3B 1958, MGR 1971–73)

1933 — Bob Bruce — B (P 1959–61)

1954 — Boston great Ted Williams returns to action, after suffering a broken collar-bone, with an astonishing performance in a doubleheader in Detroit. He goes eight for nine, hits two homers and drives in nine runs.

1956 — Jack Morris — B (P 1977–present)

1961 — Tiger ace Frank Lary gets his 100th career win and sixth of the season with a six-hit 10–4 win over the Orioles in Baltimore. Home runs by Norm Cash and Rocky Colavito lead the offense.

1966 — Manager Charlie Dressen suffers his second heart attack in two years. Coach Bob Swift is named acting manager.

May 17

1913 — The Tigers sell pitcher George Mullin to the Senators.

1932 — Billy Hoeft — B (P 1952–59)

1933 — Ozzie Virgil — B (3B–SS–2B–C 1958, 1960–61)

1968 — Outfielder Jim Northrup belts a grand slam in the bottom of the ninth to beat Washington 7–3. Joe Sparma picks up the win with a complete game three-hitter.

31

May 17 (continued)

1972 — Mickey Lolich extends his record to 7–1 with a four-hit 6–1 win over the Orioles at home. Catcher Tom Haller hits a three-run homer for his first American League hit.

May 18

1912 — A makeshift team of Tigers is forced to play the Athletics in Philadelphia after the regular team goes out on strike in support of Ty Cobb, who had been suspended three days earlier. Eight players from St. Joseph's College and a sandlotter help field a team, which the A's clobber 24–2. Ed Irvin, in his only big league appearance playing third base for Detroit, belts two triples.

1914 — Ty Cobb sustains a broken rib when he is hit with a pitch. Two days later, he leaves the lineup in favor of Harry Heilmann, who hits only .225 in his place.

1918 — Rufe Gentry — B (P 1943–44, 1946–48)

1923 — Don Lund — B (OF 1949, 1952–54)

1946 — The Tigers obtain third baseman George Kell from the Athletics for outfielder Barney McCosky. A good deal for the Tigers as Kell goes on to become the greatest third baseman in team history.

May 19

1946 — Boston buys third baseman Pinky Higgins from the Tigers.

1948 — Tiger ace Hal Newhouser ties a major league record by starting four double plays in a game.

1963 — Tiger Bill Faul pitches a three-hit 5–1 win over the Senators in Washington in his first major league start. The Tiger attack is led by Bill Bruton, who smacks four consecutive doubles and drives in three runs.

1965 — Denny McLain hurls his first major league shutout with a three-hit 4–0 victory over the Senators at home.

1968 — Al Kaline slugs a pinch-hit home run off Senator pitcher Steve Jones for his 307th career home run, surpassing former Tiger leader Hank Greenberg's 306 homers. In the same game the Senator's Frank Howard hits two home runs, setting a major league record for ten homers in six games. Tigers lose at home, 8–4.

May 20

1890 — Doc Ayers — B (P 1919–21)

1912 — At the request of Ty Cobb, the Detroit team calls off its strike in protest of his suspension and agrees to return to play.

1921 — Hal Newhouser — B (P 1939–53)

1930 — Tom Morgan — B (P 1958–60)

1947 — The Tigers trade catcher Birdie Tebbetts to Boston for catcher Hal Wagner.

1965 — A tenth-inning home run by Dick McAuliffe beats Washington 9–8 in Detroit.

May 21

1902 — Earl Averill — B (OF 1939–40)

1950 — Bob Molinaro — B (OF 1975, 1977)

1967 — Whitey Ford lasts one inning in his final major league appearance against the Tigers in Detroit. The Yankee lefthander is forced to quit because of a sore elbow.

May 22

1902 — Al Simmons — B (OF–1B 1936)

1937 — Hank Greenberg hits a home run out of Fenway Park over center field to the right of the flag pole. Boston hurler Wes Ferrell is the victim of the blast.

1970 — The Tigers obtain pitcher Bill Rohr and outfielder Russ Nagelson from Cleveland for reliever Fred Lasher.

1971 — The Tigers acquire second baseman John Donaldson from Oakland for pitcher Daryl Patterson.

May 23

1881 — Forrest (Frosty) Thomas — B (P 1905)

1905 — Charlie Sullivan — B (P 1928, 1930–31)

1969 — Mickey Lolich sets a club record by fanning 16 Angels in a 6–3 win in Detroit. Lolich breaks Paul Foytack's record of 15 strikeouts set in 1956. A grand slam by Mickey Stanley provides the winning margin.

1971 — The Tigers register a double shutout of the Senators as Mickey Lolich wins the first game 5–0 and Les Cain and Joe Niekro team up in the second game to win 11–0.

May 24

1904 — Detroit beats Washington 5–4 in a game played in Grand Rapids before a crowd of 6,000.

1927 — Milt Jordan — B (P 1953)

1929 — Tiger hurler George Uhle gets the victory in a 6–5, twenty-one-inning contest with the White Sox. Uhle pitches 20 innings before being removed for a pinch runner.

1951 — Dave Machemer — B (2B–OF 1979)

1958 — The Tigers purchase outfielder Bob "Hurricane" Hazle from the Braves. In 43 games, Hazle produces a .243 average and only two home runs.

May 24 (continued)

1962 — Oriole manager Billy Hitchcock accuses Tiger ace Jim Bunning of notching balls with his belt buckle. To add injury to insult, the Orioles lose the game in 11 innings on a passed ball.

1965 — Catcher Bill Freehan's two home runs and five RBIs pace Mickey Lolich and the Tigers to an 8-3 win over the White Sox in Chicago.

May 25

1937 — Player-manager Mickey Cochrane's playing career is ended when he receives a fractured skull from a pitch thrown by Yankee Bump Hadley in the fifth inning of a game in Yankee Stadium. Cochrane's injury opens the way for Rudy York to play more regularly.

1968 — Al Kaline suffers a broken arm when hit by a pitch from Athletic Lew Krausse. Kaline is out of action until June 30.

1979 — The Tigers obtain outfielder Champ Summers from Cincinnati for pitcher Sheldon Burnside. Summers becomes an immediate hit with Tiger fans and a valuable addition to the club.

May 26

1874 — John Cronin — B (P 1901–02)

1912 — The Tigers celebrate Cobb's return to the lineup following his suspension with a 6-2 win over the White Sox. Cobb gets a single in four at bats.

1952 — The Tigers obtain first baseman Johnny Hopp from the Yankees.

1962 — Al Kaline breaks his right collarbone while making a diving catch of an Elston Howard line drive for the final out in a 2-1 win over the Yankees in New York. Hank Aguirre is the winning pitcher.

1968 — A free-for-all brawl erupts after Jim Northrup is hit in the batting helmet by a Jack Aker pitch in Oakland. The 15-minute fight results in Aker being forced to leave the game with an injury. Despite fiery action, the Tigers still lose 7-6 in 10 innings.

May 27

1909 — Pinky Higgins — B (3B 1939–44, 1946)

1939 — Charlie Gehringer hits for the cycle against the Browns at home.

1979 — Catcher Milt May is sold to the White Sox to make room for rising young catching star Lance Parrish.

1980 — A slumping Jason Thompson is traded to California for right fielder Al Cowens. The trade appears to help both teams as each player hits well upon joining his new team.

May 28

1889 — Jim Middleton — B (P 1921)

1957 — Kirk Gibson — B (OF 1979-present)

1965 — A Don Wert home run and a two-hitter by Hank Aguirre are all that the Tigers need to beat Cleveland 1-0 at home.

May 29

1885 — Jack Lively — B (P 1911)

1931 — John Baumgartner — B (3B 1953)

1951 — Vic Wertz hits a home run to lead off the eighth inning at Briggs Stadium, ruining Bob Lemon's bid for a perfect game.

1952 — Fred Holdsworth — B (P 1972-74)

1965 — The Tigers beat the Indians 1-0 for the second day in a row at home in the tenth inning on doubles by George Thomas and Dick McAuliffe. Mickey Lolich pitches a two-hitter and retires 18 batters in a row.

1968 — Denny McLain notches his eighth win with a 3-0 shutout over the Angels. He strikes out 13 batters while pitching a four-hitter.

1969 — Five Tiger home runs (Norm Cash-2, Willie Horton, Jim Northrup and Ron Woods) give Denny McLain an 8-4 win over the A's in Oakland. Denny fans 12 and yields 7 hits in going the distance.

1975 — The Tigers give Fred Holdsworth a birthday surprise by trading him to the Orioles for pitcher Bob Reynolds.

May 30

1930 — The Tigers acquire pitcher Waite Hoyt and shortstop Mark Koenig from the Yankees in exchange for pitcher Owen Carroll, shortstop George Wuestling and outfielder Harry Rice.

1936 — Ed Rakow — B (P 1964-65)

1964 — Pitcher Frank Lary is sold to the Mets, marking the end of a distinguished 10-year stay in Detroit. Plagued by a sore arm, Lary will play only one more season after this one.

1966 — Denny McLain throws his second one-hitter of the year, this one a 5-2 win over the Athletics in Kansas City. A Phil Roof double in the fifth is the only marker, scoring Ed Charles and Ken Harrelson who had walked.

1972 — Utility man Dalton Jones is traded to the Rangers for pitcher Norm McRae.

1980 — John Hiller announces his retirement, ending a 12-year career marked by one of the greatest comebacks in sports history following a heart attack. Hiller finished as the all-time Tiger leader in games pitched with 545. Tigers smash five home

May 30 (continued)

runs to trounce California 12–1 (Richie Hebner–2, Stan Papi, Lance Parrish, Kirk Gibson). Milt Wilcox goes the distance for the win, pitching a six-hitter. The game is interrupted at the end of the third inning to announce Hiller's retirement and introduce him one last time to the Detroit fans. He receives a tumultuous ovation. Second baseman Stan Papi goes three for four in his Tiger debut, including the home run, a triple, and a single for three RBIs. Al Cowens also makes his Tiger debut, hitting two singles in five at bats. The Tigers score five runs in the sixth inning when Parrish, Hebner, and Gibson hit home runs. Hebner's second home run just misses clearing the right field roof while Gibson's drive was well hit to right center field.

May 31

1927 — First baseman Johnny Neun makes an unassisted triple play as the Tigers shut out the Indians at home 1–0. The play ends the game as Neun catches Homer Summa's liner, tags Charlie Jamieson between first and second, and touches the bag at second before Glenn Myatt can get back.

1965 — Charlie Dressen resumes his managerial duties following a heart attack, with a 5–1 win over the Yankees in New York in the second game of a doubleheader.

1968 — Lefty Mickey Lolich wins a 1–0 pitchers' duel with the Yankees' Mel Stottlemyre when Willie Horton slugs a seventh-inning home run.

1969 — Joe Sparma loses a no-hit bid in the ninth against Seattle when Don Mincher doubles. Sparma hangs on to win 3–2.

1979 — Rookie pitcher Pat Underwood hurls 8 1/3 strong innings to beat Toronto and his brother Tom 1–0 in his major league debut.

JUNE

June 1

1901 — Joyner (Jo-Jo) White — B (OF 1932–38)

1941 — Dean Chance — B (P 1971)

1976 — Relief ace John Hiller wins both ends of a doubleheader with the Brewers at home, 8–7, 6–5. Milwaukee reliever Eduardo Rodriguez winds up on the losing end in both games.

June 2

1914 — The Tigers sell infielder Del Gainor to Boston.

1932 — Lou (The Nervous Greek) Skizas — B (OF–3B 1958)

1933 — Jerry Lumpe — B (2B–3B 1964–67)

1938 — Gene Michael — B (SS–2B–3B 1975)

1948 — Jack Pierce — B (1B 1975)

36

1950 — Third sacker George Kell hits for the cycle against the Athletics in Philadelphia in the second game of a twin bill.

1980 — Tigers obtain outfielder Jim Lentine from the St. Louis Cardinals for minor league pitcher John Martin and a player to be named.

June 3

1895 — Johnny Bassler — B (C 1921–27)

1938 — Tiger ace Schoolboy Rowe, after a sterling 19–10 performance the year before, is sent to Beaumont of the Texas League to recover from an arm injury.

1952 — In one of the year's biggest trades, the Tigers send third baseman George Kell, shortstop Johnny Lipon, outfielder Hoot Evers, and pitcher Dizzy Trout to the Red Sox for first baseman Walt Dropo, third baseman Fred Hatfield, shortstop Johnny Pesky, outfielder Don Lenhardt, and pitcher Bill Wight. Although neither team derives any great advantage from the deal, the loss of Kell is a hard one for Tiger fans to accept.

1953 — Ed Glynn — B (P 1975–78)

1961 — In a home twinbill with Minnesota, eight Tigers smash homers as the Tigers win 10–5, 9–3. Norm Cash, Bill Bruton, Dick Brown, Chico Fernandez, and Jake Wood hit for the circuit in the first game. In game two, Rocky Colavito, Bubba Morton, and Mike Roarke each clear the bases once.

1966 — Hank Aguirre and Larry Sherry combine for the first shutout of the Angels in Anaheim Stadium, 1–0. Aguirre hurls the first seven innings, with Sherry mopping up. Willie Horton's homer in the seventh inning proves the margin of victory.

1980 — The Tigers sign Eduardo Cajuso, a shortstop, as the first Cuban refugee permitted under the new baseball ruling. He is assigned to the Class A Lakeland farm club.

June 4

1906 — Third baseman Bill Coughlin becomes the first Tiger to steal second, third, and home in the same inning when he turns the trick in the seventh inning of a game with the Senators.

June 5

1874 — Frank Huelsman — B (OF 1904)

1941 — Duane (Duke) Sims — B (C–OF 1972–73)

1961 — The Tigers obtain pitcher Hal Woodeshick from Washington for second baseman Chuck Cottier. Woodeshick is ineffective in relief while Cottier assumes the starting role for the Senators and performs adequately.

1970 — Al Kaline's single off A's pitcher John (Blue Moon) Odom in the fifth inning is his 2,500th major league hit. The Tigers lose 4–2 in Oakland.

June 6

1908 — Isadore (Izzy) Goldstein — B (P 1932)

1910 — Chet Morgan — B (OF 1935, 1938)

1967 — A full-scale brawl erupts between the Tigers and the A's in Kansas City when Blue Moon Odom brushes back Dick McAuliffe in the seventh inning. More than half the players from each team get involved in the melee.

June 7

1900 — Ed Wells — B (P 1923-27)

1907 — The Tigers turn their second triple play in two days against the Red Sox.

June 8

1926 — Yankee slugger Babe Ruth clubs a 626-foot home run out of Navin Field off Tiger hurler Lil Stoner. The ball lands at the intersection of Cherry Street and Brooklyn Avenue, two blocks from the ball park.

1937 — Joe Grzenda — B (P 1961)

1965 — Catcher Gene Lamont is selected as the number one Tiger draft pick in the first free agent draft held.

1975 — Shortstop Tom Veryzer's double with two out in the ninth inning at Oakland breaks up Ken Holtzman's bid for a no-hitter. Outfielder Bill North misjudges the ball, but is not charged with an error.

1976 — Following a 10–18 record in 1975 and a slow start the following year, pitcher Joe Coleman is dealt to the Chicago Cubs for cash and a player to be named.

June 9

1915 — Hookie Dauss and Bill Steen combine for a shutout over the Red Sox as the Tigers pound out a 15-0 win. Dauss hurls the first six innings, with Steen finishing the job.

1951 — Billy Baldwin — B (OF-DH 1975)

1969 — Mickey Lolich ties the club strikeout record set by himself earlier in the year by fanning 16 Seattle Pilots in a 3–2 loss.

1970 — Slugger Willie Horton thrills the home crowd with three home runs and seven RBIs in an 8–3 win over Milwaukee.

June 10

1903 — The Tigers trade shortstop Kid Elberfeld to the Yankees for shortstops Herman Long and Ernie Courtney. The Yanks best the Tigers in this deal as Elberfeld becomes a fixture at short for the next four seasons while Long and Courtney fade out after a weak 1903 season.

1929 — Hank Foiles — B (C 1960)

1958 — Bill Norman replaces Jack Tighe as manager, leads the club to a fifth place finish by winning 56 and losing 49.

1963 — Bill Faul pitches his second three-hitter in three starts by beating the Red Sox 6-1 at home. Al Kaline paces the Tiger attack with two home runs and four RBIs.

1976 — The Tigers acquire pitcher Milt Wilcox from the Cubs for their Evansville farm club.

The Tigers trade second baseman Gary Sutherland to Milwaukee for their second sacker, Pedro Garcia. Sutherland plays little before heading on to San Diego in 1977. After compiling a heady .198 average for the Tigers, Pedro heads north of the border to Toronto for his grand finale with the Blue Jays.

June 11

1892 — Archie Yelle — B (C 1917-19)

1961 — Norm Cash becomes the first Tiger to hit a home run over the right-field roof at Tiger Stadium with a tremendous clout off the Senators' Joe McClain. This blast in the sixth inning is Cash's second homer of the game.

June 12

1880 — Matty McIntyre — B (OF 1904-10)

1907 — The Tigers beat Yankees 14-6 with the aid of 11 Yankee errors. (We can all thank God George Steinbrenner wasn't around to witness that display of ineptitude.)

1932 — The Tigers trade first baseman Dale Alexander and outfielder Roy Johnson to Boston for outfielder Earl Webb. One of the worse deals from the Tigers' viewpoint as Alexander went on to win the batting title with a .367 average and Johnson played well in a starting role. For his part, Webb quickly moved on the next year to the White Sox.

1971 — The Tigers acquire second baseman Tony Taylor from the Phillies for minor league pitchers Mike Fremuth and Carl Cavanaugh. A stellar deal for the Bengals as Taylor plays a key utility role in the 1972 divisional championship.

1979 — Tiger fans are stunned when the team dismisses manager Les Moss and hires Sparky Anderson, who receives a five-year contract at $125,000 per year. Many fans feel that Moss never got a fair chance to show what he could do with a young team.

June 13

1891 — Marty Kavanagh — B (2B-1B-OF-SS-3B 1914-16)

1907 — Gene Desautels — B (C 1930-33)

1921 — In an incredible performance at the Polo Grounds, Babe Ruth personally dismantles the Tigers by pitching five innings for the win and clubbing two home runs in an 11-8 victory. As a pitcher, Ruth gives up four runs and strikes out Ty Cobb once. His second home run travels more than 460 feet to right center field.

1924 — An on-the-field brawl between the Yankees and Tigers makes 18,000 Detroit fans riot and cause a forfeit game. Tiger pitcher Bert Cole hits Yankee Bob Meusel with a pitch and the brawl ensues when Meusel charges the mound. Both Meusel and Babe Ruth are ejected from the game. According to news accounts, Ruth and Ty Cobb get into an "exchange of numerous vile epithets."

1950 — Bob Strampe — B (1972)

1954 — The Tigers trade second baseman Johnny Pesky to Washington for infielder Mel Hoderlein.

1959 — The Tigers purchase pitcher Bob Smith from Pittsburgh.

1962 — Speedy second baseman Jake Wood scores from second base on Charlie Maxwell's 400-foot sacrifice fly near the flagpole in Tiger Stadium. Indian outfielder Willie Tasby's throw to catcher John Romano is too late to catch Wood. The Bengals beat Cleveland 8–6.

1965 — The Tigers beat the Twins 5–4 before a Bat Day crowd of 50,393. Much to the disbelief of the crowd, non-hitting pitcher Hank Aguirre drives in the winning run with a single.

June 14

1917 — Hal Manders — B (P 1941–42, 1946)

1939 — The Tigers obtain outfielder Earl Averill from the Indians for pitcher Harry Eisenstat and cash. Nearing the end of a great career that will take him to the Hall of Fame, Averill proves a valuable addition, knocking out 12 pinch hits in the 1940 pennant drive.

1966 — The Tigers acquire pitcher Earl Wilson and outfielder Joe Christopher from Boston for outfielder Don Demeter and pitcher Julio Navarro. Wilson quickly proves his worth by winning 13 games in this season and leading the league with 22 wins in the near-miss run at the pennant in 1967.

1968 — The Tigers keep on the pennant track with a 6–5 win in the 14th inning over the White Sox in Chicago with a Don Wert home run. John Hiller gains his fifth win in relief by hurling two shutout innings.

1979 — Sparky Anderson assumes control of the club's managerial duties from interim manager Dick Tracewski.

June 15

1884 — Heinie Beckendorf — B (C 1909–10)

1891 — Lou North — B (P 1913)

1927 — Ben Flowers — B (P 1955)

1948 — John (Champ) Summers — B (OF–DH 1979–present)

The Tigers beat Philadelphia 4–1 in the first night game played in Detroit.

1956 — Lance Parrish — B (C 1977–present)

1958 — Yankee killer Frank Lary and teammate Jim Bunning whitewash the New Yorkers 2–0, 3–0. The Tigers trade pitcher Bob Shaw and infielder Ray Boone to the White Sox for pitcher Bill Fischer and outfielder Tito Francona.

1961 — First baseman Bobo Osborne's homer off Camilo Pascual in the bottom of the eighth beats the Twins 2–1 for Tiger pitcher Jim Bunning.

1963 — The Tigers trade pitcher Paul Foytack and infielder Frank Kostro to the Los Angeles Angels for outfielder George Thomas and cash.

1965 — In relief in the first inning, Denny McLain enters the game and proceeds to strike out the first seven Red Sox batters he faces. He winds up fanning 15 Beantowners in 6 2/3 innings as the Tigers win 6–5 at home. Catcher Bill Freehan joins McLain in the major league record books by tying the mark for the most putouts in a game by a catcher (19).

1968 — The Tigers purchase relief pitcher Johnny Wyatt from the Yankees.

1969 — The Tigers sell reliever Dick Radatz to Montreal.

1973 — The Tigers obtain pitcher Ed Farmer from Cleveland for pitcher Tom Timmerman and infielder Kevin Collins.

1975 — The Tigers sell first baseman Nate Colbert to the Expos. Tiger hopes for a productive season from the former San Diego slugger quickly evaporated and Nate was gone after 45 games and a .147 batting average.

June 16

1881 — Wish Egan — B (P 1902)

1886 — Jack Rowan — B (P 1906)

George (Kid) Speer — B (P 1909)

1888 — Jay Kirke — B (2B–OF 1910)

1948 — Ron LeFlore — B (OF–DH 1974–79)

1965 — Willie Horton gets five RBIs in a 9–4 home victory over the Red Sox with a single, double, and home run.

June 17

1881 — Claude Rossman — B (1B 1907–09)

1925 — The Tigers score 13 runs in an inning against the Yankees and go on to win 19–1 in Yankee Stadium.

June 17 (continued)

1963 — Manager Bob Scheffing is axed after the club drops into ninth place following seven straight losses. Charlie Dressen is named the manager the next day.

1967 — A doubleheader with Kansas City in Detroit is the longest ever played, lasting nine hours and five minutes in playing time. The Tigers split with the A's, 7–6, 5–6. The first game includes a rain delay and the second game goes 19 innings before a Dave Duncan home run breaks the tie and wins the game for Kansas City.

1980 — Because of growing rowdyism in the bleachers, general manager Jim Campbell announces that the team has closed the 10,500 seat area for the time being. The action followed an incident the day before when fans pelted Milwaukee's outfielders Gorman Thomas and Sixto Lezcano with assorted items. After instituting a new beer sales policy and tighter security, the club reopens the section June 30.

June 18

1911 — Losing to the White Sox 13–1 in the bottom of the fifth, the Tigers rally for four runs and go on to eventually win the game 16–15. The twelve-run deficit is the largest the team has ever overcome.

1943 — Rudy York plays a game at first base without a single putout.

1953 — The Red Sox pound the Tigers 23–3, scoring 17 runs in the bottom of the seventh inning for a modern record. Tiger hurler Steve Gromek is charged with nine of the runs. This defeat follows a 17–1 thrashing that the Red Sox had inflicted the day before.

June 19

1884 — Eddie Cicotte — B (P 1905)

1949 — Virgil Trucks and Fred Hutchinson spin double shutouts over the Senators, 9–0, 7–0.

1950 — Jim Slaton — B (P 1978)

1961 — Bill Freehan, a catching prospect out of the University of Michigan, signs a $100,000 bonus contract with Detroit.

1963 — Outfielder Gates Brown hits a home run in his first major league at bat off Boston's Don Heffner in Fenway Park.

1965 — Shortstop Dick McAuliffe hits two home runs and gets five RBIs in an 8–2 romp over Kansas City. Denny McLain goes the distance to win a six-hitter.

June 20

1874 — Win Mercer — B (P 1902)

1879 — Jim Delahanty — B (2B–1B–3B–OF 1909–12)

1891 — Charlie Grover — B (P 1913)

1939 — The Tigers win the first night game ever played in Philadelphia 5–0.

1961 — Al Kaline makes his debut as a third baseman handling two chances cleanly against the Senators in Washington. He paces the Tigers to a 5–4 win with a double and single for two RBIs. The third base experiment is very short-lived, as Kaline plays the position only one more time in his career (in 1965).

1965 — Al Kaline gets his 1,000th RBI with a two-run single in the first game of a twin bill with Kansas City. Down eight runs in the second inning, the Tigers win the first game 12–8. A loss in the second game ends an eight-game winning streak.

1968 — Denny McLain posts his 12th win of the year with a three-hitter over the Red Sox at home. Mickey Stanley's four RBIs lead the Tiger offense in the 5–1 win.

1980 — Chicago relief ace Ed Farmer vows to take criminal action against Tiger outfielder Al Cowens following a brawl during a game in the Windy City. After grounding out to shortstop, Cowens charged Farmer instead of running out the play. The incident stemmed from the fact that an errant Farmer pitch shattered Cowens' jaw a year earlier. Despite the brawl and Cowens' ejection, the Tigers go on to win 5–3 in 11 innings.

June 21

1953 — Gene Pentz — B (P 1975)

1964 — Slugger Willie Horton hits a grand slam off Washington's Casey Cox in the seventh inning to break a tie and lead the Tigers to a 9–5 home victory.

1970 — Normally light-hitting shortstop Cesar Gutierrez goes seven for seven in a twelve-inning game with Cleveland. Cesar's barrage includes six singles and a double, good for three runs and an RBI. Three of the six singles are infield hits. The Bengals win the game 9–8 in Cleveland, the second of a twin bill.

1980 — American League president Lee McPhail suspends outfielder Al Cowens for seven games following his attack on pitcher Ed Farmer in Chicago.

June 22

1920 — Walt Masterson — B (P 1956)

1937 — Jake Wood — B (2B–1B–3B–OF–SS 1961–67)

1939 — Outfielders Barney McCosky and Earl Averill lead off a game with the Athletics with back-to-back home runs off Lynn Nelson.

1973 — The Tigers purchase relief pitcher Bob Miller from San Diego.

June 23

1915 — Aaron Robinson — B (C 1949–51)

1917 — Leslie (Bubba) Floyd — B (SS 1944)

June 23 (continued)

1918 — Dutch Leonard of the Red Sox no-hits the Tigers 5–0 in Detroit. Center fielder Babe Ruth hits a home run in support of Leonard's effort.

1937 — Tom Haller — B (C 1972)

1943 — The Tigers and Indians are protected at a doubleheader by 350 armed troops, due to racial strife in Detroit. This marks the first time guards of this nature have been present at a baseball game. Tigers win the opener on Hal Newhouser's five-hitter, 3–1, but bow in the second game 9–6 on an 11th-inning home run by Jeff Heath.

1950 — A Tiger crowd of 51,400 is treated to an 11-homer barrage by the Yankees and Bengals, with the Tigers winning 10–9 in the bottom of the ninth with one out on outfielder Hoot Evers' inside-the-park home run, his second of the night. Other Tigers clearing the bases are Vic Wertz, Gerry Priddy, and pitcher Dizzy Trout, who slugs a grand slam.

1965 — Hank Aguirre wins his fifth straight game with a four-hit 2–0 shutout of the Angels at home for season win number nine.

June 24

1891 — Al Clauss — B (P 1913)

1892 — George Harper — B (OF 1916–18)

1961 — Rookie shortstop Dick McAuliffe hits a two-run homer with two out in the top of the ninth to beat Cleveland 5–4.

1962 — A two-run homer by Yankee outfielder Jack Reed, in the top of the 22nd inning off Tiger reliever Phil Regan beats the Bengals 9–7. (The blast was the only round-tripper of Reed's 222-game major league career.)

1968 — Outfielder Jim Northrup slugs two grand slam homers for a club record eight RBIs to lead the Bengals to a 14–3 romp over the Indians. Ironically, Northrup had fanned with the bases loaded in the first inning before clearing the sacks in both the fifth and sixth innings. Denny McLain garners his 13th win on the strength of this incredible power display.

1980 — First baseman Richie Hebner tallies six RBIs in leading the Tigers to their six straight win, a 9–4 victory over the Indians in Cleveland. Hebner's bases-loaded double in the seventh and bases-loaded single in the eight account for five of the six RBIs. Rookie reliever Roger Weaver gets his first major league win, while "Senor Smoke," Aurelio Lopez, racks up his eighth save.

June 25

1878 — John Deering — B (P 1903)

1905 — John Pasek — B (C 1933)

1925 — Alex Garbowski — B (PR 1952)

1935 — Don Demeter — B (OF–1B 1964–66)

1953 — Al Kaline makes his major league debut as a defensive replacement for center fielder Jim Delsing in a game in Philadelphia.

1962 — The Tigers trade outfielder Charlie Maxwell to the White Sox for first baseman-outfielder Bob Farley. A definite mistake. After 36 games and a .160 average, Farley disappeared from the Major League scene. Charlie hit .296 for the White Sox in 69 games and played another year before getting his release in 1964.

1980 — The Tigers win their seventh in a row as Milt Wilcox gets his sixth complete game in a row, beating Cleveland 13-3 at the Indians' Municipal Stadium. The Tigers tally 15 hits and receive 14 walks from the Indians as every Tiger starter gets at least one RBI. Steve Kemp's three hits and three RBIs pace the attack.

June 26

1903 — Babe Herman — B (OF 1937)

1972 — In his major league debut, Bill Slayback hurls seven no-hit innings before the Yankees' Johnny Callison hits a single in the eighth. The Tigers win 4-3 over New York at home.

June 27

1923 — Lou Kretlow — B (P 1946, 1948-49)

Gus Zernial — B (OF-1B 1958-59)

1927 — Dick Marlowe — B (P 1951-56)

1939 — The Tigers play the first night game in Cleveland history, and lose 5-0.

1961 — The Tigers attract their largest crowd for a twi-night doubleheader, 57,271, the third biggest crowd in Tiger history.

1963 — Norm Cash has no putouts or chances at first base in a 10-6 loss to the Twins in Minnesota.

1967 — In a rare display of frustration and temper, Al Kaline jams a bat into the bat rack after being struck out by Cleveland's Sam McDowell and breaks his hand. This critical injury keeps Kaline out of action for the next 28 games and severely cripples the Tigers' pennant hopes.

1972 — Three consecutive home runs in the first inning power the Bengals to a 5-2 win at home over New York. Tony Taylor walks to lead off the game, then Aurelio Rodriguez, Al Kaline, and Willie Horton hit home runs off Wade Blasingame, who was making his American League debut. Mickey Lolich gets win number 12.

June 28

1865 — Frank Scheibeck — B (2B 1906)

1903 — The Tigers lose to Chief Bender and the Athletics 7-3 before a crowd of 4,500 in Toledo.

1936 — Fred Gladding — B (P 1961-67)

June 28 (continued)

1938 — Orlando McFarlane — B (C 1966)

1942 — Tom Fletcher — B (P 1962)

1976 — Mark Fidrych beats the Yankees 5-1 at home, before a national television audience, touching off "Birdmania."

June 29

1888 — Bobby Veach — B (OF-C-P 1912-13)

1915 — Paul (Dizzy) Trout — B (P 1939-52)

1925 — Bill Connelly — B (P 1950)

1933 — Bob Shaw — B (P 1957-58)

1951 — Bruce Kimm — B (C 1976-77)

1968 — Jim Northrup hits his third grand slam in five days, against the White Sox, pacing a 5-2 Tiger win for Denny McLain's 14th season victory.

1972 — Catcher Bill Freehan's grand slam off Bill Lee in the ninth leads Detroit to an 8-4 win over the Red Sox in Fenway Park.

June 30

1880 — Davy Jones — B (OF 1906-11)

1935 — Tiger outfielder Pete Fox gets eight hits in a doubleheader.

1948 — Bob Lemon pitches a 2-0 no-hitter for the Indians against the Tigers in Detroit. A great catch by leftfielder Dale Mitchell of a George Kell line drive down the left field line in the third inning saves the no-hit bid.

1967 — The Tigers trade reliever Larry Sherry to Houston for outfielder Jim Landis.

JULY

July 1

1898 — Bert Cole — B (P 1921-25)

1900 — Lou Brower — B (SS-2B 1931)

1915 — Boots Poffenberger — B (P 1937-38)

1937 — Ron Nischwitz — B (P 1961-62, 1965)

1945 — Nearly 48,000 Tiger fans are on hand for slugger Hank Greenberg's return to action from World War II. Hammerin' Hank does not disappoint the crowd as he belts a home run to help the Tigers beat the Athletics 9-5.

1951 — Rapid Robert Feller of the Indians no-hits the Tigers 2–1 in the first game of a doubleheader. Although the third no-hitter of his career, it is his first before Cleveland fans. The Bengals score in the fourth when leadoff batter Johnny Lipon is safe at first on an error by shortstop Ray Boone. Lipon steals second, goes to third on an errant Feller pickoff attempt, and scores on George Kell's sacrifice fly.

1968 — Catcher Bill Freehan slugs two home runs to power the Bengals and Mickey Lolich to a 5–1 win over the Angels at home. Lolich strikes out 14 and throws a five-hitter.

1970 — Denny McLain is restored to active duty following his suspension for book-making activity. He pitches 5 1/3 innings against the Yankees before a home crowd of 53,863 but gets no decision.

1972 — Mickey Lolich gains his 13th season triumph with a 2–0 win over Baltimore in Detroit. Jim Northrup saves the game with one out in the ninth when he leaps against the left field fence to deny Dave Johnson of a home run.

July 2

1888 — Pat McGehee — B (P 1912)

1909 — Gil English — B (3B 1936–37)

1915 — Hal Wagner — B (C 1947–48)

1930 — Pete Burnside — B (P 1959–60)

1962 — Sad Sam Jones gets his first win as a Tiger by striking out 10 White Sox to win 2–1 at home. An Al Smith home run in the ninth ruins Jones's bid for a shutout. Norm Cash's homer in the sixth proves the winning margin for Jones, who has bounced back from treatment for cancer in his neck.

1973 — Following his parole from prison, Ron LeFlore signs with the Tigers.

July 3

1885 — Jack Dalton — B (OF 1916)

1906 — Luke Hamlin — B (P 1933–34)

Germany Schaefer wears a raincoat during the sixth inning of a soggy game in Cleveland.

1968 — Denny McLain wins his 15th of the year, striking out 10 in a four-hit, 5–2 win over the Angels. Home runs by Norm Cash, Willie Horton, and Dick Tracewski pace the offense.

1973 — Hurler Jim Perry faces his brother Gaylord and the Indians in Cleveland in the first brother pitching matchup in a regular season game in American League history. The Tigers win 5–4 as Gaylord absorbs the loss and Jim gets no decision. Two Norm Cash homers power the Tiger win.

47

July 4

1880 — George Mullin — B (P–OF 1902–13)

1912 — George Mullin hurls a birthday no-hitter against St. Louis and wins 7–0 at home. Mullin contributes two singles, a double, and two RBIs to his cause. In the fifth inning Ty Cobb steals second, third, and home.

1928 — Babe Birrer — B (P 1955)

1929 — Bill Tuttle — B (OF 1952, 1954–57)

1961 — Frank Lary beats the Yankees with his bat for the second time this season. A sacrifice bunt scores Steve Boros for a 4–3 win in the second game of a twin bill in New York.

1966 — Columnist Joe Falls reports in the Detroit *Free Press* that rumors are circulating that Casey Stengel will come out of retirement at age 76 to manage the Tigers. Both the team and Stengel deny the story.

1968 — The Tigers outslug the Angels 13–10 with six home runs and a nine-run second inning. Hitting for the circuit are Norm Cash (2), Jim Northrup (2), Bill Freehan, and Willie Horton.

July 5

1952 — Pitcher Fred Hutchinson is named manager, taking over the job from Red Rolfe.

1962 — Despite Rocky Colavito's three consecutive home runs and five RBIs, the Tigers still lose to the Indians 7–6 in Cleveland.

1968 — Bill Freehan slams two three-run homers in an 8–5 win over Oakland to give Mickey Lolich his 7th victory.

July 6

1891 — Steve O'Neill — B (MGR 1943–48)

1930 — Karl Olson — B (OF 1957)

1954 — Jason Thompson — B (1B 1976–80)

July 7

1883 — George Suggs — B (P 1908–09)

1884 — George Moriarty — B (3B–1B–OF–2B 1909–15, MGR 1927–28)

1926 — Mel Clark — B (OF 1957)

George Spencer — B (P 1958, 1960)

1938 — George Smith — B (2B–SS–3B 1963–65)

1968 — The Tigers reach the All-Star Game break in first place with a 9½ game lead over Cleveland after beating Oakland twice, 5-4, 7-6. In the first game, Denny McLain wins his 16th game with a five-hitter.

1978 — Shortstop Alan Trammell goes five for six against Texas in a 12-7 win at Arlington. His four singles and a double produce two RBIs.

July 8

1891 — Clyde Barfoot — B (P 1926)

1895 — Ray Crumpler — B (P 1920)

1913 — Francis (Salty) Parker — B (SS-1B 1936)

1941 — The American League wins the first All-Star Game played in Detroit 7-5 on a three-run homer by Boston's Ted Williams. The mid-year classic, which 54,674 Tigers fans turn out for, climaxes in dramatic fashion as Williams faces pitcher Claude Passeau with two out in the bottom of the ninth and slams the game-winner.

1948 — Lerrin LaGrow — B (P 1970, 1972-75)

1953 — Al Kaline gets his first Major League hit, a single off Luis Aloma of the White Sox in the eighth inning. The 18-year-old rookie had replaced centerfielder Jim Delsing in the field. The White Sox beat the Tigers in Chicago 14-4.

1972 — John Hiller returns to the active roster following his recovery from a January, 1971 heart attack.

July 9

1896 — Carl Holling — B (P 1921-22)

1897 — Glenn Myatt — B (C 1936)

1909 — Jimmy Shevlin — B (1B 1930)

1916 — Ned Harris — B (OF 1941-43, 1946)

1926 — First baseman Johnny Neun goes five for five, and steals five bases in an outstanding offensive display.

1932 — Bill Black — B (P 1952, 1955-56)

Coot Veal — B (SS-3B-2B 1958-60, 1963)

1961 — Tiger ace Frank Lary wins his 13th game of the year, with a three-hit, 1-0 shutout of the Angels. Catcher Mike Roarke singles in the lone run in the second inning, and Lary strikes out 10 in keeping the Angels at bay. The Tigers assume first place after winning the second game of the home twinbill 6-3 behind Jim Bunning.

1970 — Dalton Jones hits a grand slam against the Red Sox but is credited only with a single because he passes Don Wert between first and second base.

July 10

1868 — Bobby Lowe — B (2B–OF–SS–3B–1B 1904–07, MGR 1904)

1894 — Jim Walsh — B (P 1921)

1951 — In the second All-Star Game played in Detroit, the National League beats the junior circuit 8–3 on the strength of four home runs. Hometown favorites George Kell and Vic Wertz delight the Briggs Stadium crowd of 52,075 with home runs of their own. Tiger hurler Fred Hutchinson pitches innings five through seven, yielding three runs.

July 11

1917 — Boston's southpaw ace Babe Ruth hurls a one-hit, 1–0 victory over the Tigers, with shortstop Donie Bush getting the only hit.

1924 — Al Federoff — B (2B–SS 1951–52)

1973 — Jim Northrup drives in eight runs against Texas with two home runs, a sacrifice fly, and a fielder's choice. The game is noteworthy for the outfielder not only because he ties his own club RBI mark, but also because he gets his 500th career run and RBI.

July 12

1968 — Denny McLain spins his 17th win with a three-hit, 5–1 triumph over the Twins in Minnesota.

1979 — Detroit wins a forfeit in the second game of a double-header in Chicago following a riot by White Sox fans between games during an "anti-disco" rally.

July 13

1894 — George Cunningham — B (P–OF 1916–19, 1921)

1934 — Babe Ruth hits his 700th career home run over the right field wall off Tommy Bridges in Detroit. The third-inning homer paces the Yankees to a 4–2 win that puts them in first place.

1971 — The American League beats the National League in the annual All-Star Game in Detroit for the first time since 1962. The game is highlighted by six home runs, by Johnny Bench, Hank Aaron, Roberto Clemente, Reggie Jackson, Frank Robinson, and Harmon Killebrew. Jackson's homer is a titanic shot off Dock Ellis that would have cleared the stadium had it not struck a light tower projecting over the stands in right center field. Robinson's home run makes him the first player to hit a homer for each league in All-Star play. Hometown hero Mickey Lolich pitches the last two innings to get a save in preserving the 6–4 AL win before a crowd of 53,559.

1973 — Mickey Stanley ties the American League record with 11 putouts in center field.

1976 — Mark Fidrych starts the All-Star Game for the American League in Philadelphia. He yields two runs in the first inning and is charged with the loss in a 7–1 National League triumph.

50

July 14

1893 — John Peters — B(C 1915)

1952 — Walt Dropo goes five for five against the Yankees to begin a string of 12 consecutive hits. The five safeties are all singles.

1957 — Pitcher Bill Hoeft helps his own winning cause with two home runs and a single off the Orioles' Skinny Brown for three RBIs.

1966 — Manager Bob Swift is hospitalized with gastronenteritis. Coach Frank Skaff is named acting manager of the Tigers.

July 15

1893 — Red Oldham — B(P 1914-15, 1920-22)

1912 — Joe Rogalski — B(P 1938)

1935 — Bob Miller — B(P 1953-56)

1945 — Pitcher Zeb Eaton hits a pinch-hit home run for the Tigers.

1952 — First baseman Walt Dropo continues his hitting skein with four straight singles off the Senators' Walt Masterson to extend the streak to nine for nine. In the second game of the doubleheader, he runs the streak to 12 and goes four for five with five RBIs.

1966 — Pitcher Earl Wilson beats the Orioles 8-5 with a three-run pinch-hit homer with two out in the ninth off Stu Miller. The blast sends 43,647 Tiger fans home happy.

1973 — The Angels' Nolan Ryan hurls the second no-hitter of his career, beating the Bengals 6-0 in Detroit. He strikes out 17 Tigers and one of his victims, Norm Cash, comes to bat in the sixth inning with a table leg following two previous strikeouts.

1979 — Steve Kemp goes five for six in a 14-5 win over the White Sox. The five hits, all singles, lead to three RBIs.

July 16

1889 — Marv Peasley — B(P 1910)

Johnny Williams — B(P 1914)

1909 — The Tigers and Senators battle for 18 scoreless innings before darkness calls a halt to the longest scoreless game in American League history. Tiger hurler Ed Summers goes the distance, allowing only seven Senator hits. Both Ty Cobb and Sam Crawford go zero for seven.

1910 — Bill Norman — B(MGR 1958-59)

1914 — Don Ross — B(3B-OF-2B-SS-1B 1938, 1942-44)

51

July 16 (continued)

1954 — Jim Lentine — B (OF 1980–present)

1961 — The Bengals regain first place with 11-1, 8-3 wins at home over Kansas City. Phil Regan and Don Mossi both go the distance on the mound. In the double-header, Tiger fans are treated to home runs by Colavito (2), Cash, McAuliffe, Kaline, and Mossi.

1976 — "The Bird," Mark Fidrych, beats Oakland 1-0 in 11 innings in Detroit.

July 17

1882 — Simon Nicholls — B (SS 1903)

1889 — Guy Tutwiler — B (2B–OF–1B 1911, 1913)

1919 — Hal Erickson — B (P 1953)

1961 — Tiger great Ty Cobb succumbs to cancer in Emory University Hospital in Atlanta.

July 18

1916 — Johnny Hopp — B (OF–1B 1952)

1927 — Ty Cobb gets his 4,000th major league hit as a member of the Athletics against the Bengals at Navin Field. Cobb's double off Sam Gibson in the first inning skips off outfielder Harry Heilmann's glove for the historic hit. The Tigers go on to beat Lefty Grove 5-3.

1930 — The Tigers sell outfielder Bob Fothergill to the White Sox. Fats remains an effective utility player and pinch hitter for two more seasons before finishing with Boston in 1933.

1947 — Fred Hutchinson throws a two-hit, 8-0 shutout over the Yankees at home to end the New Yorkers' 19-game winning streak.

1969 — Willie Horton ties the league record for the most putouts in a game for an outfielder (11) and hits a two-run homer to pace Denny McLain and the Tigers to a 4-0 win over the Indians in Cleveland. For Denny, the victory is number 14 for the season.

July 19

1891 — Earl Hamilton — B (P 1916)

1902 — Mark Koenig — B (SS–2B–P–3B–OF 1930–31)

1915 — Catcher Steve O'Neill suffers the indignity of having the Senators steal eight bases in the first inning.

1955 — Relief pitcher Babe Birrer lives up to his nickname with two three-run homers.

1890 — Red McKee — B (C 1913–16)

1896 — Mutt Wilson — B (P 1920)

1901 — Heinie Manush — B (OF–1B 1923–27)

1942 — Mickey Stanley — B (OF–1B–SS–3B–2B 1964–78)

1947 — The Tigers draw their largest crowd ever, 58,369, for a doubleheader with the Yankees.

1958 — In the first game of a doubleheader, Tiger ace Jim Bunning no–hits the Red Sox 3–0 at Fenway Park. Bunning strikes out 12.

1961 — Slugger Rocky Colavito slams two home runs for five RBIs in leading the Tigers to a 15–8 win over the Orioles at home. Rocky's second homer of the day caps an eight-run outburst in the bottom of the eighth. The win vaults the Bengals back into first place.

1979 — After a stormy spring holdout and a slow start that produces a .236 batting average, Rusty Staub is traded to the Expos for cash and a player to be named. (The player to be named turns out to be minor league catcher Randy Schafer on December 3.) Staub plays sporadically for Montreal before going to Texas, where he regains his batting stroke during the 1980 season.

July 21

1878 — Pinky Lindsay — B (1B–2B–3B 1905–06)

1945 — The Tigers and Athletics battle to a 1–1 tie in 24 innings before darkness sets in to halt the game in Philadelphia. Tiger pitcher Les Mueller pitches 19 2/3 innings and Rudy York accepts 34 chances at first base to tie an American League record. Also contributing a record-tying performance is catcher Bob Swift, who catches 24 errorless innings.

1963 — Frank Lary posts his first win since June 19, 1962 with a four-hit, 8–2 win over the Angels in Los Angeles. The victory marks a remarkable comeback for Lary, who had been sent to the minors to recover from a shoulder ailment. The comeback will prove short-lived as Lary never fully regains his form.

1965 — Willie Horton pounds out five RBIs with a single, walk, and home run to lead the Tigers to a 10–5 win over the Indians in the first game of a home twin bill. The Bengals take the second game as well, 2–1, as Denny McLain twirls a three-hitter and strikes out 10. A Don Demeter homer with a man on provides the winning margin.

July 22

1905 — Doc Cramer — B (OF 1942–48)

1946 — Bill Zepp — B (P 1971)

1953 — "Prince Hal," lefty Hal Newhouser, is given his unconditional release after seven

July 22 (continued)

games with an 0–1 record and 7.06 earned run average. Newhouser returns to the majors the next season with Cleveland as a reliever, but never displays the brilliant form that won him 200 games with the Tigers.

1960 — Pitcher Bill Fischer is reacquired from the Senators in a waiver deal for pitcher Tom Morgan.

1967 — Norm Cash's four straight hits, including a grand slam, and five RBIs, power the Bengals to an 11–4 win over the Yankees at home for Earl Wilson's 12th victory.

July 23

1874 — Sport McAllister — B (C–1B–OF–2B–3B–SS 1901–03)

1889 — Lee Dressen — B (1B 1918)

1897 — Cy Fried — B (P 1920)

1905 — Boston and Detroit play the first of two straight games in Columbus, Ohio.

1909 — Against the Red Sox, Ty Cobb steals second, third, and home in succession.

1914 — Frank Croucher — B (SS–2B–3B 1939–41)

1917 — Ray Scarborough — B (P 1953)

1926 — Johnny Groth — B (OF 1946–52, 1957–60)

1948 — Phil Meeler — B (P 1972)

1961 — The Tigers beat the Athletics 17–14 in the second game of a twin bill in Kansas City in three hours, fifty-four minutes, a record time for a nine-inning game. First baseman Norm Cash tallies four hits and five RBIs while outfielder Rocky Colavito adds three hits and four RBIs to lead the Tiger attack.

1963 — The Tigers sell pitcher Tom Sturdivant to Kansas City.

July 24

1876 — Jesse Stovall — B (P 1904)

1939 — The Tigers sell outfielder Dixie Walker to the Brooklyn Dodgers on waivers. The team gave up on Walker too soon as he went on to eight seasons hitting .300 or better in the National League for the Dodgers and Pirates.

1961 — Rookie third baseman Steve Boros breaks his collarbone in a collision with pitcher Frank Lary in Kansas City. Lary is forced to leave the game, but he is not injured seriously. The break proves severe both for Boros and the Bengals. At the time of the injury Boros had 53 RBIs. None of his replacements provide the punch he did to the lineup.

July 25

1935 — Larry Sherry — B (P 1964–67)

54

1944 — Fred Scherman — B(P 1969–73)

1967 — Racial turmoil and rioting in the streets of Detroit force postponement of a game with the Orioles and the shifting of two more games slated with the O's for July 26–27 to Baltimore.

July 26

1894 — Larry Woodall — B(C 1920–29)

1917 — Jimmy Bloodworth — B(2B–SS 1942–43, 1946)

1924 — Milt Welch — B(C 1945)

1928 — The Bronx Bombers erupt for 11 runs in the 12th inning to beat the Tigers 11–0.

1948 — John Knox — B(2B–3B–DH 1972–75)

1968 — Reliever Daryl Patterson pitches four strong innings, including a strikeout of the side in the sixth, as the Tigers beat the Orioles 4–1 to increase their league lead to 6½ games.

The Tigers trade pitcher Dennis Ribant to the White Sox for veteran reliever Don McMahon. McMahon proves a valuable pickup for the stretch drive.

July 27

1883 — Harry Kane — B(P 1903)

1885 — Charley Hall — B(P 1918)

1923 — Ray Boone — B(3B–SS–1B 1953–58)

1938 — Hammerin' Hank Greenberg slugs two homers in his first two at bats to run his string of consecutive home runs to four in two days.

1958 — The Tigers send catcher Jim Hegan to the Philadelphia Phillies for cash and minor league catcher John Turk.

1968 — Denny McLain notches his 20th win with a three-hit 9–0 shutout of the Orioles in Baltimore. Homers by Willie Horton (2), Al Kaline, Don Wert, and Dick McAuliffe lead the Tiger attack.

1978 — Sweet Lou Whitaker hits his first major league home run, a two-run shot off Mariner reliever Enrique Romo, to beat Seattle 4–3 with two out in the ninth. The ball lands in the right field upper deck at Tiger Stadium. Dave Rozema gets the win for Detroit.

1980 — Earthquake tremors shake the upper deck and press box during a doubleheader at Oakland. A crowd of 44,093 is on hand for the unscheduled attraction and sees the Tigers split, winning 4–2, and losing 4–0.

July 28

1865 — Bob Wood — B(C 1904–05)

July 28 (continued)

1886 — Hank Perry — B (OF 1912)

1894 — John Glaiser — B (P 1920)

1921 — Ben Steiner — B (PR 1947)

1930 — Ted Lepcio — B (SS–2B–3B 1959)

1949 — Tiger hurler Dizzy Trout slugs a ninth-inning grand slam off the Senators' Al Gettel to aid his own cause.

1976 — Dave Roberts and the Tigers nip the Brewers 1–0 in the ninth to win at Milwaukee.

July 29

1887 — George Cutshaw — B (2B–3B 1922–23)

1911 — Roy Henshaw — B (P 1942–44)

1938 — Don Wert — B (3B–SS–2B 1963–70)

1974 — The Tigers hit a record four first-inning home runs, including three in a row, against the Indians in an 8–2 win. Al Kaline, Bill Freehan, and Mickey Stanley slam back-to-back homers off Fritz Peterson, then Eddie Brinkman connects off Steve Kline.

July 30

1922 — Joe Coleman — B (P 1955)

1930 — Gus Triandos — B (C 1963)

1938 — Hank Greenberg slugs his ninth home run in one week (July 24–30), tying the major league record set by Babe Ruth in 1930.

1964 — First baseman Bill Roman hits a home run in his first major league at bat.

1971 — The Tigers purchase reliever Ron Perranoski from Minnesota.

1977 — Pitcher Dave Roberts is traded to the Chicago Cubs for cash and a player to be named.

July 31

1870 — Joe Sugden — B (1B 1912)

1916 — Billy Hitchcock — B (SS–3B–2B 1942, 1946, 1953, MGR 1960)

1926 — Harry Malmberg — B (2B 1955)

1927 — Al Aber — B (P 1953–57)

1935 — Terry Fox — B(P 1961–66)

1949 — Fred Hutchinson and Ted Gray stymie the Athletics with 3–0, 6–0 shutouts.

1961 — The Tigers sell pitcher Bill Fischer to Kansas City.

1972 — Two-run home runs by Aurelio Rodriguez and Bill Freehan pace Mickey Lolich to his 18th win, a 5–2 triumph over Boston at home. The southpaw ace goes the distance, holding the Red Sox to seven hits.

AUGUST

August 1

1893 — Slim Love — B(P 1919–20)

1950 — Milt May — B(C 1976–79)

1974 — Woody Fryman hurls a one-hit, 2–0 shutout over the Brewers in Milwaukee. Outfielder Bobby Mitchell gets the only Brewer hit, a single, in the seventh inning.

August 2

1877 — Doc Nance — B(OF 1901)

1907 — Sam Crawford hits an inside-the-park home run to beat Washington's Walter Johnson in his big-league pitching debut.

1952 — Art James — B(OF 1975)

1959 — Jim Bunning, the Tigers' right-hand ace, strikes out the side in the ninth inning on nine pitches.

1961 — The Tigers send utilityman Ozzie Virgil to Kansas City for pitcher Gerry Staley and third baseman Reno Bertoia. This move completes a deal began July 31 when pitcher Bill Fischer was sent to the Athletics.

1970 — The Tigers acquire infielder-outfielder Kevin Collins from Montreal. Kevin plays little with the Bengals before ending his big league career at the end of the next season.

1972 — In a move that spurs the Tigers to a division title, the team obtains pitcher Woody Fryman from the Phillies. In 16 games, Woody wins 10 key victories and compiles a 2.05 ERA.

August 3

1894 — Harry Heilmann — B(OF–1B–2B 1914, 1916–29)

1920 — Jim Hegan — B(C 1958)

1958 — The Tigers purchase pitcher Hank Borowy from Pittsburgh. He produces little before finishing his big league career the next season.

1952 — Dan Meyer — B(OF–1B 1974–76)

1960 — Tiger general manager Bill DeWitt and his Indian counterpart, Frank (Trader) Lane, pull the most unusual deal in big league history—they swap managers! Jimmy Dykes heads to the Tribe, while Joe Gordon assumes the Bengal reins. Neither man has much impact on his new team, and Gordon is dropped after finishing the 1960 season with a 26–31, .456 record. First baseman Norm Cash reaches base safely six times with a homer, single, three walks, and by being hit by a pitch.

1962 — Minnesota slugger Harmon Killebrew becomes the first player to hit a home run over the left field roof in Tiger Stadium with a tremendous shot off ace Jim Bunning.

1969 — A Willie Horton grand slam off the White Sox' Dan Osinski in the bottom of the ninth beats Chicago 6–2.

August 4

1896 — Chick Galloway — B (SS–3B–1B–OF 1928)

1907 — George Caster — B (P 1945–46)

1910 — Tuck Stainback — B (OF 1940–41)

1918 — Don Kolloway — B (2B–1B–3B 1949–52)

1937 — Frank Kostro — B (3B–1B–OF 1962–63)

1938 — Ray Oyler — B (SS–2B–3B–1B 1965–68)

1941 — Pitcher Al Benton gets two sacrifice bunts in one inning for the Tigers.

1946 — Kevin Collins — B (3B–2B–OF–1B 1970–71)

1949 — Terry Humphrey — B (C 1975)

1967 — Four Tiger pinch hitters, Earl Wilson, Norm Cash, Jerry Lumpe, and Lenny Green, all strike out against the Indians in Cleveland to tie a major league record.

1972 — The Tigers aid their pennant drive with the purchase of catcher Duke Sims from the Dodgers. Sims contributes a .316 batting average and four home runs in 38 games.

1979 — Rookie hurler Mike Chris throws six no-hit innings against Kansas City in his first major league start, and he goes on to win 5–2 at home.

August 5

1899 — Sam Gibson — B (P 1926–28)

1904 — Vic Frasier — B (P 1933–34)

1929 — Second sacker Charlie Gehringer hits three triples in a game.

1932 — Tiger righthander Tommy Bridges retires the first 26 Senator batters safely before yielding a pinch-single to Dave Harris.

1956 — Dave Rozema — B (P 1977-present)

August 6

1905 — Chad Kimsey — B (P 1936)

1907 — Tom Hughes — B (OF 1930)

1924 — Van Fletcher — B (P 1955)

1926 — Clem Labine — B (P 1960)

1928 — Herb Moford — B (P 1958)

1938 — After several stormy disagreements with owner Walter Briggs, manager Mickey Cochrane resigns. Del Baker assumes the managerial duties.

1939 — Slugging first baseman Jimmy Foxx pitches the ninth inning for the Red Sox against the Tigers, giving up no hits or runs and recording one strikeout.

1952 — The Browns' 46-year old wonder, Satchell Paige, pitches a 12-inning, 1-0 masterpiece over the Tigers and Virgil Trucks.

1968 — Lefty John Hiller sets a Major League record by striking out the first six batters in a game with Cleveland.

August 7

1908 — Clyde Hatter — B (P 1935, 1937)

1915 — Les Fleming — B (OF 1939)

1927 — Art Houtteman — B (P 1945-50, 1952-53)

Rocky Bridges — B (SS-2B 1959-60)

1954 — Steve Kemp — B (OF-DH 1977-present)

1963 — The Tigers extend their team errorless streak to 12 games, an all-time Major League record, while defeating the Red Sox 5-4 at home. Al Kaline paces the victory going three for three and driving in four runs. Kaline wins the game with a three-run homer off Boston relief ace Dick Radatz in the seventh.

1972 — The Tigers release reliever Ron Perranoski, who in turn signs with Los Angeles. (He was washed up.)

1973 — The Tigers sell pitcher Joe Niekro to the Atlanta Braves. The Braves in turn give up on him after two seasons and send him to Houston, where he discovers the knuckleball and becomes a top pitcher.

1974 — As part of the decision to undertake a youth movement, the Bengals release 15-year veteran Norm Cash and sell outfielder Jim Northrup to Montreal.

August 8

1893 — Jack Smith — B (3B 1912)

1897 — Ken Holloway — B (P 1922–28)

1918 — Marlin Stuart — B (P 1949–52)

1920 — In the shortest game in American League history, one hour and thirteen minutes, Howard Ehmke pitches the Tigers to a 1–0 whitewash of the Yankees.

1936 — Frank Howard — B (1B–OF–DH 1972–73)

1945 — A screaming line drive off the bat of Hank Greenberg fractures the skull of Boston hurler Jim Wilson. Wilson comes back from the injury and manages to pitch another 11 seasons.

1980 — The Tigers steal six bases, the most ever in a game against the Rangers and their fine catcher Jim Sundberg. Running wild on the basepaths are Steve Kemp, with three steals, and Rick Peters, Al Cowens, and Lou Whitaker, with one each. The Tigers beat Texas 8–0 in this road game as Champ Summers contributes four RBIs with a two-run homer and two-run double.

August 9

1913 — Jack Tighe — B (MGR 1957–58)

1919 — Ralph Houk — B (MGR 1974–78)

1923 — George Vico — B (1B 1948–49)

1930 — Milt Bolling — B (SS–3B–2B 1958)

1946 — Gerry Moses — B (C 1974)

1948 — The Tigers draw their largest night game crowd ever with 56,586 against Cleveland.

1964 — The Tigers' first Bat Day promotion draws 46,342 for a doubleheader with Kansas City.

1969 — The Tigers sell reliever Don McMahon to the Giants.

1971 — Catcher Bill Freehan slams three home runs in a 12–11 loss to the Red Sox in Fenway Park.

1972 — In his American League debut, Woody Fryman pitches a six-hit, 6–0 shutout over the Yankees in New York.

August 10

1933 — Rocky Colavito — B (OF 1960–63)

1951 — Tiger great Charlie Gehringer is named vice president and general manager.

1953 — Tom Brookens — B (3B–2B 1979–present)

1961 — The Tigers purchase pitcher Ron Kline from the Los Angeles Angels. He pitches well down the stretch, winning five and compiling a 2.73 ERA.

1966 — Ailing manager Charlie Dressen dies at age 67 of a heart attack.

1969 — In a move that prompts sharp criticism from the pitching staff, manager Mayo Smith fires pitching coach Johnny Sain after several disagreements.

August 11

1907 — Bobo Newsom — B (P 1939–41)

1915 — Bob Scheffing — B (MGR 1961–63)

1936 — Bill Monbouquette — B (P 1966–67)

1942 — The first game of a twi-nighter with the Indians in Cleveland ends in a fourteen-inning scoreless tie. The rules said the game could not be continued under the lights. Tiger ace Tommy Bridges and the Tribe's Al Milnar locked horns in a pitching duel. Milnar had a no-hitter going with two out in the ninth when outfielder Doc Cramer singled to right field.

1959 — Al Kaline gets the 1,000th hit of his career, a single off the White Sox' Ken McBride in the seventh inning of an 8–1 Tiger win.

1968 — Pinch hitter extraordinaire Gates Brown belts a homer with two out in the 14th to beat Boston 5–4, then singles to cap a four-run rally in the ninth inning of the second game to beat Boston 6–5 before 49,087 delirious Tiger fans.

August 12

1877 — Bill Coughlin — B (3B 1904–08)

1887 — Marc Hall — B (P 1913–14)

1919 — Fred Hutchinson — B (P–1B 1939–41, 1946–53, MGR 1952–54)

1945 — In his Tiger debut before a home crowd of 55,000, pitcher Jim Tobin pitches three strong innings in relief and hits a three-run homer in the 11th to beat the Yankees 9–6.

1965 — Outfielder Don Demeter knocks in seven runs with a single, two-run triple, and grand slam in an 11–1 romp over the Athletics at home. Hank Aguirre strikes out 10 Kansas City batters in pitching a four-hitter.

1980 — Mark Fidrych returns once more to the big leagues for a comeback. He pitches eight innings, giving up 11 hits and 5 runs in a 5–4 loss to the Red Sox before a home crowd of 48,361.

August 13

1908 — George Susce — B (C 1932)

1969 — Denny McLain posts his eighth season shutout, tying Hal Newhouser's club record, while beating the Angels 3–0 at home for his 18th season victory. A Jim Northrup homer leads the Tiger offense.

1972 — Hoping to break a four-game losing streak, manager Billy Martin pulls the Tiger batting order out of a hat and the team beats Cleveland 3–2 in the first game of a twin bill at home. The successful batting order is: Cash 1B, Northrup RF, Horton LF, Brinkman SS, Taylor 2B, Sims C, Stanley CF, Rodriguez 3B, and Fryman P. With a regular batting order, the Tigers lose the second game 9–2.

August 14

1899 — Kyle Graham — B (P 1929)

1929 — On Charlie Gehringer Day in Detroit, the guest of honor hits three singles, a home run, and steals home.

1937 — The Tigers score 36 runs in a doubleheader with the St. Louis Browns, a Major League offensive record.

1952 — Completing a complicated waiver deal, the Bengals send first baseman Vic Wertz, outfielder Don Lenhardt, and pitchers Dick Littlefield and Marlin Stuart to the St. Louis Browns for outfielder Jim Delsing and pitchers Ned Garver, Dave Madison, and Bud Black. The transfer of Black, Stuart, and Lenhardt takes place August 11, Littlefield on August 13.

August 15

1872 — John Warner — B (C 1905–06)

1887 — Joe Casey — B (C 1909–11)

1926 — Barney Schultz — B (P 1959)

1940 — Arlo Brunsberg — B (C 1966)

1945 — Duffy Dyer — B (C 1980–present)

August 16

1890 — Baby Doll Jacobson — B (1B–OF 1915)

1897 — Bob Fothergill — B (OF 1922–30)

1900 — Billy Rhiel — B (3B–1B–OF–2B 1932–33)

1902 — Toledo native George Mullin delights 6,000 hometown fans by pitching Detroit to a 12–8 win over New York in a game played in Toledo. Sam Crawford has five hits, including two doubles and a triple.

1968 — Denny McLain extends his road record to 16-0 and wins his 25th victory with a seven-hit, 4-0 shutout of the Red Sox in Fenway Park.

1975 — Pitcher Ray Bare breaks a 19-game Tiger losing streak with a two-hit, 8-0 shutout of the Angels in Anaheim.

1978 — Reliever Steve Foucault is sold to the Royals.

August 17

1883 — Walt Justis — B (P 1905)

1906 — Hub Walker — B (OF 1931, 1935, 1945)

1910 — Pat McLaughlin — B (P 1937, 1945)

1913 — Rudy York — B (1B-C-OF-3B 1934, 1937-45)

1940 — Red Sox slugger Ted Williams blasts Boston fans and sportswriters: he asks to be traded to Detroit.

1950 — Dave Lemanczyk — B (P 1973-76)

1967 — The Tigers obtain third baseman Eddie Mathews from Houston for a player to be named (pitcher Fred Gladding is sent November 22). Although nearing the end of a Hall of Fame career, Mathews contributes greatly to the Tigers' 1968 pennant effort with his leadership.

1968 — A Bill Freehan homer with two out in the 11th leads Detroit to a 10-9 win over the Red Sox in Boston. Norm Cash belts five hits and drives in five runs in the Tiger victory.

1969 — The Tigers pound 6 home runs to tie the club record as McLain notches his 19th win in beating the A's in Oakland 9-4. Hitting for the circuit are Al Kaline (2), Mickey Stanley, Don Wert, Tom Tresh, and Jim Northrup.

1973 — The Tigers release first baseman Rich Reese, who then signs with the Twins. He was finished at age 31.

1980 — Between games of a doubleheader at home with Texas, the Tigers retire Al Kaline's number 6, the first such Tiger to be honored.

August 18

1920 — Bob Kennedy — B (3B-OF 1956)

1935 — Bob Humphreys — B (P 1962)

1964 — Southpaw Mickey Lolich notches his 13th win with a three-hit, 1-0 shutout of the Angels, striking out 10 in the second game of a home twin bill.

1972 — Mickey Lolich pitches the Tigers back into first place over the Orioles with a 2-0 whitewash of the Angels at home. Lolich outduels Nolan Ryan to gain his 19th win.

1977 — First sacker Jason Thompson belts a homer over the right field roof of Tiger Stadium off Catfish Hunter of the Yankees.

August 19

1921 — Ty Cobb gets his 3,000th hit at age 34, the youngest player ever to reach that level.

1928 — Jim Finigan — B (3B–2B 1957)

1938 — Shortstop Billy Rogell draws his seventh consecutive base on balls.

1941 — Fred Lasher — B (P 1967–70)

1951 — St. Louis owner Bill Veeck pulls his most famous and outrageous stunt, sending 3-foot, 7-inch midget Eddie Gaedel in as a pinch hitter for Frank Saucier in a game with the Tigers. Gaedel walked on four straight pitches from Tiger hurler Bob Cain.

August 20

1889 — Ross Reynolds — B (P 1914–15)

1907 — Beau Bell — B (OF 1939)

1919 — Earl Harrist — B (P 1953)

1924 — George Zuverink — B (P 1954–55)

1964 — The Tigers get their smallest crowd ever for a night game, 2,173, against the Angels.

1967 — John Hiller hurls a four-hit shutout, 4–0 win over Cleveland in his first Major League start in the second game of a doubleheader at home. Willie Horton and Al Kaline homers lead the Tiger offense. The Tigers win the first game too, 4–2, as Denny McLain gets his 16th win with the aid of a Kaline homer.

1968 — Southpaw John Hiller throws a one-hit, 7–0 win over the White Sox in the first game of a doubleheader. A single by Ron Hansen in the fifth inning is the only hit he gives up.

1974 — Despite a 19-strikeout performance, Nolan Ryan loses to the Tigers 1–0 in 11 innings at Anaheim Stadium.

1980 — Third baseman Tom Brookens goes five for five and starts a triple play to lead the Tigers to an 8–6 win over the Brewers. Brookens hits three singles, a triple, and a two-run homer in his perfect day at the plate. He also adds a stolen base to the offense. John Wockenfuss and Lance Parrish also homer in the win, which is Gerry Ujdur's first Major League victory.

August 21

1920 — Gerry Staley — B (P 1961)

1968 — Catcher Jim Price slugs a pinch hit home run in the 10th inning to beat the White Sox 3–2.

August 22

1888 — Al Bashang — B (OF 1912)

Bun Troy — B (P 1912)

1889 — Wally Schang — B (C 1931)

1968 — A Tommy John pitch at Dick McAuliffe's head precipitates a brawl between the Tigers and White Sox. John receives a torn ligament in his pitching shoulder as he is wrestled to the ground by McAuliffe, who is given a five-day suspension from the league office, as well as a $250 fine.

1978 — Speedy outfielder Ron LeFlore establishes a new American League record with his 27th consecutive stolen base. He began the streak on July 16.

August 23

1883 — Red Downs — B (2B–OF–SS–3B 1907–08)

1890 — Heinie Elder — B (P 1913)

1905 — Phil Page — B (P 1928–30)

1922 — George Kell — B (3B 1946–52)

1968 — The Tigers and Yankees play a 3–3, nineteen-inning tie in New York. The game is suspended due to curfew.

August 24

1912 — Frank Secory — B (PH 1940)

1932 — Hal Woodeshick — B (P 1956, 1961)

1940 — Ted Williams pitches the eighth and ninth innings for Boston against Detroit in Fenway Park. He allows three hits, and one run, but strikes out Rudy York on three pitches. The Bengals win 12–1 behind a strong effort by Tommy Bridges.

August 25

1952 — Virgil Trucks hurls his second no-hitter of the season, a 1–0 whitewash of New York in Yankee Stadium. The sterling performance lays to rest, at least temporarily, trade rumors involving Trucks.

August 26

1934 — Schoolboy Rowe wins his 16th straight game, tying the league record shared by Walter Johnson, Smokey Joe Wood, and Lefty Grove. He beats the Senators 4–2, driving in the winning run in the top of the 9th with a single.

1975 — The Tigers sell pitcher Bob Reynolds to Cleveland.

August 27

1885 — Baldy Louden — B (2B–SS–3B–OF 1912–13)

1935 — Em Lindbeck — B (PH 1960)

1961 — Outfielder Rocky Colavito hits three home runs in the second game of a doubleheader against the Senators in Washington as the Tigers win 10–1. He also slugs a homer in the first game as the Tigers win 7–4.

1972 — Tiger hurler Joe Coleman goes 11 innings to beat Minnesota in the second game of a doubleheader, 1–0. An Aurelio Rodriguez home run proves the winning margin. The Tigers also win the front game in the 11th inning as Willie Horton hits a homer for a 5–3 win. These two wins mark the second and third wins in a row in the 11th inning on a home run. Rodriguez had won the first game of the streak.

August 28

1875 — Joe Yeager — B (3B–P–SS–2B–OF 1901–03)

1969 — Jim Northrup goes six for six in a 5–3 win over the A's, banging out four singles and two homers.

1970 — Denny McLain runs afoul of team management once more by dousing two sportswriters, Jim Hawkins of the *Free Press* and Watson Spoelstra of the *News,* with buckets of ice water. General manager Jim Campbell immediately suspends McLain for seven days and fines him $500 per day.

August 29

1903 — Jack Warner — B (3B–SS 1925–28)

1909 — Buck Marrow — B (P 1932)

1918 — Joe Schultz — B (MGR 1973)

1924 — Wayne McLeland — B (P 1951–52)

1928 — Mickey McDermott — B (P 1958)

1934 — Philadelphia beats Schoolboy Rowe and the Tigers 13–5, ending his bid for his 17th straight win.

1947 — Pitcher Fred Hutchinson steals home after tripling in the 3rd inning of a game with the Browns. When Brown hurler Ellis Kinder takes a big windup, Hutch breaks for home and scores. He also singles in the 5–4 victory.

1948 — Star third baseman George Kell suffers a fractured lower jaw when struck by a line drive off the bat of Joe DiMaggio, his second serious injury of the campaign.

1966 — Denny McLain throws an unbelievable 229 pitches in struggling to a 6–3 win over the Orioles. McLain gives up 8 hits and walks 9, but strikes out 11 in winning his 16th game.

1967 — The Tigers remain in the thick of the pennant race with 4–2, 2–1 wins over the Angels in Anaheim behind the pitching of Denny McLain and John Hiller.

August 30

1891 — Steve Partenheimer — B(3B 1913)

1892 — Pol Perritt — B(P 1921)

1905 — Ty Cobb hits a two-run double off Jack Chesbro of the Yankees in his first big-league at bat as the Tigers win 5–3.

1912 — Earl Hamilton of the St. Louis Browns no–hits the Tigers 5–1 in Detroit.

1956 — Steve Baker — B(P 1978–79)

1968 — A crowd of 53,575 Tiger fans watch Earl Wilson put on a one-man show as he pitches a four-hitter and gets two hits and four RBIs to beat Baltimore 9–1. One of Wilson's two hits is his fifth homer of the season.

1979 — Mark Fidrych's personal caddy, catcher Bruce Kimm, is sold to the Chicago Cubs.

August 31

1907 — Jack Burns — B(1B 1936)

1931 — The Tigers trade third baseman Marty McManus to the Red Sox for catcher Muddy Ruel. Boston gets the better of the deal as McManus serves as third baseman-playing manager in 1933.

1937 — Slugging Rudy York hits his 17th and 18th home runs of the month, setting a new record for the most homers in a month. His two homers and seven RBIs off Washington's Pete Appleton lead the Tigers to a 12–3 home win.

1960 — The Tigers purchase first sacker Dick Gernert from the Cubs.

1968 — Pirate relief ace Elroy Face is bought by Detroit. Roy makes just two appearances for the Tigers before being sold to Montreal the next year.

1972 — The Tigers buy slugger Frank Howard from Texas. Hondo plays one more season with Detroit, hitting 12 homers in a part-time role.

SEPTEMBER

September 1

1876 — Jimmy Wiggs — B(P 1905–06)

1894 — Fred Nicholson — B(OF 1917)

1917 — Paul Campbell — B(1B 1948–50)

1918 — Ty Cobb pitches two innings in relief against the Browns while Brown superstar George Sisler hurls one scoreless inning in a 6-2 St. Louis win. Sisler hits a double off Cobb.

67

September 1 (continued)

1949 — Gary Ignasiak — B(P 1973)

1968 — Denny McLain wins his 27th game of the year with a 7–3 victory over the Orioles. His excellent fielding pays off when he starts a triple play in the third inning.

1970 — The Tigers stun Red Sox fans when they rally to beat Boston in Fenway Park 10-9 after trailing 8–1.

1980 — Al Cowens and White Sox' relief ace Ed Farmer end their year-long feud by shaking hands during the exchange of lineups before the game in Detroit, drawing a standing ovation from the crowd.

September 2

1880 — Fred Payne — B(C–OF 1906–08)

1943 — Luke Walker — B(P 1974)

1969 — The Tigers purchase shortstop Cesar Gutierrez from San Francisco.

1970 — In his first major league at bat, catcher Gene Lamont hits a homer against the Red Sox in Fenway Park.

1972 — Tiger 11th-inning magic strikes again as Bill Freehan and Mickey Stanley homer to beat the A's 3–1 in Oakland. The win snaps a four-game losing streak for the Bengals. Southpaw Mickey Lolich fails in his fifth bid to win his 20th game.

1973 — The Tigers fire fiery manager Billy Martin and replace him with coach Joe Schultz for the remainder of the season. The firing comes on the heels of a three-day league suspension of Martin for publicly admitting he ordered pitchers Joe Coleman and Fred Scherman to throw spitballs against the Indians in retaliation against Gaylord Perry.

1980 — Mark Fidrych gains his first win since 1978 with a seven-hit, complete game 11–2 win over the White Sox in the first game of a twin bill at home. Home runs by Champ Summers, Alan Trammell, and Tim Corcoran power the Bird to his win. Milt Wilcox pitches the Bengals to a 6–1 win in the second game.

September 3

1869 — Bill Armour — B(MGR 1905–06)

1902 — Bill Moore — B(P 1925)

1936 — Steve Boros — B(3B–SS–2B 1957–58, 1961–62)

1947 — Bill Gilbreth — B(P 1971–72)

1961 — The Yankees beat the Bengals 8–5 to sweep a key three-game series, crushing Tiger flag hopes. The wins put the New Yorkers out in front by 4½ games.

Slugger Mickey Mantle paces the win with two home runs, numbers 49 and 50, at Yankee Stadium.

1967 — The Tigers remain ½ game behind the league-leading Twins with a 5–0 Earl Wilson shutout before 43,494, the largest Twin crowd ever. Wilson's win is his 19th.

September 4

1887 — Red Corriden — B (3B–2B–SS 1912)

1913 — Cleveland's Vean Gregg fans Ty Cobb the first three times he faces him.

1949 — Paul Jata — B (1B–OF–C 1972)

September 5

1876 — Pete LePine — B (OF–1B 1902)

1900 — Merv Shea — B (C 1927–29, 1939)

1915 — Bob Maier — B (3B–OF 1945)

The Tigers beat St. Louis 6–5 as George Sisler pitches a complete game in a losing effort.

1920 — Gene Bearden — B (P 1951)

1967 — Joe Sparma hurls a two-hit, 4–0 whitewash over Kansas City at home for his 14th win and fifth shutout.

September 6

1905 — Chicago's Frank Smith pitches a 15–0 no-hitter against the Tigers in Detroit, the first no-hit game ever played there.

1921 — Jack Phillips — B (1B–3B–OF–2B 1955–57)

1967 — Earl Wilson becomes the season's first 20-game winner with a 6–3 win over Kansas City in Detroit in the second game of a doubleheader. In the first game, Eddie Mathews slugs two home runs for three RBIs.

1968 — Denny McLain racks up his 28th win, striking out 12 and yielding 9 hits in an 8–3 win over Minnesota. Willie Horton paces the Tiger attack with five RBIs on a double and his 32nd homer of the year.

1972 — Mickey Lolich wins his 20th game with the aid of reliever Chuck Seelbach, beating the Orioles in Baltimore 4–3.

The Tigers sell pitcher Bill Gilbreth to California.

September 7

1943 — Tommy Matchick — B (SS–2B–3B–1B 1967–69)

69

September 7 (continued)

1950 — Outfielder Hoot Evers hits for the cycle in a ten-inning tie with Cleveland in Detroit.

1971 — Jim Northrup goes five for five, with two homers and two RBIs, in a 3–2 eleven-inning win over the Senators in Washington.

1977 — In the second start of his career, catcher Lance Parrish walks, singles, and doubles with the bases loaded, and homers in a 12–5 win over Baltimore.

September 8

1926 — Lou Sleater — B (P 1957–58)

1932 — Casey Wise — B (2B–SS–3B 1960)

1949 — The Tigers play their first day-night doubleheader and beat Cleveland twice.

1961 — The Tigers obtain first baseman Vic Wertz from Boston for cash and a player to be named.

1967 — The Tigers move into a first place tie with the Twins with a 4-1 win in Chicago. Homers by Eddie Mathews and Jim Northrup lead the attack.

September 9

1872 — John Eubank — B (P 1905–07)

1899 — Waite Hoyt — B (P 1930–31)

1910 — Bud Thomas — B (P 1939–41)

1935 — Jim Proctor — B (P 1959)

1949 — Reggie Sanders — B (1B–DH 1974)

1959 — Al Kaline beats the Red Sox 3–1 with a home run, belting his 10th homer of the year against the Red Sox.

1967 — The Tigers explode for seven runs in the ninth to beat the White Sox 7–3 in Comiskey Park and stay in a first place tie with Minnesota. Catcher Bill Freehan is hit by a pitch from Chicago's Roger Nelson, the 18th time of the year for the Tiger catcher, breaking the 1924 club record set by Heinie Manush.

1970 — Trouble-plagued hurler Denny McLain is suspended for the third time in the season by Commissioner Kuhn for carrying a gun and breaking his probationary status. The suspension holds till the end of the season.

September 10

1896 — Sammy Hale — B (3B–OF–2B 1920–21)

1899 — Augie Johns — B (P 1926–27)

1959 — Bruce Robbins — B (P 1979–present)

1961 — More than 8,000 fans turn out at the airport to greet the Tigers following a disastrous road trip in which the Bengals lost nine of ten.

1967 — Joel Horlen of the White Sox no-hits the Tigers 6–0 in the first game of a twin bill in Detroit.

1968 — Denny McLain gains his 29th victory and aids his own cause with a triple, two singles and two RBIs in a 7–2 win over the Angels. He gives up 9 hits but strikes out 12.

September 11

1914 — Clay Smith — B(P 1940)

1944 — Dave Roberts — B(P 1976–77)

1958 — Reliever Bill Fischer is sold to Washington on waivers.

September 12

1880 — Boss Schmidt — B(C–OF 1906–11)

1891 — Pepper Peploski — B(3B 1913)

1894 — Arthur Olsen — B(P 1922–23)

1919 — Charlie Keller — B(OF 1950–51)

1926 — George Freese — B(PH 1953)

1940 — Mickey Lolich — B(P 1963–75)

1961 — Frank Lary notches his 20th win with a five-hit, 3–1 triumph at home over Kansas City.

1980 — Mark Fidrych leaves the mound after throwing only six pitches, complaining of shoulder pain. The Tigers go on to beat the Indians 6–3 in Cleveland behind the solid pitching of Roger Weaver and Aurelio Lopez.

September 13

1931 — George Susce — B(P 1958–59)

1969 — Willie Horton slugs his third grand slam of the season, the blast coming off Dennis Higgins in a losing battle with Washington.

1974 — John Hiller gains his 17th win, breaking the American League record of 16 for relievers set in 1964 by Boston's Dick Radatz. The Tigers beat the Brewers 9–7 as shortstop Tom Veryzer belts a two-run homer into the left field upper deck in the bottom of the 10th off Tom Murphy.

September 14

1912 — Icehouse Wilson — B(PH 1934)

September 14 (continued)

1947 — Outfielder Vic Wertz hits for the cycle against the Senators in the first game of a twin bill in Washington.

1968 — Denny McLain becomes the majors' first 30-game winner since Dizzy Dean in 1934, beating Oakland 5-4 with a six-hitter and 10 strikeouts. The Tigers rallied for two runs in the bottom of the 9th to win, as Willie Horton singled in Mickey Stanley with the game-winner.

September 15

1901 — Detroit wallops Cleveland 21-0 at home in the most lopsided victory in Tiger history. Because the game is the second in a doubleheader, it is called after 7½ innings to permit the Tribe to catch a train. Pitcher Ed Siever is the beneficiary of the offensive explosion.

1968 — Five Tiger home runs crush Oakland 13-0 as southpaw Mickey Lolich hurls a three-hitter and strikes out 12. Providing the power are Jim Northrup (2), Bill Freehan (2), and Willie Horton.

1969 — Denny McLain sets a new club record with his 9th shutout of the season, a 2-0 win over New York in Yankee Stadium.

September 16

1915 — Ty Cobb loses his temper and throws his bat at Boston hurler Carl Mays after a close pitch. Fenway Park fans are so riled by Cobb's action that the police have to give him an escort from the field.

1928 — Vito Valentinetti — B (P 1958)

1968 — First baseman Norm Cash drives in five runs to lead the Bengals to a 9-1 win over the Yankees. Cash supplies the offense with a double, single, and home run as southpaw John Hiller goes the distance to win his 9th of the year.

September 17

1888 — Jean Dubuc — B (P-OF 1912-16)

1898 — Earl Webb — B (OF-1B 1932-33)

1913 — Bob Uhle — B (P 1940)

1920 — Outfielder Bobby Veach hits for the cycle, going six for six in a twelve-inning game against the Red Sox in Detroit.

1933 — Chuck Daniel — B (P 1957)

1968 — The Tigers clinch their first pennant since 1945 with a 2-1 win over New York at home. Joe Sparma goes the distance with a five-hitter for the win. The key hit is a Don Wert single with the bases loaded and two out in the bottom of the 9th.

1977 — First baseman Jason Thompson hits the second home run over the right field roof in Detroit in his career off Dick Tidrow of the Yankees.

72

1972 — Second baseman Dick McAuliffe hits two homers and drives in four runs to pace the Bengals to a 6–2 triumph over the Brewers in Milwaukee to keep Detroit within one percentage point of division-leading Boston. Joe Coleman throws a six-hitter for his 17th win and the team's fifth win in a row.

September 18

1898 — George Uhle — B (P 1929–33)

1966 — Three Cleveland pitchers (Sam McDowell, John O'Donoghue, and Luis Tiant) strike out 19 Tigers in nine innings and a total of 21 in a 6–5 ten-inning Tiger loss at home. Tiger hurlers record 10 strikeouts of their own.

September 19

1890 — Ralph Young — B (2B–SS–3B 1915–21)

1909 — Frank Reiber — B (C–OF 1933–36)

1931 — Ron Shoop — B (C 1959)

1944 — Russ Nagelson — B (OF–1B 1970)

September 20

1898 — Chuck Dressen — B (MGR 1963–66)

1902 — Jimmy Callahan of the White Sox pitches a 3–0, no-hitter against Detroit in Chicago.

1912 — The Tigers end the 16–game winning streak of Boston's Smokey Joe Wood with a 6–4 triumph in Fenway Park.

1915 — Tiger pennant hopes fade as Boston wins the third of a four-game set.

1937 — Tom Tresh — B (SS–OF–3B 1969)

1941 — Dennis Ribant — B (P 1968)

1962 — Al Kaline gets his 1,500th hit, a two-run homer off Minnesota southpaw Jim Kaat in the fifth inning of a 5–1 Tiger win at home.

1965 — Indian second baseman Pedro Gonzalez goes after Tiger reliever Larry Sherry with a bat following a brushback pitch in the fifth inning. When play resumes after a brief brawl, the Tigers lose 5–4 in 14 innings of a four-hour, 58-minute game. Gonzalez is fined $500 for his action and suspended for the rest of the season.

1980 — Steve Kemp gets six RBIs with a grand slam and a two-run triple as the Tigers pound Cleveland 13–3 at home.

September 21

1875 — Frank McManus — B (C 1904)

1900 — John Bogart — B (P 1920)

1910 — Eldon Auker — B (P 1933–38)

1921 — John McHale — B (1B 1943–45, 1947–48)

1946 — The Tigers beat Cleveland 5–3 in the last game played at the Indians' League Park.

1954 — Frank MacCormack — B (P 1976)

1972 — The Tigers move into a virtual tie for first place with the Red Sox with a 10–3 win in Boston. Joe Coleman wins his 18th with a seven-hitter, striking out 10 and driving in three runs.

September 22

1889 — George Dauss — B (P 1912–26)

1893 — Ira Flagstead — B (OF–SS–2B–3B 1917, 1919–23)

1894 — Frank Walker — B (OF 1917–18)

1903 — Chuck Hostetler — B (OF 1944–45)

1908 — Tiger hurler George Mullin wins both games of a doubleheader with the Senators, 5–3, 4–3.

1917 — Anse Moore — B (OF 1946)

1936 — Eldon Auker and Tommy Bridges score the biggest double shutout win ever with 12–0 and 4–0 triumphs over the St. Louis Browns.

1967 — The Tigers sweep a doubleheader from Washington on the road, 8–3 and 4–0, to stay one game behind the league-leading Twins. In game one, Earl Wilson notches his 22nd win, while in the second Mickey Lolich throws a four-hitter to win his 12th.

1973 — John Hiller gets his record 38th save by pitching 3 2/3 scoreless innings in a 5–1 Tiger win over the Red Sox in Detroit.

1977 — The Tigers sell outfielder Bob Molinaro to the White Sox.

September 23

1889 — Biff Schaller — B (OF–1B 1911)

1900 — Lefty Stewart — B (P 1921)

1942 — Jim Rooker — B (P 1968)

1973 — Joe Coleman hurls a one-hit, 3–0 win over the Red Sox. The only Boston hit comes in the fifth when catcher Bob Montgomery singles.

The Tigers sell relief pitcher Bob Miller to the Mets.

September 24

1893 — Joe Sargent — B (2B–3B–SS 1921)

1910 — Dixie Walker — B (OF 1938–39)

1911 — Tom Seats — B (P 1940)

1928 — The Tigers draw their smallest crowd ever, 404, for a game with Boston.

1963 — Don Wert's solo homer gives Jim Bunning and the Bengals a 1–0 victory over Claude Osteen and the Washington Senators.

1965 — The Tigers observe their 10,000th American League game with ceremonies honoring outfielder Davy Jones, sportswriter E. A. Batchelor, and grounds crew member Gilbert Claeys. The Tigers lose in 10 innings to Cleveland, 3-2.

1973 — The Tigers sell catcher Duke Sims to the New York Yankees.

1974 — Al Kaline enters one of baseball's most select circles, the 3,000 hit club, with a double down the right field line off the Orioles' Dave McNally in the fourth inning of a game in Baltimore.

September 25

1872 — Dick Harley — B (OF 1902)

1908 — Ed Summers pitches two complete game wins over Philadelphia, 7–2 and 1–0. The second game is a ten-inning two-hitter.

1940 — Bobo Newsom wins both games of a doubleheader with the White Sox by hurling two innings in relief in one game and going the distance in the other.

1953 — Ed Putman — B (C–1B 1979)

1955 — Although hitless in one at bat before leaving the game after two innings with a sore wrist, Al Kaline becomes the youngest (20) American League batting champion ever, with a .340 average. The Tigers end their season with a 6–2 win over the Indians.

1967 — A 2–0 shutout by lefty Al Downing of the Yankees is a big setback in the Tigers' pennant drive.

1977 — The Tigers get 18 hits off Boston's Reggie Cleveland but still manage to lose at home 12-5.

September 26

1903 — Outfielder Billy Lush gets three triples in one game.

1910 — Joe Sullivan — B (P 1935–36)

1926 — Bob (Fats) Fothergill hits for the cycle against Boston in Detroit.

1935 — Walt Streuli — B (C 1954–56)

1947 — Norm McRae — B (P 1969–70)

1948 — The Tigers draw their biggest crowd in history, 57,888, against the Indians.

1953 — Rookie Al Kaline hits his first major league home run off Dave Hoskins in Cleveland.

1966 — Denny McLain wins his 20th game with a 2–1 triumph over the Angels in Anaheim. A Gates Brown pinch single drives in the winning run in the 9th.

September 27

1878 — Cy Ferry — B (P 1904)

1890 — Frank Gibson — B (C–OF 1913)

1897 — Chick Gagnon — B (SS–3B 1922)

1907 — Haskell Billings — B (P 1927–29)

Whitlow Wyatt — B (P 1929–33)

1912 — Tiger pitcher Charlie Wheatley throws five wild pitches in a game.

1919 — Johnny Pesky — B (SS–3B–2B 1952–54)

1933 — Manager Bucky Harris resigns, with Del Baker assuming the reins for the remaining two games.

Jerry Casale — B (P 1961–62)

1935 — Dave Wickersham — B (P 1964–67)

1938 — In the nightcap of a twin bill with the Browns, Hank Greenberg hits his 57th and 58th homers of the year. The Tigers win both games, 5–4, 10–2. Greenberg's 58th homer is a controversial inside-the-park hit that involves a close play at home plate.

1940 — The Tigers clinch the pennant as Floyd Giebell throws a six-hit, 2–0 whitewash over Bob Feller and the Indians in Cleveland. The Bengals score on a Rudy York home run that travels 320 feet down the left field line. The Cleveland crowd of 45,553 is unruly, pelting the Tigers with fruit, vegetables, and eggs. Tiger catcher Birdie Tebetts is forced to leave the game after being hit with a basket of green tomatoes thrown from the upper deck.

1944 — Gary Sutherland — B (2B–SS–3B–1B–DH 1974–76)

1972 — Trailing 5–1, the Tigers rally for three runs in the eighth and two more in the bottom of the ninth to beat the Yankees and Sparky Lyle. Duke Sims singles in the winning run.

September 28

1905 — Paul Easterling — B (OF 1928, 1930)

1928 — Dick Gernert — B (1B–OF 1960–61)

1935 — Bob Dustal — B (P 1963)

September 29

1901 — Tony Rensa — B (C 1930)

1928 — The Tigers pound out 28 hits in a 19–10 win over the Yankees. Combined with 17 Yankee hits, the 45-hit total for a nine-inning game is an American League record.

1935 — Bob Anderson — B (P 1963)

1941 — Rich Reese — B (1B–OF 1973)

1950 — Jim Crawford — B (P 1976–78)

1972 — Jim Northrup goes four for four and drives in five runs with a double and two singles in a 12–5 home win over the Brewers.

September 30

1907 — The Tigers and Athletics play a 9–9, 17-inning tie in Philadelphia that breaks the A's pennant drive. Ty Cobb ties the game at 8–8 in the top of the 9th with a home run off Rube Waddell. Then in the 11th inning, his double puts the Tigers ahead, but the Athletics rally to tie. A crowd of 24,000 watches the showdown, the largest crowd yet for a regular season game.

1913 — Frank Skaff — B (MGR 1966)

1924 — Bennie Taylor — B (1B 1952)

1932 — Johnny Podres — B (P 1966–67)

1945 — The Tigers win their seventh American League pennant when Hank Greenberg slugs a grand slam in the 9th to beat the Browns in St. Louis, 6–3.

1949 — Ike Blessitt — B (OF 1972)

1953 — Dan Gonzales — B (OF 1979–80)

1968 — The Tigers sell pitcher Jim Rooker to the New York Yankees.

1972 — The Tigers pound 16 hits for the second night in a row to beat the Brewers 13–4 at home. Al Kaline leads the attack with four hits, including a double and homer, and two RBIs. Joe Coleman notches his 19th win with the aid of Chuck Seelbach's 13th save.

1973 — The Tigers win the last game played in the old Yankee Stadium 8–5, with John Hiller getting the win in relief.

1907 DETROIT TIGERS

Front Row — Siever, Archer, Jennings (manager), Schmidt, O'Leary
Middle Row — D. Jones, Downs, Cobb, Coughlin, Schaefer, B. Jones
Back Row — Eubank, Rossman, Crawford, Donovan, Mullin, Willett, Payne, Killian

1908 DETROIT TIGERS

Front Row — McIntyre, Malloy, D. Jones, Suggs, Schmidt, Killefer
Middle Row — Schaefer, Donovan, Winter, Navin (president), Jennings (manager), Coughlin, O'Leary, Bush, Cobb
Back Row — Tuthill (trainer), Stanage, Killian, Downs, Thomas, Rossman, Summers, Willett, Crawford, Mullin

1909 DETROIT TIGERS

Front Row — Tuthill (trainer), Lelivelt, Donovan, Works, McIntyre, Beckendorf, Speer
Middle Row — Delahanty, T. Jones, Killian, D. Jones, Jennings (manager), Moriarty, O'Leary, Bush
Back Row — Summers, Schmidt, Stanage, Gainor, Willett, Crawford, Cobb, Mullin

1934 DETROIT TIGERS

Front Row — Fischer, Greenberg, batboy, Clifton, Baker (coach), Cochrane (manager), Perkins (coach), Goslin
Middle Row — Owen, Doljack, Hayworth, Rogell, White, Auker, Gehringer, Fox
Back Row — Marberry, Carroll (trainer), G. Walker, Rowe, Hamlin, Hogsett, Bridges, Sorrell, Schuble

1935 DETROIT TIGERS

Front Row — Fox, Gehringer, Baker (coach), Cochrane (manager), Perkins (coach), White, Greenberg, Roggins (batboy)
Middle Row — Goslin, Rogell, Owen, Hayworth, Crowder, Auker, Rowe, Clifton
Back Row — Schuble, Reiber, Carroll (trainer), Hogsett, G. Walker, unidentified, Bridges, Sorrell

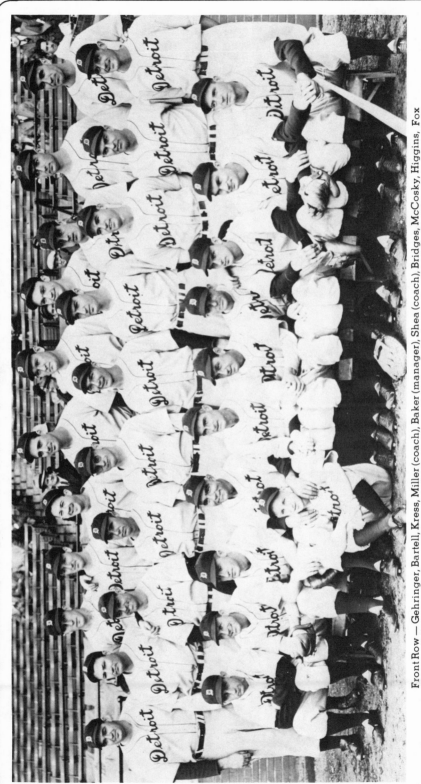

Front Row — Gehringer, Bartell, Kress, Miller (coach), Baker (manager), Shea (coach), Bridges, McCosky, Higgins, Fox
Middle Row — Newsom, York, Averill, Croucher, Trout, Newhouser, Rowe, Meyer, McKain, Stainback
Back Row — Hutchinson, Sullivan, Tebbetts, Greenberg, Benton, Gorsica, Seats, Smith, Campbell

1945 DETROIT TIGERS

Front Row — Cramer, Maier, Trout, Mills (coach), O'Neill (manager), Newhouser, Richards, Mayo
Second Row — Wilson, Mueller, Outlaw, Benton, McHale, Overmire, Orrell
Third Row — Webb, Borom, Pierce, H. Walker, Houtteman, Swift, York, Cullenbine
Back Row — Hoover, Hostetler, Welch, Forsyth (trainer)

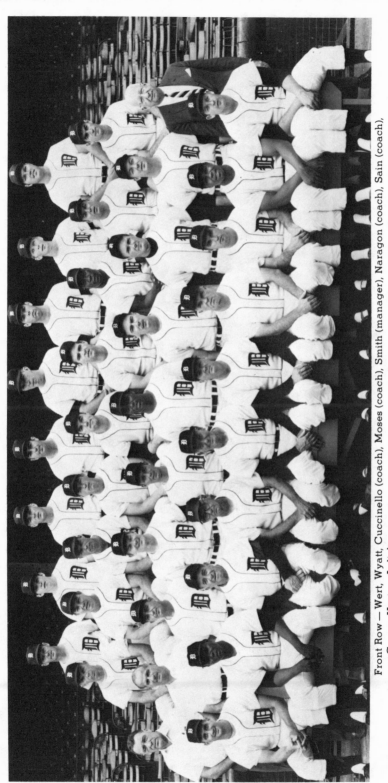

Front Row — Wert, Wyatt, Cuccinello (coach), Moses (coach), Smith (manager), Naragon (coach), Sain (coach), Comer, Horton, Lolich

Second Row — Hand (equipment mgr.), Behm (trainer), Moreno (batting practice pitcher), Northrup, Oyler, Wilson, Lasher, McMahon, Kaline, Creedon (traveling secretary)

Third Row — Tracewski, Cash, Mathews, Price, Warden, McLain, Brown, Hiller, McAuliffe

Back Row — Face, Christian, Stanley, Sparma, Patterson, Dobson, Matchick, Freehan

1972 DETROIT TIGERS

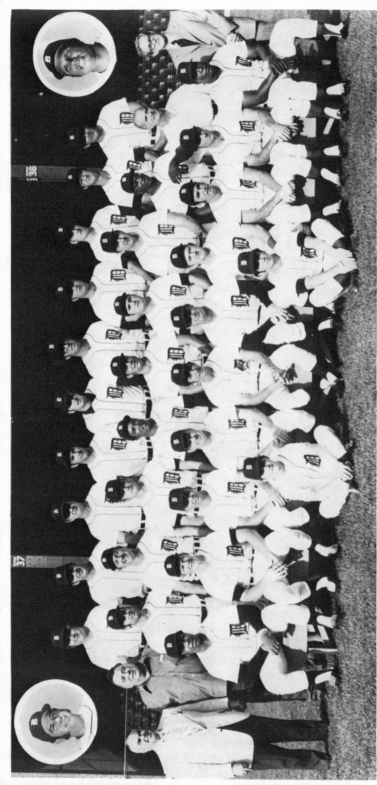

Front Row — Horton, Northrup, Tracewski (coach), Schultz (coach), Martin (manager), Fowler (coach), Silvera (coach), Jones, McAuliffe, G. Brown

Middle Row — Desmond (traveling secretary), Hand (equipment manager), Seelbach, Kaline, Niekro, Taylor, Hiller, unidentified, Haller, I. Brown, Behm (trainer), Livingood (physician)

Back Row — Perranoski, Lolich, Cash, Scherman, Coleman, Timmerman, Zachary, Kilkenny, Brinkman, Stanley

Left Inset — Rodriguez   Right Inset — Freehan

DETROIT TIGERS—1980

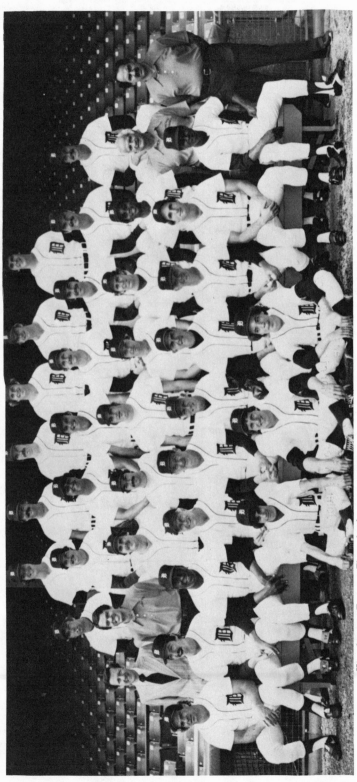

Kneeling in Front — Three batboys

First Row — Steve Kemp, Jason Thompson, Gates Brown, Alex Grammas, Roger Craig, Sparky Anderson, Billy Consolo, Dick Tracewski, Dave Stegman, Lou Whitaker

Second Row — Bill Brown, Jim Schmackel, Richie Hebner, Tom Brookens, Kirk Gibson, Tim Corcoran, Alan Trammell, Rick Peters, Bill Behm, Pio DiSalvo

Third Row — John Wockenfuss, Mark Wagner, Aurelio Lopez, Dave Tobik, Lance Parrish, Dan Schatzeder, Duffy Dyer, Champ Summers

Fourth Row — Pat Underwood, John Hiller, Jack Morris, Dan Petry, Milt Wilcox, Dave Rozema

ALL-TIME TIGER GREATS

Selected the greatest Tiger southpaw in a 1969 fan vote, Hal Newhouser compiled 200 career wins for Detroit.

Right-hander Denny McLain joined Newhouser on the all-time team in 1969.

Now a city councilman, Billy Rogell is remembered as the greatest shortstop in Tiger history.

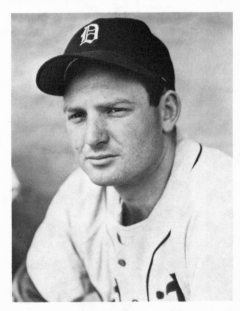

George Kell is the all-time Tiger third baseman and a popular television broadcaster today.

FOUR WINNING MANAGERS

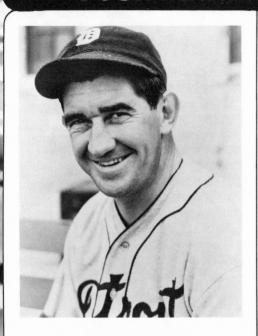

Mickey Cochrane
(1934-1935)

Del Baker
(1940)

Mayo Smith
(1968)

Billy Martin
(1972 divisional)

George (Hookie) Dauss is the all-time Tiger leader in games won (223) and second in innings pitched (3,391).

Ed Summers won 24 games in his rookie year of 1908, pacing the Tiger pennant effort.

George Mullin pitched the first no-hitter for the Tigers on his birthday (July 4) in 1912.

Outfielder Bobby Veach led the American League in RBIs three different times in his 12 season with Detroit.

THE GEORGIA PEACH

Known chiefly as a great hitter, Ty Cobb was a better than average fielder, tying for the league lead in 1924.

Beneath the smiling exterior was the fiercest competitor who ever stepped on a diamond.

The Ty Cobb display at the Hall of Fame features old photographs, uniforms, balls and trophies from his illustrious career. (Photo courtesy of Hall of Fame)

THE EARLY YEARS

Manager Hughie Jennings led the Tigers to three consecutive pennants in 1907, 1908 and 1909.

Sam Crawford was considered the most powerful hitter of his day, the only man ever to lead both leagues in homers.

Heinie Manush won a batting title for the Tigers in 1926 with a .378 average.

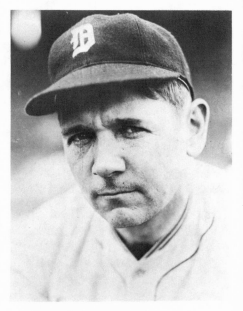

Harry Heilmann proved an apt student for Manager Ty Cobb, compiling a .342 career average.

TIGERS OF THE THIRTIES

Schoolboy Rowe's 24 wins in 1934 paced the Tigers to their first pennant in 25 years.

Joining Rowe as an ace for the Thirties' pennant-winners was right-hander Tommy Bridges.

Flyhawk Pete Fox led the Tigers in hits, doubles, triples and stolen bases in 1938.

Gee Walker was a great favorite of Tiger fans. He hit .353 as a starting outfielder in 1936.

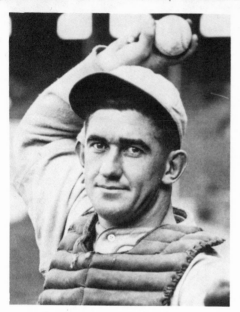

Playing manager Mickey Cochrane was the heart of the 1934-35 champions with his fiery leadership and catching ability.

Goose Goslin drove in 334 runs in a three-year period with the Bengals (1934-36).

Slugger Hank Greenberg holds the all-time league record for the most home runs by a right-handed batter in a season, 58 in 1938.

Silent Charlie Gehringer was not only a great fielder but also a standout batter with a lifetime .320 average.

A GALAXY OF SUPERSTARS

Detroit's "G" men, Hank Greenberg (left) and Charlie Gehringer, are shown here with the cream of the Bronx Bombers, Babe Ruth and Lou Gehrig (right).

The 1937 American League All-Star team boasted these notables, from left: Lou Gehrig, Joe Cronin, Bill Dickey, Joe DiMaggio, Charlie Gehringer, Jimmy Foxx and Hank Greenberg.

October 1

1944 — Tiger flag hopes are dashed when Dutch Leonard and the Senators beat Dizzy Trout 4–1 at home before a crowd of 45,565. That same day, St. Louis beats the Yankees 5–2 to clinch the pennant.

1946 — Jon Warden — B (P 1968)

1956 — Under a court order, the Briggs heirs sell their Tiger stock to a syndicate of eleven radio and television men headed by John Fetzer, Fred Knorr, and Kenyon Brown for $5.5 million. Fred Knorr is named the new president.

1967 — The Tigers fall short of the pennant by ½ game as they lose the second game of a doubleheader to the Angels 8–5 at home. The Tigers have a chance in the bottom of the 9th, but Dick McAuliffe grounds into a double play with two men on. The Tigers had won the first game 6–4.

1970 — Immediately after the final game, manager Mayo Smith is fired. Hiller fans seven Indians in a row to tie the American League record as the Tigers win 1–0.

1972 — As the season draws to a close, the Tigers pick up a key win as Aurelio Rodriguez belts a three-run homer to fuel a 5–1 win over Milwaukee. John Hiller pitches a five-hitter to get the win.

1976 — Southpaw relief ace John Hiller pitches a four-hit, 5–0 shutout at Milwaukee in a rare start after 215 consecutive relief appearances.

October 2

1934 — Earl Wilson — B (P 1966–70)

1938 — Bob Feller of the Indians fans 18 Tigers, including outfielder Chet Laabs five times, but he still loses to Detroit 4–1 as his counterpart, Harry Eisenstat, pitches a four-hitter.

1940 — Bobo Newsom opens the 1940 World Series for the Tigers with a 7–2 win over the Reds in Cincinnati.

1968 — In game one of the World Series, Cardinal ace Bob Gibson strikes out 17 Tigers to set a new Series record and wins 4–0.

1970 — Billy Martin is named Tiger manager for the 1971 season.

1972 — Southpaw ace Mickey Lolich fires a six-hitter and fans 15 Red Sox in a 4–1 win at home, part of a crucial three-game series. A crowd of 51,518 Tiger fans watch Al Kaline and Aurelio Rodriguez bang out three hits each and Rodriguez drive in three runs to lead Lolich to his 22nd win.

1974 — After a truly great 22-year career exclusively in the Major Leagues, Al Kaline announces his retirement.

October 3

1874 — Al Shaw — B (C–1B–3B–SS 1901)

1919 — Joe Wood — B (2B–3B 1943)

1935 — Hank Greenberg's homer paces an 8–3 Tiger win over the Cubs in game two of the World Series at Detroit.

1936 — Jim Perry — B (P 1973)

1937 — Whistlin' Jake Wade beats Cleveland 1–0 at home on a one-hitter. A single by the Indians' first baseman Hal Trosky with two out in the 7th spoils Wade's bid for a no-hitter. The Tiger win breaks a 15-game win streak of Cleveland hurler Johnny Allen, who threw a five-hitter. The Tiger run scores when Pete Fox doubles and Hank Greenberg singles him home.

1947 — Chuck Scrivener — B (SS–2B–3B 1975–77)

1948 — A five-hit effort by Hal Newhouser paces the Tigers to a 7–1 win over the Indians, forcing a playoff between Cleveland and Boston. Rightfielder Vic Wertz leads the attack with three doubles and three RBIs.

1949 — Steve Foucault — B (P 1977–78)

1960 — Joe Gordon is fired as Tiger manager after a half season.

1966 — Mayo Smith is named the new Tiger manager and given a two-year contract.

1968 — Mickey Lolich leads the Tigers to an 8–1 win over the Cardinals in game two of the World Series. Lolich hits his first major league home run in the victory.

1972 — The Tigers clinch the division title on the next-to-last day of the season, 3–1, as Woody Fryman and Chuck Seelbach combine to turn back the Red Sox and Luis Tiant. Al Kaline singles in the winning run as Fryman gets his 10th win and Seelbach his 14th save.

October 4

1922 — Don Lenhardt — B (OF 1952)

1925 — Harry Heilmann wins the batting title with a .393 average after going six for nine in a doubleheader with the Browns, thus edging out Cleveland's Tris Speaker, who hit .389. Manager Ty Cobb pitches one perfect inning in the 11–6 win over the Browns while George Sisler hurls two scoreless innings for St. Louis.

1934 — Goose Goslin's single in the 12th wins the second game of the World Series for the Tigers in Detroit. Rowe pitches a no-hitter against the Cardinals for seven innings.

1935 — Jo-Jo White's single in the 11th scores Marv Owen with the winning run to beat the Cubs 6–5 in the third game of the World Series in Chicago.

1940 — A four-run 7th inning propels the Tigers to a 7–4 win over the Reds in game three of the World Series in Detroit. Rudy York and Pinky Higgins hit homers to pace the Tiger attack.

1945 — Hank Greenberg's three-run home run in the 5th leads the Bengals to a 4–1 win over the Cubs at home in game two of the World Series.

October 4 (continued)

1965 — The Tigers acquire pitcher Bill Monbouquette from Boston for outfielder George Thomas and infielder George Smith. All of the principals perform unspectacularly for their new teams.

October 5

1875 — Davey Crockett — B (1B 1901)

1907 — Frank Doljack — B (OF–1B 1930–34)

1915 — Ty Cobb steals his 96th base of the season in a 5–0 loss to the Indians in Cleveland.

1935 — Two Cub errors give General Crowder and the Tigers a 2–1 win in the fourth game of the World Series at Chicago.

1948 — Aurelio Lopez — B (P 1979–present)

October 6

1889 — Carl Zamloch — B (P 1913)

1915 — Dutch Meyer — B (2B 1940–42)

1917 — Paul Calvert — B (P 1950–51)

1934 — The Tigers beat the Cardinals 10–4 in game four of the World Series at St. Louis as Hank Greenberg has four hits and shortstop Billy Rogell drives in four runs.

1940 — Bobo Newsom gets his second Series win against the Reds in game five at Detroit, 8–0, paced by Hank Greenberg's three-run homer.

1945 — A four-run 4th inning gives the Tigers a 4–1 win over the Cubs in game four of the World Series at Chicago.

1954 — Roger Weaver — B (P 1980–present)

1971 — The Tigers give pitcher Dean Chance his unconditional release.

October 7

1908 — The Tigers beat the White Sox 7–0 to win the American League pennant.

1928 — Joe Presko — B (P 1957–58)

1935 — The Tigers win their first World Championship before the home fans with a 4–3 seventh game victory over the Cubs. Tommy Bridges gets his second win of the Series as Goose Goslin drives in the winning run. A crowd of 500,000 parade and party downtown until dawn to celebrate the win.

1945 — Hal Newhouser strikes out 9 Cubs in game five of the World Series as the Tigers beat the Cubs 8–4. Hank Greenberg's three doubles lead the Bengal offense.

1968 — Mickey Lolich gains his second Series victory in game five with a 5–3 defeat of the Cardinals in Detroit. Al Kaline singles in the tying and go-ahead runs in the 7th inning.

October 8

1887 — Donie Bush — B (SS–2B–3B 1908–21)

1892 — Harry Baumgartner — B (P 1920)

1907 — Boss Schmidt's passed ball on a third strike lets the Cubs tie the score in the 9th inning of the first game of the 1907 World Series. The game ends in a 3–3 tie in the 12th.

1918 — Bob Gillespie — B (P 1944)

1940 — The Tigers lose a heartbreaker and the world title to Cincinnati, 2–1, in the seventh game of the World Series as Paul Derringer outduels Bobo Newsom.

1943 — Don Pepper — B (1B 1966)

1972 — In game two of the American League Championship Series, A's shortstop Bert Campaneris throws his bat at Tiger pitcher Lerrin LaGrow after being hit with a pitch in the 7th inning. Both principals are ejected as the A's go on to win 5–0.

1974 — The Tigers give an unconditional release to utilityman Ike Brown.

October 9

1909 — Ty Cobb's theft of home sparks a three-run inning in a 7–2 win over the Pirates in Pittsburgh in game two of the World Series.

1934 — Dizzy Dean shuts out the Bengals 11–0 in the final game of the World Series to lead the Gashouse Gang to the World Championship.

1964 — The Tigers release catcher Mike Roarke.

1968 — Denny McLain wins game six of the World Series, beating the St. Louis Cardinals 13–1. Tiger fans are thrilled with a grand slam by Jim Northrup and an Al Kaline home run.

1970 — In a blockbuster deal that paves the way for a 1972 divisional title, General Manager Jim Campbell sends trouble-prone pitcher Denny McLain, pitcher Norm McRae, and third baseman-outfielder Elliott Maddox to the Washington Senators for shortstop Eddie Brinkman, third baseman Aurelio Rodriguez, and pitchers Joe Coleman and Jim Hannan.

October 10

1905 — John Stone — B (OF 1928–33)

1915 — Harry Eisenstat — B (P 1938–39)

1921 — Hank Riebe — B (C 1942, 1947–49)

October 10 (continued)

1922 — Saul Rogovin — B (P 1949–51)

1945 — Hal Newhouser gets his second Series win as the Tigers win the World Championship by beating the Cubs in Chicago 9–3.

1968 — Mickey Lolich pitches the Tigers to a World Championship, notching his third Series win, as the Bengals beat the Cards 4–1 in game seven. A Jim Northrup triple drives in two key runs. This Series victory is voted as the most memorable moment in Tiger history in a poll of fans as the Tigers overcome a 3–1 deficit to win the title.

1972 — Joe Coleman strikes out 14 A's in a 3–0 win in game three of the American League Championship Series at home. The win is paced by a Bill Freehan home run.

1975 — All-time Tiger great pinch hitter Gates Brown announces his retirement.

October 11

1926 — Joe Ginsberg — B (C 1948, 1950–53)

1930 — Bill Fischer — B (P 1958, 1960–61)

1938 — Bill Roman — B (1B 1964–65)

1943 — The Tigers trade outfielder Rip Radcliff to the Philadelphia Athletics for catcher Bob Swift and second baseman Don Heffner. Radcliff is returned to the Tigers upon his entry into the U.S. Navy. A cash settlement is made to complete the deal.

1960 — John Fetzer announces that he is acquiring majority stock control, securing the interest of Kenyon Brown, and soon becomes the new president.

1972 — The Tigers rally in the 10th to beat Oakland 4–3 in game four of the league playoffs at home.

1973 — Ralph Houk signs a three-year contract as the new skipper of the Tigers.

October 12

1907 — The Cubs beat the Tigers 2–0 to sweep the World Series.

1908 — In game three of the World Series, Ty Cobb's four hits lead the Tigers to a come-from-behind 8–3 win over the Cubs.

1909 — George Mullin strikes out 10 Pirates in shutting out the National League Champs 5–0 in game four of the World Series in Detroit.

1912 — Al Unser — B (C–2B 1942–44)

1927 — Doc Daugherty — B (PH 1951)

1935 — Larry Osborne — B (1B–3B–OF–C 1957–59)

1972 — Oakland takes the American League pennant in game five of the playoffs by downing Detroit 2-1.

October 13

1876 — Wild Bill Donovan — B (P–SS–2B–OF–1B 1903–12, 1918)

1888 — Jack Onslow — B (C 1912)

1891 — Fred McMullin — B (SS 1914)

1926 — Eddie Yost — B (3B–2B 1959–60)

1931 — Eddie Mathews — B (3B–1B 1967–68)

1941 — Jim Price — B (C 1967–71)

1943 — Jerry Robertson — B (P 1970)

1966 — The Tigers send catcher Jackie Moore to the Red Sox to complete a prior deal for pitcher Bill Monbouquette.

October 14

1908 — The Cubs beat the Tigers in Detroit 2–0 to win the World Series four games to one.

1909 — George Mullin gains his second Series win in a 5–4 triumph over Pittsburgh in game five in Detroit.

October 15

1875 — Emil Frisk — B (P–OF 1901)

1881 — Charlie O'Leary — B (SS–2B–3B–OF 1904–12)

1931 — Gail Harris — B (1B 1958–60)

1959 — The Tigers trade catcher Charlie Lau and pitcher Don Lee to the Milwaukee Braves for catcher Mike Roarke, second baseman Casey Wise, and pitcher Don Kaiser.

October 16

1900 — Goose Goslin — B (OF–1B 1934–37)

1904 — Walter Beck — B (P 1944)

1909 — Pittsburgh wins the World Series by beating Detroit 8–0.

1921 — Matt Batts — B (C 1952–54)

1924 — Bob Cain — B (P 1951)

1931 — Dave Sisler — B (P 1959–60)

October 16 (continued)

1936 — Manny Montejo — B (P 1961)

October 17

1873 — Frank Dillon — B (1B 1901–02)

1908 — Red Rolfe — B (MGR 1949–52)

1927 — Johnny Klippstein — B (P 1967)

1945 — Bob Christian — B (OF–1B 1968)

1966 — Bob Swift dies of lung cancer in Detroit.

October 18

1895 — Babe Pinelli — B (3B–SS–2B 1920)

1903 — George Wuestling — B (SS–3B–2B 1929–30)

1914 — Roy Cullenbine — B (OF–1B–3B 1938–39, 1945–47)

1922 — The Tigers trade pitchers Howard Ehmke and Carl Holling and first baseman Babe Herman to the Red Sox for pitcher Rip Collins and second baseman Del Pratt. It is a losing proposition for the Tigers as Ehmke becomes a 20-game winner with Boston and the ace of their staff.

1942 — Willie Horton — B (OF–DH–3B 1963–77)

   Vern Holtgrave — B (P 1965)

1949 — Ed Farmer — B (P 1973)

October 19

1933 — Ossie Alvarez — B (PH–PR 1959)

1945 — Gary Taylor — B (P 1969)

October 20

1909 — Bruce Campbell — B (OF 1940–41)

1930 — Bill Froats — B (P 1955)

1960 — John Fetzer assumes the presidency of the ball club following the resignation of Bill DeWitt.

1967 — The Tigers release pitcher Johnny Podres.

October 21

1884 — Bill Lelivelt — B (P 1909–10)

84

1898 — Roy Moore — B (P 1922–23)

1913 — Mark Christman — B (3B–SS 1938–39)

October 22

1888 — Chick Lathers — B (3B–2B–SS–1B 1910–11)

1975 — The Tigers give infielder Gene Michael his release.

October 23

1910 — Billy Sullivan, Jr. — B (C 1940–41)

1931 — Jim Bunning — B (P 1955–63)

1973 — The Tigers trade second baseman Dick McAuliffe to the Red Sox for outfielder Ben Oglivie. It is another good deal by Jim Campbell as Oglivie provides four seasons of solid play for the Tigers, while McAuliffe ends his career in 1974 on a weak note, hitting .210.

October 24

1871 — Heinie Smith — B (2B 1903)

1887 — Hugh High — B (OF 1913–14)

1905 — Jack Russell — B (P 1937)

1928 — George Bullard — B (SS 1954)

1967 — Tiger second baseman Jerry Lumpe announces his retirement. Lumpe spent four seasons in Detroit out of a 12-year career, providing a solid starter at the keystone for three of those years.

October 25

1951 — Al Cowens — B (OF 1980–present)

1972 — The Tigers sell catcher Tom Haller and pitcher Don Leshnock to the Philadelphia Phillies.

1973 — Outfielder-first baseman Frank Howard is given his unconditional release.

October 26

1866 — Kid Gleason — B (2B 1901–02)

1910 — Hugh Shelley — B (OF 1935)

October 27

1901 — George Smith — B (P 1926–29)

1917 — Bob Patrick — B (OF 1941–42)

October 28

1896 — Frank Okrie — B (P 1920)

1897 — Clarence Huber — B (3B 1920–21)

1900 — Johnny Neun — B (1B 1925–28)

1904 — Liz Funk — B (OF 1930)

October 29

1882 — Frank Browning — B (P 1910)

1891 — Happy Finneran — B (P 1918)

1929 — Tiger great Harry Heilmann is sold on waivers to the Cincinnati Reds. Heilmann enjoys one good season for the Reds, hitting .333, before ending his 17-year Hall of Fame career in 1932.

1954 — Kip Young — B (P 1978–79)

October 30

1891 — Charlie Deal — B (3B 1912–13)

1896 — Clyde Manion — B (C 1920–24, 1926–27)

1915 — Red Borom — B (2B–3B–SS 1944–45)

October 31

1938 — Jim Donohue — B (P 1961)

1977 — Construction begins on a $15 million, three-year modernization project at Tiger Stadium for renovated clubhouses, a new press box, luxury boxes, and an electronic scoreboard. The work is planned after the team sells the stadium to the city of Detroit and signs a 30-year lease. This transaction enables the project to qualify for federal funds.

1979 — The Tigers acquire first baseman-third baseman Richie Hebner from the Mets for third baseman Phil Mankowski and outfielder Jerry Morales. This deal works well for the Bengals, giving them flexibility at two positions and a solid RBI man in Hebner.

NOVEMBER

November 1

1880 — Tom Fisher — B (P 1902)

1906 — Heinie Schuble — B (SS–3B–2B 1929, 1932–35)

1917 — Pat Mullin — B (OF 1940–41, 1946–53)

November 2

1903 — Chief Hogsett — B(P 1929–36, 1944)

1926 — After six seasons without a finish above second place, Ty Cobb draws his release as the Tiger manager. The Georgia Peach compiled a 479–444 record for a .519 winning percentage during his tenure. His best season was 1923 when the Bengals finished second, 16 games behind Miller Huggins' New York Yankees.

November 3

1895 — Jim Walkup — B(P 1927)

1908 — Red Phillips — B(P 1934, 1936)

1949 — Ed Brookens — B(P 1975)

November 4

1893 — Bill Leinhauser — B(OF 1912)

1933 — Tito Francona — B(OF 1958)

1942 — Jack Whillock — B(P 1971)

November 5

1905 — Carl Fischer — B(P 1933–35)

November 6

1919 — Frank Carswell — B(OF 1953)

1976 — The Tigers purchase second baseman Luis Alvarado from the St. Louis Cardinals. Luis played only two games for the '77 Tigers before shuffling off to the Mets.

November 7

1944 — Joe Niekro — B(P 1970–72)

1948 — Tom Walker — B(P 1975)

November 8

1896 — Bucky Harris — B(2B–SS 1929–33, MGR 1929–33, 1955–56)

1930 — Mike Roarke — B(C 1961–64)

November 9

1888 — Jim McGarr — B(2B 1912)

1915 — Benny McCoy — B(2B–3B–SS 1938–39)

1919 — Jerry Priddy — B (2B–3B–1B–SS 1950–53)

1931 — Whitey Herzog — B (1B–OF 1963)

1954 — Al Greene — B (OF–DH 1979)

November 10

1873 — Billy Lush — B (OF–3B–SS 1903)

1886 — Del Gainor — B (1B 1909, 1911–14)

1895 — Slicker Parks — B (P 1921)

1896 — Jimmy Dykes — B (MGR 1959–60)

1912 — Birdie Tebbetts — B (C 1936–42, 1946–47)

1920 — Russ Kerns — B (PH 1945)

1922 — Johnny Lipon (SS–3B–2B 1942, 1946, 1948–52)

1930 — Charlie King — B (OF 1954–56)

1934 — Norm Cash — B (1B–OF–DH 1960–74)

1948 — In one of the worst trades in baseball history, the Bengals send pitcher Billy Pierce to the White Sox for catcher Aaron Robinson. Robinson fades after two mediocre seasons behind the plate, while Pierce goes on to become the mainstay of the Chicago pitching staff for the next 13 seasons, including two 20-game years in 1956–57.

November 11

1885 — Jack Ness — B (1B 1911)

1887 — Bill Steen — B (P 1915)

1902 — Ownie Carroll — B (P 1925, 1927–30)

1948 — Outfielder Doc Cramer draws his release from Detroit after seven seasons, including four as a starter.

November 12

1876 — Ed Killian — B (P 1904–10)

1889 — Red McDermott — B (OF 1912)

1900 — Herm Merritt — B (SS 1921)

November 13

1925 — Jim Delsing — B (OF 1952–56)

1928 — Steve Bilko — B (1B 1960)

1935 — Owner Frank Navin suffers a heart attack while horseback riding and dies a few hours later in a Detroit hospital. Walter Briggs assumes sole ownership of the club following the settling of the estate.

1958 — Dan Petry — B (P 1979–present)

November 14

1881 — Fred Carisch — B (C 1923)

1938 — Johnnie Seale — B (P 1964–65)

1961 — John Fetzer becomes sole owner of the Tigers, purchasing the remaining interest held by the Fred Knorr estate. Fetzer goes on to build the club into one of baseball's more solid franchises, and transforms the game with his key role in obtaining network television contracts.

November 15

1896 — Babe Ellison — B (1B–2B–OF–3B–SS 1916–20)

1937 — Bob Farley — B (1B–OF 1962)

November 16

1930 — Paul Foytack — B (P 1953, 1955–63)

1931 — Frank Bolling — B (2B 1954–60)

1932 — Harry Chiti — B (C 1960–61)

November 17

1867 — George Stallings — B (MGR 1901)

1927 — Dick Weik — B (P 1954)

1933 — Orlando Pena — B (P 1965–67)

November 18

1863 — Deacon McGuire — B (C–1B 1902–03, 1912)

1882 — Jack Coombs — B (P 1920)

1897 — Danny Claire — B (SS 1920)

1912 — Charlie Fuchs — B (P 1942)

1963 — The Tigers trade outfielder Rocky Colavito, pitcher Bob Anderson, and $50,000 to Kansas City for second baseman Jerry Lumpe and pitchers Dave Wickersham and Ed Rakow. The trade produces immediate dividends for the Tigers as Wickersham wins 19 games the next season and Lumpe performs well at second. The Rock enjoys one season in Kansas City before heading back to Cleveland.

November 18 (continued)

1974 — In a three-team deal that proves a bust for all concerned, the Tigers obtain first baseman Nate Colbert from San Diego for shortstop Eddie Brinkman, outfielder Dick Sharon, and pitcher Bob Strampe. The Padres in turn send Brinkman and catcher Danny Breeden to the St. Louis Cardinals for pitchers Alan Foster, Rich Folkers, and Sonny Siebert. Never has so much effort proven so fruitless.

November 19

Nothing of significance happened on this date.

November 20

1888 — Ray Powell — B (OF 1913)

1902 — Augie Prudhomme — B (P 1929)

1929 — Lou Berberet — B (C 1959–60)

1949 — Ron Cash — B (1B–3B–OF 1973–74)

1957 — In a giant 13-player deal, the Tigers obtain second baseman Billy Martin, outfielders Gus Zernial and Lou Skizas, catcher Tim Thompson, and pitchers Tom Morgan and Mickey McDermott from Kansas City for catcher Frank House, first basemen Kent Hadley and Jim McManus, outfielders Jim Small and Bill Tuttle, and pitchers Duke Maas and John Tsitouris. (Hadley transfers January 8, 1958 and McManus April 2, 1958, to complete the transaction.)

November 21

1885 — Gus Hetling — B (3B 1906)

1908 — Paul Richards — B (C 1943–46)

1943 — Daryl Patterson — B (P 1968–71)

1955 — Rick Peters B (OF–2B–3B–DH 1979–present)

1960 — Bob Scheffing signs a two-year contract as the new Tiger manager, succeeding Joe Gordon.

November 22

1901 — Harry Rice — B (OF–3B 1928–30)

1907 — Dick Bartell — B (SS–3B 1940–41)

1967 — Pitcher Fred Gladding is sent to Houston to complete the August 17, 1967 deal for Eddie Mathews.

November 23

1888 — Bill Jensen — B (P 1912)

November 24

1890 — Ralph Comstock — B (P 1913)

1904 — Billy Rogell — B (SS–3B–2B–OF 1930–39)

1913 — Walter Wilson — B (P 1945)

1939 — Jim Northrup — B (OF–1B 1964–74)

November 25

1928 — Ray Narleski — B (P 1959)

1945 — Wayne Redmond — B (OF 1965, 1969)

1946 — Don Leshnock — B (P 1972)

November 26

1898 — John Kerr — B (SS–3B–OF 1923–24)

1947 — Richie Hebner — B (1B–3B–DH 1980–present)

1962 — The Tigers trade catcher Dick Brown to Baltimore for catcher Gus Triandos and outfielder Whitey Herzog.

November 27

1923 — Bob Schultz — B (P 1955)

November 28

1891 — Frank O'Rourke — B (2B–3B–SS 1924–26)

1937 — Purnal Goldy — B (OF 1962–63)

1941 — Fritz Fisher — B (P 1964)

1962 — The Tigers trade third baseman Steve Boros to the Cubs for pitcher Bob Anderson.

1967 — The Tigers obtain hometown boy Dennis Ribant from Pittsburgh in exchange for another pitcher, Dave Wickersham.

November 29

1914 — Joe Orengo — B (SS–3B–1B–2B 1944)

1937 — George Thomas — B (OF–2B–3B–SS 1957–58, 1961, 1963–65)

1939 — Dick McAuliffe — B (2B–SS–3B–DH 1960–73)

1941 — Bill Freehan — B (C–1B–OF–DH 1961, 1963–76)

91

November 30

1898 — Firpo Marberry — B (P 1933–35)

1955 — Veteran hurler Virgil Trucks is obtained from the White Sox for third baseman-outfielder Bubba Phillips. Chicago gets the better of this deal as Trucks proves to be over-the-hill.

1958 — In a deal that solidifies the pitching staff, Detroit obtains hurlers Don Mossi and Ray Narleski and infielder Ossie Alvarez from Cleveland for second baseman Billy Martin and pitcher Al Cicotte.

1972 — The Tigers buy first baseman Rich Reese from Minnesota. Outfielder Dick Sharon and a player to be named are obtained from Pittsburgh for pitchers Jim Foor and Norm McRae.

DECEMBER

December 1

1888 — Willie Mitchell — B (P 1916–19)

1894 — Ernie Alten — B (P 1920)

1919 — Pete Wojey — B (P 1956–57)

1922 — George Lerchen — B (OF 1952)

1944 — Jim Ray — B (P 1974)

1954 — Dan Schatzeder — B (P 1980–present)

1960 — Detroit *Free Press* sports writer Hal Middlesworth is named public relations director, inaugurating a 20-year period in which the Tigers' publicity operation becomes one of the finest in baseball.

December 2

1876 — Roscoe Miller — B (P 1901–02)

1889 — Bob Jones — B (3B–2B–1B–SS 1917–25)

1927 — In an ill-considered move, the Tigers trade future Hall of Fame outfielder Heinie Manush and first baseman Lu Blue to the St. Louis Browns for pitcher Elam Vangilder, infielder Chick Galloway, and outfielder Harry Rice.

1937 — The Tigers obtain outfielder Dixie Walker, second baseman Tony Piet, and pitcher Vern Kennedy from the White Sox for third baseman Marv Owen, outfielder Gee Walker, and minor league catcher Mike Tresh. Tiger fans react bitterly to the trading of their favorite, Gee Walker. Dixie, not related, spends one unhappy season with Detroit before being waived to Brooklyn.

1958 — Catcher Lou Berberet is obtained from the Red Sox for pitcher Herb Moford.

1971 — The Tigers obtain catcher Tom Haller from the Los Angeles Dodgers for cash and a player to be named.

December 3

1886 — Delos Drake — B (OF–1B 1911)

1969 — The Tigers trade a fading Joe Sparma to the Expos for pitcher Jerry Robertson.

1973 — Reliever Fred Scherman is sent to Houston for reliever Jim Ray and second sacker Gary Sutherland.

December 4

1896 — Allen Conkwright — B (P 1920)

1930 — Harvey Kuenn — B (SS–OF–3B–1B 1952–59)

1952 — Double no-hitter ace Virgil Trucks is traded to the St. Louis Browns, along with pitcher Hal White and outfielder Johnny Groth, for second baseman Owen Friend, outfielder Bob Nieman, and catcher J. W. Porter.

1963 — The Tigers trade ace hurler Jim Bunning and catcher Gus Triandos to the Phillies for outfielder Don Demeter and pitcher Jack Hamilton. Bunning continues his winning ways in the National League, racking up 106 wins over the next eight seasons.

1969 — The Tigers obtain pitcher Joe Niekro from San Diego for pitcher Pat Dobson and infielder Dave Campbell.

1974 — In the mistaken notion that he is washed up, the Tigers send ageless Woody Fryman to Montreal for pitcher Tom Walker and catcher Terry Humphrey. Fryman remains an effective reliever to this day.

1978 — The Tigers score a coup for their bullpen by obtaining Aurelio Lopez (Senor Smoke) and outfielder Jerry Morales from the St. Louis Cardinals for pitchers Bob Sykes and Jack Murphy. On this same day, the Tigers draft outfielder Lynn Jones from Cincinnati and infielder Dave Machemer from California, while releasing Chuck Scrivener.

December 5

1884 — Ed Summers — B (P 1908–12)

1956 — The Tigers trade pitchers Virgil Trucks, Ned Garver, and Gene Host, first baseman Wayne Belardi, and $20,000 to Kansas City for first baseman Eddie Robinson, third baseman Jim Finigan, and pitchers Jack Crimian and Bill Harrington.

1973 — Pitcher Luke Walker is bought from the Pirates.

1979 — The Tigers trade pitcher Fernando Arroyo to Minnesota for pitcher Jeff Holly.

December 6

1881 — Joe Lake — B (P 1912–13)

1939 — Tiger favorite Billy Rogell, a fixture at shortstop for the past eight seasons, is sent to the Cubs for shortstop Dick Bartell. Rogell ends his career with the Cubs in 1940 playing sparingly, while Bartell mans short in the Tigers' pennant drive.

1958 — The Tigers obtain third baseman Eddie Yost, shortstop Rocky Bridges, and outfielder Neil Chrisley from Washington for third baseman Reno Bertoia, shortstop Ron Samford, and outfielder Jim Delsing.

1974 — Reliever Jim Ray is sent to Pittsburgh for a player to be named.

1975 — The Tigers acquire catcher Milt May and pitchers Dave Roberts and Jim Crawford from Houston for outfielder Leon Roberts, catcher Terry Humphrey, and pitchers Gene Pentz and Mark Lemongello.

December 7

1906 — Tony Piet — B (3B–2B 1938)

1927 — Dick Donovan — B (P 1954)

1942 — Alex Johnson — B (OF–DH 1976)

1949 — Outfielder Charlie (King Kong) Keller is signed by the Tigers following his release by the Yankees. Keller proves to be a valuable pinch hitter for the next two seasons.

1960 — The Tigers trade second baseman Frank Bolling and outfielder Neil Chrisley to the Milwaukee Braves for outfielder Bill Bruton, catcher Dick Brown, second baseman Chuck Cottier, and relief pitcher Terry Fox. The Bengals gain a solid performer in Bruton, and Fox is their relief ace for the next five years.

1966 — The Tigers send pitchers Ed Rakow and Julio Navarro to Atlanta for catcher Chris Cannizzaro and utilityman John Herrnstein.

1979 — The Tigers obtain pitcher Dan Schatzeder from Montreal for outfielder Ron LeFlore.

The Tigers send third baseman Aurelio Rodriquez to the Padres for a player to be named (and eventually settle for cash).

December 8

1894 — Razor Ledbetter — B (P 1915)

1941 — Ed Brinkman — B (SS 1971–74)

1951 — Steve Dillard — B (2B–DH 1978)

December 9

1910 — Steve Larkin — B (P 1934)

1921 — Charlie Kress — B (1B–OF 1954)

1925 — The Tigers trade third baseman Fred Haney to Boston for infielder Homer Ezzell and outfielder Ted Vache.

1930 — Bob Hazle — B (OF 1958)

1939 — The Tigers obtain outfielder Wally Moses from the Athletics for second baseman Benny McCoy and pitcher Slick Coffman. The deal is cancelled January 14, 1940 when Judge Landis declares McCoy a free agent because of irregularities in the Tiger farm system.

1977 — A dark day for Tiger fans as two trades are made that turn out unsuccessfully. Shortstop Tom Veryzer is sent to Cleveland for outfielder Charlie Spikes, and outfielder Ben Oglivie goes to the Milwaukee Brewers for pitchers Jim Slaton and Rich Folkers. The failure to sign free agent Slaton after a 17-victory season in '78 turns this deal in the Brewers favor, as Milwaukee re-signs him.

December 10

1883 — Art Griggs — B (1B 1918)

1907 — Bots Nekola — B (P 1933)

1908 — Earl Cook — B (P 1941)

1909 — Floyd Giebell — B (P 1939–41)

1926 — Leo Crisante — B (P 1955)

1935 — Outfielder Al Simmons is purchased from the White Sox for $75,000. Despite a .327 season the next year, Bucketfoot Al moves on to Washington.

1936 — Jack Feller — B (C 1958)

1943 — Dalton Jones — B (2B–3B–1B–OF 1970–72)

1980 — The Tigers trade shortstop Mark Wagner to Texas for pitcher Kevin Saucier.

December 11

1895 — Erwin Renfer — B (P 1913)

1910 — Slick Coffman — B (P 1937–39)

1928 — Pitcher George Uhle is acquired from the Indians for shortstop Jackie Tavener and pitcher Ken Holloway. A good deal for Detroit as Uhle becomes a mainstay on the pitching staff for the next four seasons.

1954 — Bob Sykes — B (P 1977–78)

December 12

1893 — Les Hennessy — B (2B 1913)

1907 — Catcher Ira Thomas is purchased from New York

1909 — Flea Clifton — B (3B–SS–2B 1934–37)

1933 — In the key deal to the Tigers' glory years of '34 and '35, catcher Mickey Cochrane is obtained from Philadelphia for catcher Johnny Pasek and $100,000. Cochrane's fiery leadership as a playing manager proves the ingredient needed to take the·Bengals to the top.

1940 — The Tigers sell outfielder Pete Fox to the Red Sox.

1941 — The Tigers obtain outfielder Doc Cramer and second baseman Jimmy Bloodworth from Washington for outfielder Bruce Campbell and shortstop Frank Croucher.

1946 — Five years after his acquisition, Jimmy Bloodworth is sold to Pittsburgh.

1969 — The Tigers obtain infielder Dalton Jones from Boston for infielder Tom Matchick.

1975 — In a deal that ends an era, Detroit sends veteran southpaw Mickey Lolich and outfielder Billy Baldwin to the Mets for outfielder Rusty Staub and pitcher Bill Laxton. Lolich compiled 207 wins in his 13 seasons with the Tigers and remains the all-time Tiger leader in career games started, in strikeouts, and shutouts.

1976 — Catcher Bill Freehan draws his release, ending a 15-year career as one of the finest catchers in Tiger history.

1980 — Detroit obtains pitcher Dennis Kinney in a deal with San Diego for outfielder Dave Stegman.

December 13

1876 — Rube Kissinger — B (P 1902–03)

1913 — Scat Metha — B (2B–3B 1940)

1923 — Larry Doby — B (OF 1959)

1931 — Bubba Morton — B (OF–1B 1961–63)

1978 — Mickey Stanley ends his 15-year career after being released.

December 14

1892 — Rudy Kallio — B (P 1918–19)

1909 — Jim Walkup — B (P 1939)

1925 — Sam Jones — B (P 1962)

1929 — Carl Linhart — B (PH 1952)

1932 — The Tigers obtain pitchers Firpo Marberry and Carl Fischer from the Senators for pitcher Earl Whitehill. The change of scene helps Whitehill to his only 20-game season in 1933, as he leads the pennant-winning Senators with 22 wins.

1933 — In a deal that places another piece in the pennant puzzle, the Tigers trade outfielder John Stone to Washington for outfielder Goose Goslin.

December 15

1920 — Eddie Robinson — B (1B 1957)

1929 — Ray Herbert — B (P 1950–51, 1953–54)

1938 — The Tigers trade pitchers Eldon Auker and Jake Wade and outfielder Chet Morgan to the Red Sox for third baseman Pinky Higgins and pitcher Archie McKain.

1964 — Owner John Fetzer, chairing the major league television committee, announces a historic first: a complete network television package, worth $12.2 million for two seasons.

1965 — Infielder Dick Tracewski is acquired from the Dodgers for pitcher Phil Regan.

December 16

1931 — Neil Chrisley — B (OF–1B 1959–60)

1976 — Outfielder Alex Johnson and second baseman Pedro Garcia are released by Detroit.

December 17

1949 — The Tigers trade first baseman Dick Wakefield to the Yankees for first sacker Dick Kryhoski.

December 18

1881 — Clay Perry — B (3B 1908)

1886 — Ty Cobb — B (OF–1B–2B–3B 1905–26, MGR 1921–26)

1899 — Sam Barnes — B (1B 1921)

1902 — Les Burke — B (2B–3B–SS–C 1923–26)

December 19

1934 — Al Kaline — B (OF–1B–3B–DH 1953–74)

1935 — Tony Taylor — B (2B–3B–1B–DH 1971–73)

1973 — Tony Taylor is released, then signs with Philadelphia.

December 20

1885 — Paddy Baumann — B (2B–3B–OF 1911–14)

1893 — Deacon Jones — B (P 1916–18)

December 20 (continued)

1897 — Snooks Dowd — B (PR 1919)

December 21

1948 — Elliott Maddox — B (3B–OF–SS–2B 1970)

December 22

1885 — Tex Erwin — B (C 1907)

1922 — Johnny Bero — B (2B 1948)

1929 — Bill Bruton — B (OF 1961–64)

1950 — Tom Makowski — B (P 1975)

1954 — Sheldon Burnside — B (P 1978–79)

December 23

1879 — Frank Owen — B (P 1901)

1880 — Doc Gessler — B (OF 1903)

December 24

1937 — Larry Foster — B (P 1963)

1953 — Jerry Manuel — B (2B–SS–DH 1975–76)

December 25

1904 — Bill Akers — B (SS–2B 1929–31)

1925 — Ned Garver — B (P 1952–56)

1938 — Jack Hamilton — B (P 1964–65)

1946 — Gene Lamont — B (C 1970–72, 1974, 75)

December 26

1889 — Pug Cavet — B (P 1911, 1914–15)

1895 — Herman Pillette — B (P 1922–24)

December 27

1876 — Charlie Carr — B (1B 1903–04)

1897 — Jackie Tavener — B (SS 1921, 1925–28)

1912 — Jim Tobin — B (P 1945)

1913 — Red Lynn — B (P 1939)

December 28

1906 — Tommy Bridges — B (P 1930–43, 1945–46)

1947 — Aurelio Rodriguez — B (3B–SS–1B 1971–79)

December 29

1892 — Dave Skeels — B (P 1910)

1904 — Bill Sweeney — B (1B–OF 1928)

1954 — Pitcher Bob Schultz is purchased from Pittsburgh.

December 30

Nothing of significance happened on this date.

December 31

1900 — Syl Johnson — B (P 1922–25)

1918 — Al Lakeman — B (C 1954)

1924 — Ted Gray — B (P 1946, 1948–54)

UNKNOWN BIRTHDATES

???? — Harry Lockhead (SS 1901)
???? — Ed High (P 1901)
???? — E. Poste (OF 1902)
???? — Arch McCarthy (P 1902)
???? — Samuel McMackin (P 1902)
???? — John Terry (P 1902)
???? — Rabbit Robinson (SS–3B–OF–2B 1904)
???? — Herm Malloy (P 1907–08)
???? — Daniel McGarvey (OF 1912)
???? — Hap Ward (OF 1912)
1867 — Alex Jones (P 1903)
1879 — Soldier Boy Murphy (SS 1903)
        Ernie Courtney (SS–3B–2B–1B 1903)
1882 — Ed Irvin (3B 1912)
        Charlie Jackson (P 1905)
1885 — Art Loudell (P 1910)
1889 — Alex Remneas (P 1912)
1891 — Fred House (P 1913)
        Ed McCreery (P 1914)
1892 — Pat Meany (SS 1912)
1893 — Charlie Wheatley (P 1912)
1894 — Herb Hall (P 1918)

99

2. NICKNAMES

More than any other sport, baseball holds the distinction for players with nicknames—funny, unusual, insulting, or downright strange.

Whoever heard of Lynwood Rowe? Or Paul Trout? Tiger fans knew and loved them as Schoolboy and Dizzy. Their nicknames, as much as their performance on the field, have forever burnished them in the memories of every Tiger follower.

So here goes—a listing of the common and not-so-common monickers hung on our heroes over the years:

Al Aber	Lefty
Dale Alexander	Moose
Ernie Alten	Lefty
George Alusik	Turk, Glider
Luis Alvarado	Pimba
George Anderson	Sparky
Eldon Auker	Big Six
Yancy Ayers	Doc
Robert Baldwin	Billy
Ed Barrow	Cousin Ed
Dick Bartell	Rowdy Richard
Charles Baumann	Paddy
Erwin Beck	Erve, Dutch
Walter Beck	Boom-Boom
Henry Beckendorf	Heinie
Wayne Belardi	Footsie
Roy Bell	Beau
Jack Billingham	The Blade
Werner Birrer	Babe
William Black	Bud
John Bogart	Big John
Ray Boone	Ike
Edward Borom	Red
Jim Brady	Diamond Jim
Ralph Branca	Hawk
Everett Bridges	Rocky
Edward Brookens	Ike
William Brown	Gates, Gator
Les Burke	Buck
Bill Burns	Sleepy Bill
George Burns	Tioga George
Jack Burns	Slug
Owen Bush	Donie
Bob Cain	Sugar
Guy Cantrell	Gunner
Owen Carroll	Ownie
Frank Carswell	Tex, Wheels
James Casey	Doc
Tiller Cavet	Pug
Al Cicotte	Bozo
Jay Clarke	Nig
Al Clauss	Lefty
Herman Clifton	Flea

Nicknames (continued)

Ty Cobb	The Georgia Peach
Gordon Cochrane	Mickey, Black Mike
George Coffman	Slick
Rocco Colavito	Rocky, The Rock
Kevin Collins	Casey
Harry Collins	Rip
Ralph Comstock	Commy
Allen Conkwright	Red
Bill Connelly	Wild Bill
Duff Cooley	Sir Richard, Dick
Jack Coombs	Colby Jack
Tim Corcoran	Corky
John Corriden	Red
Harry Coveleski	The Giant Killer
Bill Covington	Tex
Plateau Cox	Red
Roger Cramer	Doc, Flit
Sam Crawford	Wahoo Sam
Frank Croucher	Dingle
Alvin Crowder	General
George Cutshaw	Clancy
Talbot Dalton	Jack
Harold Daugherty	Doc
George Dauss	Hookie
Harry Davis	Stinky
Woodrow Davis	Woody, Babe
Clyde DeFate	Tony
Gene Desautels	Red
Frank Dillon	Pop
Francis Donahue	Red
William Donovan	Wild Bill
Raymond Dowd	Snooks
Jerome Downs	Red
Walt Dropo	Moose
Jean Dubuc	Chauncey
Joseph Dugan	Jumping Joe
Don Dyer	Duffy
Mal Eason	Kid
Zeb Eaton	Red
Aloysius Egan	Wish
Howard Ehmke	Bob
Norman Elberfeld	Kid, The Tabasco Kid
Henry Elder	Heinie
Herbert Ellison	Babe
Ross Erwin	Tex
John Eubank	Honest John
Walter Evers	Hoot
Ferris Fain	Burrhead
Ed Farmer	Eatin' Ed
Al Federoff	Whitey

Alfred Ferry	Cy
Mark Fidrych	The Bird
Joseph Finneran	Happy, Smokey Joe
Tom Fisher	Red
Ira Flagstead	Pete
Les Fleming	Moe
Leslie Floyd	Bubba
Bob Fothergill	Fats
Ervin Fox	Pete
John Francona	Tito
Murray Franklin	Moe
George Freese	Bud
Arthur Fried	Cy
Owen Friend	Red
Frank Fuller	Rabbit
Elias Funk	Liz
Harold Gagnon	Chick
Del Gainor	Sheriff
Clarence Galloway	Chick
Charlie Gehringer	The Mechanical Man
Harry Gessler	Doc
Kirk Gibson	Hall of Famer, Gib
Bob Gillespie	Bunch
Myron Ginsberg	Joe
John Glaiser	Bert
William Gleason	Kid
Isadore Goldstein	Izzy
Joe Gordon	Flash
Leon Goslin	Goose
Johnny Grabowski	Nig
Hank Greenberg	Hammerin' Hank
Patrick Greene	Willie
Ed Gremminger	Battleship
Charlie Grover	Bert, Buggs
Cesar Gutierrez	Coca
Charley Hall	Sea Lion
Jack Hamilton	Hairbreadth Harry
Luke Hamlin	Hot Potato
Fred Haney	Pudge
Charlie Harding	Slim
William Hargrave	Pinky
Stanley Harris	Bucky
Earl Harrist	Irish
Clyde Hatter	Mad
Bob Hazle	Hurricane
Richie Hebner	Digger, Hacker
Don Heffner	Jeep
Harry Heilmann	Slug
Floyd Herman	Babe
Art Herring	Sandy
Dorrel Herzog	Whitey

Charles Hickman	Piano Legs
Ed High	Lefty
Hugh High	Bunny, Lefty
John Hiller	Ratso
Elon Hogsett	Chief
James Holmes	Ducky
Vern Holtgrave	Woody
Johnny Hopp	Hippity
Gene Host	Twinkles, Slick
Ralph Houk	Major
Frank House	Pig
Frank Howard	Hondo
Waite Hoyt	Schoolboy
Clarence Huber	Gilly
William Jacobson	Baby Doll
Bill James	Big Bill
Hughie Jennings	Ee-Yah
Augie Johns	Lefty
Earl Johnson	Lefty
Ken Johnson	Hooks
Bob Jones	Ducky
Carroll Jones	Deacon
Davy Jones	Kangaroo
Ken Jones	Broadway
Sam Jones	Sad Sam, Toothpick Sam
Walter Justis	Smoke
Harry Kane	Klondike
Charlie Keller	King Kong
Wade Killefer	Red, Lollypop
Ed Killian	Twilight Ed
Charlie King	Chick
Charles Kisinger	Rube
Don Kolloway	Butch, Cab
George Korince	Moose
Ralph Kress	Red
Ed Lafitte	Doc
Al Lakeman	Moose
Frank Lary	The Yankee Killer, Mule
Charles Lathers	Chick
Alfred Lawson	Roxie
Ralph Ledbetter	Razor
Don Lenhardt	Footsie
Hubert Leonard	Dutch
Louis Lepine	Pete
Christian Lindsay	Pinky
Johnny Lipon	Skids
Henry Lively	Jack
Bob Logan	Lefty
Herman Long	Germany
Auerlio Lopez	Senor Smoke, El Lanzallama

Adolph Lorenzen	Lefty
William Louden	Baldy
Elmer Love	Slim
Grover Lowdermilk	Slim
Bobby Lowe	Link
Willie Ludloph	Wee Willie
Japhet Lynn	Red
Duane Maas	Duke
Miles Main	Alex
Harry Malmberg	Swede
Clyde Manion	Pete
Henry Manush	Heinie
Cliff Mapes	Tiger
Fred Marberry	Firpo
Charles Marrow	Buck
Alfred Martin	Billy, Billy the Kid
Charlie Maxwell	Smokey
Lewis McAllister	Sport
Frank McDermott	Red
Maurice McDermott	Mickey
Jim McGarr	Reds
James McGuire	Deacon
Archie McKain	Happy
Raymond McKee	Red
Wayne McLeland	Nubbin
Carl McNabb	Skinny
Eric McNair	Boob
George Mercer	Win
Frank Metha	Scat
Lambert Meyer	Dutch
Gene Michael	Stick
Jim Middleton	Rifle Jim
Ed Mierkowicz	Butch
James Miller	Hack
Roscoe Miller	Roxy, Rubberlegs
Manny Montejo	Pete
Chet Morgan	Chick
Tom Morgan	Plowboy
Wycliffe Morton	Bubba
Don Mossi	The Sphinx
George Mullin	Wabash George
John Murphy	Soldier Boy
William Nance	Doc, Kid
Julio Navarro	Whiplash
Francis Nekola	Bots
Lynn Nelson	Line Drive
Hal Newhouser	Prince Hal
Norman Newsom	Bobo, Buck
Jim Northrup	The Gray Fox
Henry Oana	Prince

Frank Okrie	Lefty
John Oldham	Red
Arthur Olsen	Ole
Karl Olson	Ole
Frank O'Rourke	Blackie
Forrest Orrell	Joe
Larry Osborne	Bobo
Frank Overmire	Stubby
Frank Owen	Yip
Francis Parker	Salty
Vernon Parks	Slicker
Edward Parsons	Dixie
Harold Partenheimer	Steve
Joseph Peploski	Pepper
Ralph Perkins	Cy
Henry Pernoll	Hub
William Perritt	Pol
William Perry	Hank, Socks
John Peters	Shotgun
Daniel Petry	Peaches
Clarence Phillips	Red
Jack Phillips	Stretch
John Phillips	Bubba
Herman Pillette	Old Folks
Ralph Pinelli	Babe
Henry Pippen	Cotton
Cletus Poffenberger	Boots
Ray Powell	Rabbit
Joseph Presko	Little Joe
John Prudhomme	Augie
Dick Radatz	The Monster
Raymond Radcliff	Rip
Ed Rakow	Rock
Jim Ray	Sting
Arthur Raymond	Bugs
Phil Regan	The Vulture
Frank Reiber	Tubby
Tony Rensa	Pug
Emory Rigney	Topper
Clyde Robinson	Rabbit
Robert Rolfe	Red
Lynwood Rowe	Schoolboy
Dave Rozema	The Rose
Herold Ruel	Muddy
Joe Sargent	Horse Belly
Herman Schaefer	Germany
Walter Schaller	Biff
Charles Schmidt	Boss
Henry Schuble	Heinie
Bob Schultz	Bill

George Schultz	Barney
Joe Schultz	Dode
Wayne Scrivener	Chuck
Johnny Seale	Durango Kid
Roman Semproch	Ray, Baby
Truett Sewell	Rip
Ivey Shiver	Chick
Charles Shorten	Chick
Al Simmons	Bucketfoot Al
George Simmons	Hack
Duane Sims	Duke
Lou Skizas	The Nervous Greek
John Skopec	Buckshot
George Smith	Heinie
Willie Smith	Wonderful Willie
Steve Souchock	Bud
George Speer	Kid
Edward Spencer	Tubby
George Stainback	Tuck
Joe Staton	Slim
Daniel Staub	Rusty
Walter Stewart	Lefty
John Stone	Rocky
Ulysses Stoner	Lil
Jesse Stovall	Scout
Ralph Stroud	Sailor
Tom Sturdivant	Snake
Carl Sullivan	Jack
Ed Summers	Kickapoo
John Summers	Champ
George Susce	Good Kid
Gary Sutherland	Suds
Harvey Sutherland	Suds
Bill Taylor	Cash
George Tebbetts	Birdie
Forrest Thomas	Frosty
Luther Thomas	Bud
Charles Thompson	Tim
Sam Thompson	Big Sam
Dave Tobik	Tobe
Jim Tobin	Abba Dabba
Earl Torgeson	The Earl of Snohomish
Aloysius Travers	Allan
Paul Trout	Dizzy
Robert Troy	Bun
Virgil Trucks	Fire
Bob Uhle	Lefty
George Uhle	The Bull
Orville Veal	Coot
George Vico	Sam

Nicknames (continued)

Jacob Wade	Whistlin' Jake
Mark Wagner	Peanut
Fred Walker	Dixie
Gerald Walker	Gee
Harvey Walker	Hub
Jon Warden	Warbler
James Webb	Skeeter
Dick Weik	Legs
Lou Whitaker	Sweet Lou
Joyner White	Jo-Jo
Jimmy Wiggs	Big Jim
Bill Wight	Lefty
Claud Williams	Lefty
Johnny Williams	Honolulu Johnny
George Wilson	Icehouse
George Wilson (catcher)	Squanto
Jack Wilson	Black Jack
Robert Wilson	Red
William Wilson	Mutt
Al Wingo	Red
George Winter	Sassafras
Kendall Wise	Casey
John Wockenfuss	Fuss
Ralph Works	Judge
George Wuestling	Yats
Joe Yeager	Little Joe
Tom Yewcic	Kibby
Eddie Yost	The Walking Man
Gus Zernial	Ozark Ike

3. ALL-TIME TIGER ROSTER (1901–1980)

—A—

Aber, Al, P, 1953–57
Adams, Bob, C, 1977
Aguirre, Hank, P, 1958–67
Ainsmith, Eddie, C, 1919–21
Akers, Bill, IF, 1929–31
Alexander, Dale, IF-OF, 1929–32
Alten, Ernie, P, 1920
Alusik, George, OF, 1958, 1961–62
Alvarado, Luis, IF, 1977
Alvarez, Ossie, IF, 1959
Amoros, Sandy, OF, 1960
Anderson, Bob, P, 1963
Archer, Jimmy, C-IF, 1907
Archie, George, IF, 1938
Arndt, Harry, IF-OF, 1902
Arroyo, Fernando, P, 1975, 1977–79

Auker, Eldon, P, 1933–38
Averill, Earl, OF, 1939–40
Ayers, Doc, P, 1919–21

—B—

Bailey, Bill, P, 1918
Baker, Del, C, 1914–16
Baker, Steve, P, 1978
Baldwin, Billy, OF, 1975
Bare, Ray, P, 1975–77
Barfoot, Clyde, P, 1926
Barnes, Frank, P, 1929
Barnes, Sam, IF, 1921
Barrett, Jimmy, OF, 1901–05
Bartell, Dick, IF, 1940–41
Bashang, Al, OF, 1912
Bassler, Johnny, C, 1921–27
Batts, Matt, C, 1952–54
Baumann, Paddy, IF–OF, 1911–14
Baumgartner, Harry, P, 1920
Baumgartner, John, IF, 1953
Bearden, Gene, P, 1951
Beck, Erve, IF–OF, 1902
Beck, Walter, P, 1944
Beckendorf, Heinie, C, 1909–10
Belardi, Wayne, IF–OF, 1954–56
Bell, Beau, OF, 1939
Benton, Al, P, 1938–42, 1945–48
Berberet, Lou, C, 1959–60
Bero, Johnny, IF, 1948
Berry, Neil, IF, 1948–52
Bertoia, Reno, IF–OF, 1953–58, 1961–62
Beville, Monte, C–IF, 1904
Bilko, Steve, IF, 1960
Billingham, Jack, P, 1978–80
Billings, Haskell, P, 1927–29
Birrer, Babe, P, 1955
Black, Bud, P, 1952, 1955–56
Blessitt, Ike, OF, 1972
Bloodworth, Jimmy, IF, 1942–43, 1946
Blue, Lu, IF–OF, 1921–27
Boehler, George, P, 1912–16
Bogart, John, P, 1920
Boland, Bernie, P, 1915–20
Bolling, Frank, IF, 1954, 1956–60
Bolling, Milt, IF, 1958
Bolton, Cliff, C, 1937
Boone, Danny, P, 1921
Boone, Ray, IF, 1953–58
Borom, Red, IF, 1944–45
Boros, Steve, IF, 1957–58, 1961–62
Borowy, Hank, P, 1950–51

Boswell, Dave, P, 1971
Brady, Jim, P, 1956
Branca, Ralph, P, 1953-54
Brideweser, Jim, IF, 1956
Bridges, Rocky, IF, 1959-60
Bridges, Tommy, P, 1930-43, 1945-46
Brinkman, Ed, IF, 1971-74
Brookens, Ike, P, 1975
Brookens, Tom, IF, 1979-80
Brower, Lou, IF, 1931
Brown, Dick, C, 1961-62
Brown, Gates, OF-IF, 1963-75
Brown, Ike, IF-OF, 1969-74
Browning, Frank, P, 1910
Bruce, Bob, P, 1959-61
Bruckmiller, Andy, P, 1905
Brunsberg, Arlo, C, 1966
Bruton, Billy, OF, 1961-64
Bucha, Johnny, C, 1953
Buddin, Don, IF, 1962
Buelow, Fritz, C-IF, 1901-04
Bullard, George, IF, 1954
Bunning, Jim, P, 1955-63
Burke, Les, IF-C, 1923-26
Burns, Bill, P, 1912
Burns, George, IF, 1914-17
Burns, Jack, IF, 1936
Burns, Joe, OF, 1913
Burns, John, IF, 1903-04
Burnside, Pete, P, 1959-60
Burnside, Sheldon, P, 1978-79
Bush, Donie, IF, 1908-21
Byrd, Harry, P, 1957

—C—

Cain, Bob, P, 1951
Cain, Les, P, 1968, 1970-72
Calvert, Paul, P, 1950-51
Campbell, Bruce, OF, 1940-41
Campbell, Dave, IF, 1967-68
Campbell, Paul, IF, 1948-50
Cantrell, Guy, P, 1930
Carisch, Fred, C, 1923
Carr, Charlie, IF, 1903-04
Carroll, Ownie, P, 1925, 1927-30
Carswell, Frank, OF, 1953
Casale, Jerry, P, 1961-62
Casey, Doc, IF, 1901-02
Casey, Joe, C-OF, 1909-11
Cash, Norm, IF-OF, 1960-74
Cash, Ron, IF-OF, 1973-74
Caster, George, P, 1945-46

Cavet, Pug, P, 1911, 1914–15
Chance, Dean, P, 1971
Chiti, Harry, C, 1960–61
Chris, Mike, P, 1979
Chrisley, Neil, OF–IF, 1959–60
Christian, Bob, IF–OF, 1968
Christman, Mark, IF, 1938–39
Cicotte, Al, P, 1958
Cicotte, Eddie, P, 1905
Claire, Danny, IF, 1920
Clark, Danny, IF-OF, 1922
Clark, Mel, OF, 1957
Clarke, Nig, C, 1905
Clarke, Rufe, P, 1923–24
Clauss, Al, P, 1913
Clifton, Flea, IF, 1934–37
Cobb, Joe, PH, 1918
Cobb, Ty, OF–IF, P, 1905–26
Cochrane, Mickey, C, 1934–37
Coffey, Jack, IF, 1918
Coffman, Slick, P, 1937–39
Colavito, Rocky, OF, 1960–63
Colbert, Nate, IF, 1975
Cole, Bert, P, 1921–25
Coleman, Joe, P, 1955
Coleman, Joe, P, 1971–76
Collier, Orlin, P, 1931
Collins, Kevin, IF–OF, 1970–71
Collins, Rip, P, 1923–27
Comer, Wayne, OF–C, 1967–68, 1972
Comstock, Ralph, P, 1913
Conger, Dick, P, 1940
Conkwright, Allen, P, 1920
Connelly, Bill, P, 1950
Cook, Earl, P, 1941
Cooley, Dick, OF, 1905
Coombs, Jack, P, 1920
Cooper, Wilbur, P, 1926
Corcoran, Tim, OF, 1977–80
Corriden, Red, IF, 1912
Cottier, Chuck, IF, 1961
Couch, Johnny, P, 1917
Coughlin, Bill, IF, 1904–08
Courtney, Ernie, IF, 1903
Coveleski, Harry, P, 1914–18
Covington, Bill, P, 1911–12
Cowens, Al, OF, 1980
Cox, Red, P, 1920
Cramer, Doc, OF, 1942–48
Crawford, Jim, P, 1976–78
Crawford, Sam, OF–IF, 1903–17
Crimian, Jack, P, 1957
Cristante, Leo, P, 1955

Crockett, Davey, IF, 1901
Cronin, Jack, P, 1901–02
Croucher, Frank, IF, 1939–41
Crowder, General, P, 1934–36
Crumpler, Roy, P, 1920
Cullenbine, Roy, OF–IF, 1938–39, 1945–47
Cunningham, George, P–OF, 1916–19, 1921
Curry, Jimmy, IF, 1918
Cutshaw, George, IF, 1922–23

—D—

Dalton, Jack, OF, 1916
Daniel, Chuck, P, 1957
Daugherty, Doc, PH, 1951
Dauss, Hookie, P, 1912–26
Davie, Jerry, P, 1959
Davis, Harry, IF, 1932–33
Davis, Woody, P, 1938
Deal, Charlie, IF, 1912–13
Derring, John, P, 1903
DeFate, Tony, IF, 1917
Delahanty, Jim, IF, 1909–12
Delsing, Jim, OF, 1952–56
Demeter, Don, OF–IF, 1964–66
Demeter, Steve, IF, 1959
Demmit, Ray, OF, 1914
Denehy, Bill, P, 1971
Desautels, Gene, C, 1930–33
DeViveiros, Bernie, IF, 1927
Didier, Bob, C, 1973
Dillard, Steve, IF, 1978
Dillon, Pop, IF, 1901–02
Disch, George, P, 1905
Dittmer, Jack, IF, 1957
Dobson, Pat, P, 1967–69
Doby, Larry, OF, 1959
Doljack, Frank, OF–IF, 1930–34
Donahue, Red, P, 1906
Donohue, Jim, P, 1961
Donovan, Dick, P, 1954
Donovan, Wild Bill, P–IF–OF, 1903–12, 1918
Doran, Tom, C, 1905
Dowd, Snooks, IF, 1919
Downs, Red, IF–OF, 1907–08
Doyle, Jess, P, 1925–27
Drake, Delos, OF–IF, 1911
Dressen, Lee, IF, 1918
Drill, Lew, C–OF–IF, 1904–05
Dropo, Walt, IF, 1952–54
Dubuc, Jean, P–OF, 1912–16
Dugan, Joe, IF, 1931
Dustal, Bob, P, 1963

Dyer, Ben, IF-OF-P, 1916-19
Dyer, Duffy, C, 1980

—E—

Eason, Mel, P, 1903
Easterling, Paul, OF, 1928, 1930
Eaton, Zeb, P, 1944-45
Egan, Dick, P, 1963-64
Egan, Wish, P, 1902
Ehmke, Howard, P, 1916-17, 1919-22
Eisenstat, Harry, P, 1938-39
Elberfeld, Kid, IF, 1901-03
Elder, Heinie, P, 1913
Ellison, Bert, IF-OF, 1916-20
English, Gil, IF, 1936-37
Erickson, Eric, P, 1916, 1918-19
Erickson, Hal, P, 1953
Erwin, Tex, C, 1907
Eubank, John, P, 1905-07
Evers, Hoot, OF, 1941, 1946-52, 1954

—F—

Face, Roy, P, 1968
Fain, Ferris, IF, 1955
Farley, Bob, IF-OF, 1962
Farmer, Ed, P, 1973
Faul, Bill, P, 1962-64
Federoff, Al, IF, 1951-52
Feller, Jack, C, 1958
Fernandez, Chico, IF, 1960-63
Ferry, Cy, P, 1904
Fidrych, Mark, P, 1976-80
Finigan, Jim, IF, 1957
Finneran, Happy, P, 1918
Fischer, Bill, P, 1958, 1960-61
Fischer, Carl, P, 1933-35
Fisher, Fritz, P, 1964
Fisher, Tom, P, 1902
Flagstead, Ira, OF-IF, 1917, 1919-23
Fleming, Les, OF, 1939
Fletcher, Tom, P, 1962
Fletcher, Van, P, 1955
Flowers, Ben, P, 1955
Floyd, Bubba, IF, 1944
Foiles, Hank, C, 1960
Foor, Jim, P, 1971-72
Ford, Gene, P, 1905
Foster, Larry, P, 1963
Fothergill, Bob, OF, 1922-30
Foucault, Steve, P, 1977-78
Fox, Pete, OF, 1933-40

Fox, Terry, P, 1961–66
Foytack, Paul, P, 1953, 1955–63
Francis, Ray, P, 1923
Francona, Tito, OF, 1958
Franklin, Murray, IF, 1941–42
Frasier, Vic, P, 1933–34
Freehan, Bill, C–IF–OF, 1961, 1963–76
Freese, George, PH, 1953
Fried, Cy, P, 1920
Friend, Owen, IF, 1953
Frisk, Emil, P–OF, 1901
Froats, Bill, P, 1955
Fryman, Woodie, P, 1972–74
Fuchs, Charlie, P, 1942
Fuentes, Tito, IF, 1977
Fuller, Frank, IF, 1915–16
Funk, Liz, OF, 1930

—G—

Gagnon, Chick, IF, 1922
Gainor, Del, IF, 1909, 1911–14
Gallagher, Doug, P, 1962
Galloway, Chick, IF–OF, 1928
Gamble, John, IF, 1972–73
Garbowski, Alex, PR, 1952
Garcia, Pedro, IF, 1976
Garver, Ned, P, 1952–56
Gehringer, Charlie, IF, 1924–42
Gelbert, Charley, IF, 1937
Gentry, Rufe, P, 1943–44, 1946–48
Gernert, Dick, IF–OF, 1960–61
Gessler, Doc, OF, 1903
Gibson, Frank, C–OF, 1913
Gibson, Kirk, OF, 1979–80
Gibson, Sam, P, 1926–28
Giebell, Floyd, P, 1939–41
Gilbreth, Bill, P, 1971–72
Gill, George, P, 1937–39
Gillespie, Bob, P, 1944
Ginsberg, Joe, C, 1948, 1950–53
Gladding, Fred, P, 1961–67
Glaiser, John, P, 1920
Gleason, Kid, IF, 1901–02
Glynn, Ed, P, 1975
Goldstein, Izzy, P, 1932
Goldy, Purnal, OF, 1962–63
Gonzales, Dan, OF, 1979–80
Gorsica, Johnny, P, 1940–44, 1946–47
Goslin, Goose, OF, 1934–37
Grabowski, Johnny, C, 1931
Graham, Bill, P, 1966
Graham, Kyle, P, 1929

Gray, Ted, P, 1946, 1948-54
Green, Lenny, OF, 1967-68
Greenberg, Hank, IF-OF, 1930, 1933-41, 1945-46
Greene, Altar, OF, 1979
Greene, Willie, IF, 1903
Gremminger, Ed, IF, 1904
Griggs, Art, IF, 1918
Grilli, Steve, P, 1975-77
Grissom, Marv, P, 1949
Gromek, Steve, P, 1953-57
Groth, Johnny, OF, 1946-52, 1957-60
Grover, Bert, P, 1913
Grzenda, Joe, P, 1961
Gutierrez, Cesar, IF, 1969-71

—H—

Hale, Sammy, IF-OF, 1920-21
Hall, Charley, P, 1918
Hall, Herb, P, 1918
Hall, Marc, P, 1913-14
Haller, Tom, C, 1972
Hamilton, Earl, P, 1916
Hamilton, Jack, P, 1964-65
Hamlin, Luke, P, 1933-34
Haney, Fred, IF, 1922-25
Hankins, Don, P, 1927
Hannan, Jim, P, 1971
Harding, Charlie, P, 1913
Hargrave, Pinky, C, 1928-30
Harley, Dick, OF, 1902
Harper, George, OF, 1916-18
Harrington, Andy, PH, 1925
Harris, Bob, P, 1938-39
Harris, Ned, OF, 1941-43, 1946
Harris, Bucky, IF, 1929, 1931
Harris, Gail, IF, 1958-60
Harrist, Earl, P, 1953
Hatfield, Fred, IF, 1952-56
Hatter, Clyde, P, 1935, 1937
Hayworth, Ray, C, 1926, 1929-38
Hazle, Bob, OF, 1958
Heath, Bill, C, 1967
Hebner, Richie, IF, 1980
Heffner, Don, IF, 1944
Hegan, Jim, C, 1958
Heilmann, Harry, OF-IF, 1914, 1916-29
Hennessy, Les, IF, 1913
Henshaw, Roy, P, 1942-44
Herbert, Ray, P, 1950-51, 1953-54
Herman, Babe, OF, 1937
Herring, Art, P, 1929-33
Herzog, Whitey, OF-IF, 1963

Hetling, Gus, IF, 1906
Hickman, Piano Legs, IF–OF, 1904–05
Hicks, Buddy, IF, 1956
Higgins, Pinky, IF, 1939–44, 1946
High, Ed, P, 1901
High, Hugh, OF, 1913–14
Hiller, John, P, 1965–70, 1972–80
Hitchcock, Billy, IF, 1942, 1946, 1953
Hoeft, Billy, P, 1952–59
Hogsett, Chief, P, 1929–36, 1944
Holdsworth, Fred, P, 1972–74
Holloway, Ken, P, 1922–28
Holling, Carl, P, 1921–22
Holmes, Ducky, OF, 1901–02
Holtgrave, Vern, P, 1965
Hoover, Joe, IF, 1943–45
Hopp, Johnny, IF–OF, 1952
Horton, Willie, OF, 1963–77
Hosley, Tim, C–IF, 1970–71
Host, Gene, P, 1956
Hostetler, Chuck, OF, 1944–45
House, Frank, C, 1950–51, 1954–57, 1961
House, Will, P, 1913
Houtteman, Art, P, 1945–50, 1952–53
Howard, Frank, IF–OF, 1972–73
Hoyt, Waite, P, 1930–31
Huber, Clarence, IF, 1920–21
Huelsman, Frank, OF, 1904
Hughes, Tom, OF, 1930
Humphrey, Terry, C, 1975
Humphreys, Bob, P, 1962
Hutchinson, Fred, P, 1939–41, 1946–53

—I—

Ignasiak, Gary, P, 1973
Irvin, Ed, IF, 1912

—J—

Jackson, Charlie, P, 1905
Jacobson, Baby Doll, OF–IF, 1915
Jaeger, Charlie, P, 1904
James, Art, OF, 1975
James, Bill, P, 1915–19
Jata, Paul, IF–OF, 1972
Jennings, Hughie, IF, 1907, 1909, 1912, 1918
Jensen, Bill, P, 1912
Johns, Augie, P, 1926–27
Johnson, Alex, OF, 1976
Johnson, Earl, P, 1951
Johnson, Ken, P, 1952
Johnson, Roy, OF, 1929–32

Johnson, Syl, P, 1922–25
Jones, Alex, P, 1903
Jones, Bob, IF, 1917–25
Jones, Dalton, IF–OF, 1970–72
Jones, Davy, OF, 1906–12
Jones, Deacon, P, 1916–18
Jones, Elijah, P, 1907, 1909
Jones, Ken, P, 1924
Jones, Lynn, OF, 1979–80
Jones, Sam, P, 1962
Jones, Tom, IF, 1909–10
Jordon, Milt, P, 1953
Justis, Walt, P, 1905

—K—

Kaline, Al, OF–IF, 1953–74
Kallio, Rudy, P, 1918–19
Kane, Harry, P, 1903
Kavanagh, Marty, IF–OF, 1914–16
Kell, George, IF, 1946–52
Keller, Charlie, OF, 1950–51
Kemp, Steve, OF, 1977–80
Kennedy, Bob, IF–OF, 1956
Kennedy, Vern, P, 1938–39
Kerns, Russ, PH, 1945
Kerr, John, IF–OF, 1923–24
Kilkenny, Mike, P, 1969–72
Killefer, Red, IF–OF, 1907–09
Killian, Ed, P, 1904–10
Kimm, Bruce, C, 1976–77
Kimsey, Chad, P, 1936
King, Chick, OF, 1954–56
Kirke, Jay, IF–OF, 1910
Kisinger, Rube, P, 1902–03
Kitson, Frank, P, 1903–05
Klawitter, Al, P, 1913
Kline, Ron, P, 1961–62
Klippstein, Johnny, P, 1967
Kniesch, Rudy, P, 1926
Knox, John, IF, 1972–75
Koch, Al, P, 1963–64
Kocher, Brad, C, 1912
Koenig, Mark, IF–P, 1930–31
Kolloway, Don, IF, 1949–52
Koplitz, Howie, P, 1961–62
Korince, George, P, 1966–67
Kostro, Frank, IF–OF, 1954
Kress, Charlie, IF–OF, 1954
Kress, Red, IF, 1939–40
Kretlow, Lou, P, 1946, 1948–49
Kryhoski, Dick, IF, 1950–51
Kuenn, Harvey, IF–OF, 1952–59

—L—

Laabs, Chet, OF, 1937–39
Labine, Clem, P, 1960
Lafitte, Ed, P, 1909, 1911–12
LaGrow, Lerrin, P, 1970, 1972–75
Lake, Eddie, IF, 1946–50
Lake, Joe, P, 1912–13
Lakeman, Al, C, 1954
Lamont, Gene, C, 1970–72, 1974–75
Landis, Jim, OF, 1967
Lane, Marvin, OF, 1971–74, 1976
Larkin, Steve, P, 1934
Lary, Frank, P, 1954–64
Lasher, Fred, P, 1967–70
Lathers, Chick, IF, 1910–11
Lau, Charlie, C, 1956, 1958–59
Lawrence, Bill, OF, 1932
Lawson, Roxie, P, 1933, 1935–39
Laxton, Bill, P, 1976
Ledbetter, Razor, P, 1915
Lee, Don, P, 1957–58
LeFlore, Ron, OF, 1974–79
Leinhauser, Bill, OF, 1912
Lelivelt, Bill, P, 1909–10
Lemanczyk, Dave, P, 1973–76
Lenhardt, Don, OF, 1952
Lentine, Jim, OF, 1980
Leonard, Dutch, P, 1919–21, 1924–25
Lepcio, Ted, IF, 1959
Lepine, Peter, OF–IF, 1902
Lerchen, George, OF, 1952
Leshnock, Don, P, 1972
Lindbeck, Em, PH, 1960
Lindsay, Pinky, IF, 1905–06
Linhart, Carl, PH, 1952
Lipon, Johnny, IF, 1942, 1946, 1948–52
Littlefield, Dick, P, 1952
Lively, Jack, P, 1911
Lockhead, Harry, IF, 1901
Logan, Bob, P, 1937
Lolich, Mickey, P, 1963–75
Long, Herman, IF, 1903
Lopez, Aurelio, P, 1979–80
Lorenzen, Lefty, P, 1913
Loudell, Art, P, 1910
Louden, Baldy, IF–OF, 1912–13
Love, Slim, P, 1919–20
Lowdermilk, Grover, P, 1915–16
Lowe, Bobby, IF–OF, 1904–07
Ludolph, Willie, P, 1924
Lumpe, Jerry, IF, 1964–67
Lund, Don, OF, 1949, 1952–54

Lush, Billy, OF–IF, 1903
Lynn, Red, P, 1939

—M—

Maas, Duke, P, 1955–57
MacCormack, Frank, P, 1976
Machemer, Dave, IF, 1979
Maddox, Elliott, IF–OF, 1970
Madison, Dave, P, 1952–53
Maharg, Billy, IF, 1912
Maier, Bob, IF–OF, 1945
Main, Alex, P, 1914
Maisel, George, IF, 1916
Makowski, Tom, P, 1975
Malloy, Herm, P, 1907–08
Malmberg, Harry, IF, 1955
Manders, Hal, P, 1941–42, 1946
Manion, Clyde, C–IF, 1920–24, 1926–27
Mankowski, Phil, IF, 1976–79
Manuel, Jerry, IF, 1975–76
Manush, Heinie, OF–IF, 1923–27
Mapes, Cliff, OF, 1952
Marberry, Firpo, P, 1933–35
Marentette, Leo, P, 1965
Marlowe, Dick, P, 1951–56
Marrow, Buck, P, 1932
Marshall, Mike, P, 1967
Martin, Billy, IF, 1958
Masterson, Walt, P, 1956
Matchick, Tom, IF, 1967–69
Mathews, Eddie, IF, 1967–68
Mavis, Bob, PR, 1949
Maxwell, Charlie, OF–IF, 1955–62
May, Milt, C, 1976–79
Mayo, Eddie, IF, 1944–48
McAllister, Sport, OF–IF–C, 1901–03
McAuliffe, Dick, IF, 1960–73
McCarthy, Arch, P, 1902
McCosky, Barney, OF, 1939–42, 1946
McCoy, Benny, IF, 1938–39
McCreery, Ed, P, 1914
McDermott, Mickey, P, 1958
McDermott, Red, OF, 1912
McFarlane, Orlando, C, 1966
McGarr, Jim, IF, 1912
McGarvey, Dan, OF, 1912
McGehee, Pat, P, 1912
McGuire, Deacon, C–IF, 1902–03, 1912
McHale, John, IF, 1943–45, 1947–48
McIntyre, Matty, OF, 1904–10
McKain, Archie, P, 1939–41
McKee, Red, C, 1913–16

McLain, Denny, P, 1963–70
McLaughlin, Pat, P, 1937, 1945
McLeland, Wayne, P, 1951–52
McMackin, Sam, P, 1902
McMahon, Don, P, 1968–69
McManus, Frank, C, 1904
McManus, Marty, IF, 1927–31
McMullin, Fred, IF, 1914
McNabb, Carl, PH, 1945
McNair, Eric, IF, 1941–42
McRae, Norm, P, 1969–70
McTigue, Bill, P, 1916
Meany, Pat, IF, 1912
Meeler, Phil, P, 1972
Mercer, Win, P, 1902
Merritt, Herm, IF, 1921
Metha, Scat, IF, 1940
Metro, Charlie, OF, 1943–44
Meyer, Dan, OF–IF, 1974–76
Meyer, Dutch, IF, 1940–42
Michael, Gene, IF, 1975
Middleton, Jim, P, 1921
Mierkowicz, Ed, OF, 1945, 1947–48
Miller, Bob, P, 1953–56
Miller, Bob, P, 1973
Miller, Hack, C, 1944–45
Miller, Roscoe, P, 1901–02
Mitchell, Clarence, P, 1911
Mitchell, Willie, P, 1916–19
Moford, Herb, P, 1958
Mohardt, John, OF, 1922
Molinaro, Bob, OF, 1975, 1977
Monbouquette, Bill, P, 1966–67
Montejo, Manny, P, 1961
Moore, Anse, OF, 1946
Moore, Bill, P, 1925
Moore, Jackie, C, 1965
Moore, Roy, P, 1922–23
Mooty, Jake, P, 1944
Morales, Jerry, OF, 1979
Moran, Harry, P, 1912
Morgan, Chet, OF, 1935, 1938
Morgan, Tom, P, 1958–60
Moriarty, George, IF–OF, 1905–15
Morris, Jack, P, 1977–80
Morrisette, Bill, P, 1920
Morton Bubba, OF–IF, 1961–63
Moses, Jerry, C, 1974
Mossi, Don, P, 1959–63
Mueller, Les, P, 1941, 1945
Mullen, Billy, IF, 1926
Mullin, George, P–OF, 1902–13
Mullin, Pat, OF, 1940–41, 1946–53

Murphy, Soldier Boy, IF, 1903
Myatt, Glenn, C, 1936

—N—

Nagelson, Russ, OF–IF, 1970
Nance, Doc, OF, 1901
Narleski, Ray, P, 1959
Navarro, Julio, P, 1964–66
Nekola, Bots, P, 1933
Nelson, Lynn, P, 1940
Ness, Jack, IF, 1911
Nettles, Jim, OF, 1974
Neun, Johnny, IF, 1925–28
Newhouser, Hal, P, 1939–53
Newsom, Bobo, P, 1939–41
Nicholls, Simon, IF, 1903
Nicholson, Fred, OF, 1917
Niekro, Joe, P, 1970–72
Nieman, Bob, OF, 1953–54
Nischwitz, Ron, P, 1961–62, 1965
North, Lou, P, 1913
Northrup, Jim, OF–IF, 1964–74

—O—

Oana, Prince, P, 1943, 1945
O'Connell, John, IF, 1902
Oglivie, Ben, IF–OF, 1974–77
Okrie, Frank, P, 1920
Oldham, Red, P, 1914–15, 1920–22
O'Leary, Charley, IF–OF, 1904–12
Olsen, Ole, P, 1922–23
Olson, Karl, OF, 1957
O'Mara, Ollie, IF, 1912
Onslow, Eddie, IF, 1912–13
Onslow, Jack, C, 1912
Orengo, Joe, IF, 1944
O'Rourke, Frank, IF, 1924–26
Orrell, Joe, P, 1943–45
Osborne, Bobo, IF–OF–C, 1957–59, 1961–62
Outlaw, Jimmy, OF–IF, 1943–49
Overmire, Stubby, P, 1943–49
Owen, Frank, P, 1901
Owen, Marv, IF, 1931, 1933–37
Oyler, Ray, IF, 1965–68

—P—

Page, Phil, P, 1928–30
Papi, Stan, IF, 1980

Parker, Salty, IF, 1936
Parks, Slicker, P, 1921
Parrish, Lance, C, 1977–80
Parsons, Dixie, C, 1939, 1942–43
Partenheimer, Steve, IF, 1913
Pasek, Johnny, C, 1933
Patrick, Bob, OF, 1941–42
Patterson, Daryl, P, 1968–71
Payne, Fred, C–OF, 1906–08
Peasley, Marv, P, 1910
Pena, Orlando, P, 1965–67
Pentz, Gene, P, 1975
Peploski, Pepper, IF, 1913
Pepper, Don, IF, 1966
Perkins, Cy, PH, 1934
Pernoll, Hub, P, 1910, 1912
Perranoski, Ron, P, 1971–72
Perritt, Pol, P, 1921
Perry, Boyd, IF, 1941
Perry, Clay, IF, 1908
Perry, Hank, OF, 1912
Perry, Jim, P, 1973
Pesky, Johnny, IF, 1952–54
Peters, John, C, 1915
Peters, Rick, IF–OF, 1979–80
Petry, Dan, P, 1979–80
Philley, Dave, IF–OF, 1957
Phillips, Bubba, IF–OF, 1955, 1963–64
Phillips, Eddie, C, 1929
Phillips, Jack, IF–OF, 1955–57
Phillips, Red, P, 1934, 1936
Pierce, Billy, P, 1945, 1948
Pierce, Jack, IF, 1975
Piet, Tony, IF, 1938
Pillette, Herman, P, 1922–24
Pinelli, Babe, IF, 1920
Pipp, Wally, IF, 1913
Pippen, Cotton, P, 1939–40
Platte, Al, OF, 1913
Podres, Johnny, P, 1966–67
Poffenberger, Boots, P, 1937–39
Porter, J. W., C–OF–IF, 1955–57
Poste, E., OF, 1902
Powell, Ray, OF, 1913
Pratt, Del, IF, 1923–24
Presko, Joe, P, 1957–58
Price, Jim, C, 1967–71
Priddy, Jerry, IF, 1950–53
Proctor, Jim, P, 1959
Prudhomme, Johnny, P, 1929
Purtell, Billy, IF, 1914
Putman, Ed, C, 1979

—Q—

Quellich, George, OF, 1931

—R—

Radatz, Dick, P, 1969
Radcliff, Rip, OF–IF, 1941–43
Rakow, Ed, P, 1964–65
Rapp, Earl, OF, 1949
Ray, Jim, P, 1974
Raymond, Bugs, P, 1904
Redmond, Wayne, OF, 1965, 1969
Reed, Bob, P, 1969–70
Reese, Rich, IF–OF, 1973
Regan, Phil, P, 1960–65
Reiber, Frank, C–OF, 1933–36
Remneas, Alex, P, 1912
Renfer, Erwin, P, 1913
Rensa, Tony, C, 1930
Reynolds, Bob, P, 1975
Reynolds, Ross, P, 1914–15
Rhiel, Billy, IF–OF, 1932–33
Ribant, Dennis, P, 1968
Rice, Harry, OF–IF, 1928–30
Richards, Paul, C, 1943–46
Richardson, Nolen, IF, 1929, 1931–32
Riebe, Hank, C, 1942, 1947–49
Rigney, Topper, IF, 1922–25
Roarke, Mike, C, 1961–64
Robbins, Bruce, P, 1979–80
Roberts, Dave, P, 1976–77
Roberts, Leon, OF, 1974–75
Robertson, Jerry, P, 1970
Robinson, Aaron, C, 1949–51
Robinson, Eddie, IF, 1957
Robinson, Rabbit, IF–OF, 1904
Rodriguez, Aurelio, IF, 1971–79
Rogalski, Joe, P, 1938
Rogell, Billy, IF–OF, 1930–39
Rogovin, Saul, P, 1949–51
Roman, Bill, IF, 1964–65
Rondeau, Henri, C–IF, 1913
Rooker, Jim, P, 1968
Ross, Don, IF–OF, 1938, 1942–45
Rossman, Claude, IF, 1907–09
Rowan, Jack, P, 1906
Rowe, Schoolboy, P, 1933–42
Rozema, Dave, P, 1977–80
Ruble, Art, OF, 1927
Ruel, Muddy, C, 1931–32
Ruhle, Vern, P, 1974–77
Russell, Jack, P, 1937

—S—

Samford, Ron, IF, 1955, 1957
Samuels, Joe, P, 1930
Sanders, Reggie, IF, 1974
Sargent, Joe, IF, 1921
Saunders, Dennis, P, 1970
Scarborough, Ray, P, 1953
Schaefer, Germany, IF–OF, 1905–09
Schaller, Bliff, OF–IF, 1911
Schang, Wally, C, 1931
Schatzeder, Dan, P, 1980
Scheibeck, Frank, IF, 1906
Scherman, Fred, P, 1969–73
Schiappacasse, Lou, OF, 1902
Schmidt, Boss, C–OF, 1906–11
Schuble, Heinie, IF, 1929, 1932–35
Schultz, Barney, P, 1959
Schultz, Bob, P, 1955
Scrivener, Chuck, IF, 1975–77
Seale, Johnnie, P, 1964–65
Seats, Tom, P, 1940
Secory, Frank, OF, 1940
Seelbach, Chuck, P, 1971–74
Semproch, Ray, P, 1960
Sewell, Rip, P, 1932
Sharon, Dick, OF, 1973–74
Shaw, Al, C–IF, 1901
Shaw, Bob, P, 1957–58
Shea, Merv, C, 1927–29, 1939
Shelley, Hugh, OF, 1935
Sherry, Larry, P, 1964–67
Shevlin, Jimmy, IF, 1930
Shiver, Ivey, OF, 1931
Shoop, Ron, C, 1959
Shorten, Chick, OF–C, 1919–21
Siever, Ed, P, 1901–02, 1906–08
Sigafoos, Frank, IF, 1929
Simmons, Al, OF–IF, 1936
Simmons, Hack, IF–OF, 1910
Sims, Duke, C–OF, 1972–73
Sisler, Dave, P, 1959–60
Skeels, Dave, P, 1910
Skizas, Lou, OF–IF, 1958
Skopec, John, P, 1903
Slaton, Jim, P, 1978
Slayback, Bill, P, 1972–74
Sleater, Lou, P, 1957–58
Small, Jim, OF, 1955–57
Smith, Bob, P, 1959
Smith, Clay, P, 1940
Smith, George, P, 1926–29
Smith, George, IF, 1963–65

Smith, Heinie, IF, 1903
Smith, Jack, IF, 1912
Smith, Rufus, P, 1927
Smith, Willie, P, 1963
Sorrell, Vic, P, 1928-37
Souchock, Steve, OF-IF, 1951-55
Sparma, Joe, P, 1964-69
Speer, Kid, P, 1909
Spencer, George, P, 1958, 1960
Spencer, Tubby, C-IF, 1916-18
Spikes, Charlie, OF, 1978
Stainback, Tuck, OF, 1940-41
Staley, Gerry, P, 1961
Stanage, Oscar, C-IF, 1909-20, 1925
Stanley, Mickey, OF-IF, 1964-78
Staton, Joe, IF, 1972-73
Staub, Rusty, OF, 1976-79
Steen, Bill, P, 1915
Stegman, Dave, OF, 1978-80
Steiner, Ben, PR, 1947
Stewart, Walter, P, 1921
Stone, John, OF, 1928-33
Stoner, Lil, P, 1922, 1924-29
Stovall, Jesse, P, 1904
Strahler, Mike, P, 1973
Strampe, Bob, P, 1972
Streuli, Walt, C, 1954-56
Stroud, Sailor, P, 1910
Stuart, Marlin, P, 1949-52
Stump, Jim, P, 1957, 1959
Sturdivant, Tom, P, 1963
Sugden, Joe, IF, 1912
Suggs, George, P, 1908-09
Sullivan, Billy, C, 1916
Sullivan, Billy, C-IF, 1940-41
Sullivan, Charlie, P, 1928, 1930-31
Sullivan, Jack, IF, 1944
Sullivan, Joe, P, 1935-36
Sullivan, John, C, 1905
Sullivan, John, C, 1963-65
Sullivan, Russ, OF, 1951-53
Summers, Champ, OF, 1979-80
Summers, Ed, P, 1908-12
Susce, George, C, 1932
Susce, George, P, 1958-59
Sutherland, Gary, IF, 1974-76
Sutherland, Suds, P, 1921
Sweeney, Bill, IF-OF, 1928
Swift, Bob, C, 1944-53
Sykes, Bob, P, 1977-78
Szotkiewicz, Ken, IF, 1970

—T—

Tavener, Jackie, IF, 1921, 1925–28
Taylor, Bennie, IF, 1952
Taylor, Bill, OF, 1957–58
Taylor, Bruce, P, 1977–79
Taylor, Gary, P, 1969
Taylor, Tony, IF–OF, 1971–73
Taylor, Wiley, P, 1911
Tebbetts, Birdie, C, 1936–42, 1946–47
Terry, John, P, 1902
Thomas, Bud, P, 1939–41
Thomas, Frosty, P, 1905
Thomas, George, IF–OF, 1957–58, 1961, 1964–65
Thomas, Ira, C, 1908
Thompson, Jason, IF, 1976–80
Thompson, Sam, OF, 1906
Thompson, Tim, C, 1958
Timmerman, Tom, P, 1969–73
Tobik, Dave, P, 1978–80
Tobin, Jim, P, 1945
Torgeson, Earl, IF, 1955–57
Tracewski, Dick, IF, 1966–69
Trammell, Alan, IF, 1977–80
Travers, Allan, P, 1912
Tresh, Tom, IF–OF, 1969
Triandos, Gus, C, 1963
Trout, Dizzy, P, 1939–52
Troy, Bun, P, 1912
Trucks, Virgil, P, 1941–43, 1945–52, 1956
Tsitouris, John, P, 1957
Tuttle, Bill, OF, 1952, 1954–57
Tutwiler, Guy, IF–OF, 1911, 1913

—U—

Uhle, Bob, P, 1940
Uhle, George, P, 1929–33
Ujdur, Gerry, P, 1980
Underwood, Pat, P, 1979–80
Unser, Al, C–IF, 1942–44

—V—

Valentinetti, Vito, P, 1958
Vangilder, Elam, P, 1928–29
Veach, Bobby, OF–C–P, 1912–23
Veal, Coot, IF, 1958–60, 1963
Vedder, Lou, P, 1920
Veryzer, Tom, IF, 1973–77
Vico, George, IF, 1948–49
Virgil, Ozzie, IF–C, 1958, 1960–61
Vitt, Ossie, IF–OF, 1912–18

—W—

Wade, Jake, P, 1936-38
Wagner, Hal, C, 1947-48
Wagner, Mark, IF, 1976-80
Wakefield, Dick, OF, 1941, 1943-44, 1946-49
Walker, Dixie, OF, 1938-39
Walker, Frank, OF, 1917-18
Walker, Gee, OF, 1931-37
Walker, Hub, OF, 1931, 1935, 1945
Walker, Luke, P, 1974
Walker, Tom, P, 1975
Walkup, Jim, P, 1939
Walsh, Jim, P, 1921
Ward, Hap, OF, 1912
Warden, Jon, P, 1968
Warner, Jack, IF, 1925-28
Warner, John, C, 1905-06
Watson, Johnny, IF, 1930
Weaver, Roger, P, 1980
Webb, Earl, OF-IF, 1932-33
Webb, Skeeter, IF, 1945-57
Wehmeier, Herm, P, 1958
Weik, Dick, P, 1954
Welch, Milt, C, 1945
Wells, Ed, P, 1923-27
Wert, Don, IF, 1963-70
Wetz, Vic, OF-IF, 1947-52, 1961-63
Wheatley, Charlie, P, 1912
Whillock, Jack, P, 1971
Whitaker, Lou, IF, 1977-80
White, Hal, P, 1941-43, 1946-52
White, Jo-Jo, OF, 1932-38
Whitehill, Earl, P, 1932-38
Wickersham, Dave, P, 1964-67
Wiggs, Jimmy, P, 1905-06
Wight, Bill, P, 1952-53
Wilcox, Milt, P, 1977-80
Willett, Ed, P, 1906-13
Williams, Johnny, P, 1914
Williams, Lefty, P, 1913-14
Wilson, Earl, P, 1966-70
Wilson, Icehouse, PH, 1934
Wilson, Jack, P, 1942
Wilson, Mutt, P, 1920
Wilson, Red, C, 1954-60
Wilson, Squanto, C, 1911
Wilson, Walter, P, 1945
Wingo, Red, OF-IF, 1924-28
Winter, George, P, 1908
Wise, Casey, IF, 1960
Wise, Hughie, C, 1930
Wockenfuss, John, C-OF, 1974-80

Wojey, Peter, P, 1956–57
Wood, Bob, C, 1904–05
Wood, Jake, IF–OF, 1961–67
Wood, Joe, IF, 1943
Woodall, Larry, C, 1920–29
Woodeshick, Hal, P, 1956, 1961
Woods, Ron, OF, 1969
Works, Ralph, P, 1909–12
Wuestling, Yats, IF, 1929–30
Wyatt, John, P, 1968
Wyatt, Whitlow, P, 1929–33

—Y—

Yde, Emil, P, 1929
Yeager, Joe, IF–P–OF, 1901–03
Yelle, Archie, C, 1917–19
Yewcic, Tom, C, 1957
York, Rudy, IF–C–OF, 1934, 1937–45
Yost, Eddie, IF, 1959–60
Young, John, IF, 1971
Young, Kip, P, 1978–79
Young, Ralph, IF, 1915–21

—Z—

Zachary, Chris, P, 1972
Zamloch, Carl, P, 1913
Zepp, Bill, P, 1971
Zernial, Gus, OF–IF, 1958–59
Zuverink, George, P, 1954–55

4. DETROIT IN THE AMERICAN LEAGUE

YEAR	POS	W–L	PCT	GA GB	MANAGER	ATTENDANCE
1901	3	74–61	.548	8½	George Stallings	259,430
1902	7	52–83	.385	30½	Frank Dwyer	189,469
1903	5	65–71	.478	25	Ed Barrow	224,523
1904	7	62–90	.408	32	Ed Barrow–Bobby Lowe	177,796
1905	3	79–74	.516	15½	Bill Armour	193,384
1906	6	71–78	.477	21	Bill Armour	174,043
1907	1	92–58	.613	1½	Hughie Jennings	297,079
1908	1	90–63	.588	½	Hughie Jennings	436,199
1909	1	98–54	.645	3½	Hughie Jennings	490,490
1910	3	86–68	.558	18	Hughie Jennings	391,288
1911	2	89–65	.578	13½	Hughie Jennings	484,988
1912	6	69–84	.451	36½	Hughie Jennings	402,870
1913	6	66–87	.431	30	Hughie Jennings	398,502
1914	4	80–73	.523	19½	Hughie Jennings	416,225
1915	2	100–54	.649	2½	Hughie Jennings	476,105

YEAR	POS	W–L	PCT	GA GB	MANAGER	ATTENDANCE
1916	3	87–67	.565	4	Hughie Jennings	616,772
1917	4	78–75	.510	21½	Hughie Jennings	457,289
1918	7	55–71	.437	20	Hughie Jennings	203,719
1919	4	80–60	.571	8	Hughie Jennings	643,805
1920	7	61–93	.396	37	Hughie Jennings	579,650
1921	6	71–82	.464	27	Ty Cobb	661,527
1922	3	79–75	.513	15	Ty Cobb	861,206
1923	2	83–71	.539	16	Ty Cobb	911,377
1924	3	86–68	.558	6	Ty Cobb	1,015,136
1925	4	81–73	.526	16½	Ty Cobb	820,766
1926	6	74–75	.513	12	Ty Cobb	711,914
1927	4	82–71	.536	27½	George Moriarty	773,716
1928	6	68–86	.442	33	George Moriarty	474,323
1929	6	70–84	.455	36	Bucky Harris	869,318
1930	5	75–79	.487	27	Bucky Harris	649,450
1931	7	61–93	.396	47	Bucky Harris	434,056
1932	5	76–75	.503	29½	Bucky Harris	397,157
1933	5	75–79	.487	25	Bucky Harris-Del Baker	320,972
1934	1	101–53	.656	7	Mickey Cochrane	919,161
1935	1	93–58	.616	3	Mickey Cochrane	1,034,929
1936	2	83–71	.539	19½	Mickey Cochrane	875,948
1937	2	89–65	.578	13	Mickey Cochrane	1,072,276
1938	4	84–70	.545	16	Mickey Cochrane-Del Baker	799,557
1939	5	81–73	.526	26½	Del Baker	836,279
1940	1	90–64	.584	1	Del Baker	1,112,693
1941	T4	75–79	.487	26	Del Baker	684,915
1942	5	73–81	.474	30	Del Baker	580,087
1943	5	78–76	.506	20	Steve O'Neill	606,287
1944	2	88–66	.571	1	Steve O'Neill	923,176
1945	1	88–65	.575	1½	Steve O'Neill	1,280,341
1946	2	92–62	.597	12	Steve O'Neill	1,722,590
1947	2	85–69	.552	12	Steve O'Neill	1,398,093
1948	5	78–76	.506	18½	Steve O'Neill	1,743,035
1949	4	87–67	.565	10	Red Rolfe	1,821,204
1950	2	95–59	.617	3	Red Rolfe	1,951,474
1951	5	73–81	.474	25	Red Rolfe	1,132,641
1952	8	50–104	.325	45	Red Rolfe-Fred Hutchinson	1,026,846
1953	6	60–94	.390	40½	Fred Hutchinson	884,658
1954	5	68–86	.442	43	Fred Hutchinson	1,079,842
1955	5	79–75	.513	17	Bucky Harris	1,181,838
1956	5	82–72	.532	15	Bucky Harris	1,051,182
1957	4	78–76	.506	20	Jack Tighe	1,272,346
1958	5	77–77	.500	15	Jack Tighe-Bill Norman	1,098,924
1959	4	76–78	.494	18	Bill Norman-Jimmie Dykes	1,221,221
1960	6	71–83	.461	26	Jimmie Dykes-Billy Hitchcock-Joe Gordon	1,167,669

YEAR	POS	W–L	PCT	GA GB	MANAGER	ATTENDANCE
1961	2	101–61	.623	8	Bob Scheffing	1,600,710
1962	4	85–76	.528	10½	Bob Scheffing	1,207,881
1963	T5	79–83	.488	25½	Bob Scheffing-Chuck Dressen	821,952
1964	4	85–77	.525	14	Chuck Dressen	816,139
1965	4	89–73	.549	13	Chuck Dressen	1,029,645
1966	3	88–74	.543	10	Chuck Dressen-Bob Swift-Frank Skaff	1,124,293
1967	T2	91–71	.562	1	Mayo Smith	1,447,143
1968	1	103–59	.636	12	Mayo Smith	2,031,847
1969	2	90–72	.556	19	Mayo Smith	1,577,481
1970	4	79–83	.487	29	Mayo Smith	1,501,293
1971	2	91–71	.562	12	Billy Martin	1,591,073
1972	1	86–70	.551	½	Billy Martin	1,892,386

(2–3 vs. Oakland in East-West Series. Att. (3G) at Detroit 129,047)

YEAR	POS	W–L	PCT	GA GB	MANAGER	ATTENDANCE
1973	3	85–77	.525	12	Billy Martin-Joe Schultz	1,724,146
1974	6	72–90	.444	19	Ralph Houk	1,243,080
1975	6	57–102	.358	37½	Ralph Houk	1,058,836
1976	5	74–87	.460	24	Ralph Houk	1,467,020
1977	4	74–88	.457	26	Ralph Houk	1,359,856
1978	5	86–76	.531	13½	Ralph Houk	1,714,893
1979	5	85–76	.528	18	Les Moss-Dick Tracewski-Sparky Anderson	1,630,929
1980	T4	84–78	.519	19	Sparky Anderson	1,785,293

5. TIGER MANAGERS AND THEIR RECORDS

Manager	Years	Wins	Losses	Pct.	Pennants	Champs.
George Stallings	1901	74	61	.548	0	0
Frank Dwyer	1902	52	83	.385	0	0
Ed Barrow	1903–04	97	117	.453	0	0
Bobby Lowe	1904	30	44	.405	0	0
Bill Armour	1905–06	150	152	.497	0	0
Hughie Jennings	1907–20	1131	972	.538	3	0
Ty Cobb	1921–26	479	444	.519	0	0
George Moriarty	1927–28	150	157	.489	0	0
Bucky Harris	1929–33 1955–56	516	557	.481	0	0
Mickey Cochrane	1934–38	413	297	.582	2	1
Del Baker	1933 1938–42	358	317	.530	1	1
Steve O'Neill	1943–48	509	414	.551	1	1
Red Rolfe	1949–52	278	256	.521	0	0
Fred Hutchinson	1952–54	155	235	.397	0	0
Jack Tighe	1957–58	99	104	.488	0	0
Bill Norman	1958–59	58	64	.475	0	0
Jimmie Dykes	1959–60	118	115	.506	0	0

Tiger Managers and Their Records (continued)

Manager	Years	Wins	Losses	Pct.	Pennants	Champs.
Billy Hitchcock	1960	1	0	1.000	0	0
Joe Gordon	1960	26	31	.456	0	0
Bob Scheffing	1961–63	210	173	.548	0	0
Charlie Dressen	1963–66	245	207	.540	0	0
Bob Swift	1966	32	25	.561	0	0
Frank Skaff	1966	40	39	.506	0	0
Mayo Smith	1967–70	363	285	.560	1	1
Billy Martin	1971–73	248	206	.546	1*	0
Joe Schultz	1973	14	12	.538	0	0
Ralph Houk	1974–78	363	443	.450	0	0
Les Moss	1979	27	26	.509	0	0
Dick Tracewski	1979	2	0	1.000	0	0
Sparky Anderson	1979–80	140	128	.522	0	0

*Division title

6. DETROIT OWNERSHIP

1901 — JAMES D. BURNS, hotel man and Wayne County sheriff, is owner-president of charter franchise in American League.

1902 — SAMUEL F. ANGUS, insurance man, buys franchise; FRANK J. NAVIN enters the business office as a bookkeeper.

1904 — WILLIAM HOOVER YAWKEY, son and heir of William Clymer Yawkey, Michigan lumber-ore magnate, buys franchise for $50,000. Navin gets $5,000 and Edward G. Barrow, team manager, $2,500 in stock for arranging sale.

1905 — Yawkey buys Barrow's interest for $1,400.

1907 — Navin acquires the rest of the team half-interest from Yawkey for $40,000 and becomes president.

1920 — WALTER O. BRIGGS, SR. and JOHN KELSEY, auto industrialists, buy quarter shares from the heirs of Yawkey (dec. March 5, 1919) for $250,000 each.

1927 — Briggs becomes half-owner by buying Kelsey stock from his estate.

1935 — Briggs gains complete ownership and becomes president, acquiring Navin stock from his estate (dec. Nov. 13, 1935).

1952 — Briggs's stock goes into estate following his death Jan. 17, 1952; WALTER O. BRIGGS, JR. becomes president.

1956 — All stock is sold by court order Oct. 1, 1956 by Briggs heirs to syndicate of eleven radio-television men headed by JOHN E. FETZER, FRED A. KNORR, and KENYON BROWN for $5,500,000. Knorr is made president; he is succeeded by HARVEY R. HANSEN (April 19, 1957), and WILLIAM O. DeWITT (Sept. 30, 1959).

1960 — JOHN E. FETZER buys out Brown group, becomes president (Oct. 11).

1961 — Fetzer becomes sole owner (Nov. 14), purchasing interest held by Knorr estate (dec. Dec. 27, 1960).

1978 — Fetzer becomes chairman of the board and yields the title of president to James A. Campbell (already general manager).

7. THE BALLPARKS

American League baseball has always been played on one site in Detroit—the present-day site of Tiger Stadium was also the location of the original Bennett Park.

From the first American League season in 1901, Tiger fans have come to the intersection of Michigan and Trumbull Avenues for baseball. The old wooden grandstand held 8,000 fans. With the rise of Ty Cobb as a superstar and the assumption of the club leadership by Frank Navin in 1911, it became apparent that the team was ready for more expansive quarters.

As a result, Navin Field was opened in 1912 with a concrete and steel grandstand. This facility still stands today as Tiger Stadium, although it has undergone considerable renovation over the years.

The original Navin Field seated 29,000 and its dimensions favored right-hand hitters. The right field line was just over 370 feet, the left field line ran 345 feet, and center field stretched to 467 feet.

After the championship years of the thirties, when Walter Briggs assumed control of the team, the facility was expanded in time for the 1938 season to 54,900 seats and renamed Briggs Stadium. New stands in right field cut the length in the corner from 372 to 325 feet, its current dimension. The park remained virtually unchanged for the next forty years except for being renamed Tiger Stadium in 1961.

A renovation was begun in November, 1977 to install new plastic seats, modern broadcast facilities, and a 2 million dollar electronic scoreboard. These improvements were all undertaken by the new ownership of the City of Detroit, which purchased the park for $1 and then leased it back to the Tigers for 30 years, with a 30-year renewal option.

The current capacity of the stadium is 52,067. The seating breaks down as follows: 11,753 box seats; 23,544 reserved; 6,270 general admission; and 10,500 bleachers. The stadium site and parking grounds cover 8½ acres, of which the playing field occupies approximately half. The dimensions are: left field, 340 feet from home plate; left center, 365 feet; center field, 440 feet; right center, 370 feet; and right field, 325 feet. All outfield fences are uniformly nine feet high.

Tiger Stadium was the last American League park to have lights installed. The first night game was not played in Detroit until July 15, 1948, when the Bengals beat the Athletics 4–1. A new $500,000 multi-vapor field lighting system was installed in 1977.

8. THE TOP 20 CROWDS AT TIGER STADIUM

1	58,369	July 20, 1947	New York (dh)
2	57,888	Sept. 26, 1948	Cleveland
3	57,271	June 27, 1961	Chicago (tn)
4	57,235	Aug. 18, 1946	St. Louis (dh)
5	57,149	April 28, 1946	Cleveland
6	57,130	May 19, 1946	Boston (dh)
7	56,787	June 8, 1947	Boston
8	56,586	Aug. 9, 1948	Cleveland (n)
9	56,548	Sept. 16, 1950	New York
10	56,367	May 30, 1947	St. Louis (dh)
11	56,038	Sept. 8, 1946	Chicago (dh)
12	55,875	May 31, 1948	Chicago (dh)
13	55,857	June 5, 1949	Boston (dh)
14	55,787	Sept. 22, 1940	Cleveland
15	55,628	June 25, 1950	New York (dh)
16	55,537	May 30, 1950	Cleveland (dh)
17	55,255	Sept. 19, 1948	Boston (dh)
18	55,189	Oct. 6, 1940	Cincinnati (World Series)
19	55,145	July 7, 1950	Cleveland (n)
20	54,875	July 8, 1945	New York (dh)

9. DETROIT ATTENDANCE RECORDS

Season	1968	3,383,452	Finished First
Home	1968	2,031,847	Finished First
Road	1979	1,548,897	Finished Fifth
Single Game	Sept. 26, 1948	57,888	Cleveland
Doubleheader	Sunday, July 20, 1947	58,369	New York
Single Night Game	August 9, 1948	56,586	Cleveland
Twi-Night Doubleheader	June 27, 1961	57,271	Chicago
Opening Day	April 6, 1971	54,089	Cleveland
Smallest Crowd	Sept. 24, 1928	404	Boston
Smallest Night Game	Aug. 20, 1964	2,173	Los Angeles

10. TIGER SPRING TRAINING SITES

1901 Detroit
1902 Ypsilanti
1903–04 Shreveport, La.
1905–07 Augusta, Ga.
1908 Hot Springs, Ark.
1909–10 San Antonio, Tex.
1911–12 Monroe, La.
1913–15 Gulfport, Miss.
1916–18 Waxahachie, Tex.
1919–20 Macon, Ga.
1921 San Antonio, Tex.

1922–26 Augusta, Ga.
1927–28 San Antonio, Tex.
1929 Phoenix, Ariz.
1930 Tampa, Fla.
1931 Sacramento, Calif.
1932 Palo Alto, Calif.
1933 San Antonio, Tex.
1934–42 Lakeland, Fla.
1943–45 Evansville, Ind.
1946–present Lakeland, Fla.

11. TIGERS WHO SERVED IN WORLD WAR II

Pitchers	**Full Seasons Missed**
Al Benton	1943–44
Tommy Bridges	1944
Johnny Gorsica	1945
Fred Hutchinson	1942–45
Les Mueller	1942–44
Virgil Trucks	1944
Hal White	1944–45

Catchers	
Hank Riebe	1943–45
Birdie Tebbetts	1943–45

Infielders	
Jimmy Bloodworth	1944–45
Murray Franklin	1943–45
Charlie Gehringer	1943–45
Pinky Higgins	1945
Bill Hitchcock	1943–45
Johnny Lipon	1943–45
Dutch Meyer	1943–44
Joe Wood	1944–45

Outfielders

Hoot Evers	1943–45
Hank Greenberg	1942–44
Ned Harris	1944–45
Barney McCosky	1943–45
Pat Mullin	1942–45
Bob Patrick	1943–45
Rip Radcliff	1944–46
Dick Wakefield	1945
Hub Walker	1942–44

12. TIGERS SELECTED IN EXPANSION DRAFTS

December, 1960

Los Angeles Angels—Pitchers Aubrey Gatewood and Bob Sprout, Catcher Bob Rodgers, Infielders Eddie Yost and Steve Bilko

Washington Senators—Pitchers Pete Burnside and Dave Sisler, Infielder Coot Veal

October, 1968

Kansas City Royals—Pitchers Jon Warden, Bill Butler, and Dick Drago

Seattle Pilots—Pitcher Mike Marshall, Infielder Ray Oyler, Outfielder Wayne Comer

November, 1976

Seattle Mariners—Infielder Dan Meyer, Pitchers Frank MacCormack and Bill Laxton

Toronto Blue Jays—Pitchers Dennis DeBarr and Dave Lemanczyk

13. TIGER TALES

A collection of Tiger trivia, tidbits, and down-right amusing incidents from the past 80 years.

* * *

On May 31, 1927, the day Johnny Neun made his unassisted triple play, the pitcher for Cleveland was Garland Buckeye. Garland's sister, Virginia, was married to Russ Dawson, the foremost automobile dealer in Detroit.

* * *

Arithmetic projections using average season statistics indicate that Hank Greenberg would have finished his career with 581 home runs instead of 331 had he not had his career interrupted by military service or suffered a broken wrist in 1936.

* * *

The 1937 Tigers were the only team in baseball history to have four players with 200 hits or more in a season. They were: Hank Greenberg (200), Charlie Gehringer (209), Pete Fox (208), and Gee Walker (213).

* * *

The Tiger outfield of the 1920s was the best hitting outfield of all time, compiling a combined average of .350. Eight of the players hit better than .300 in a season (Ty Cobb, Harry Heilmann, Bobby Veach, Heinie Manush, Al Wingo, Bob Fothergill, Harry Rice, and Roy Johnson). Heinie Manush was the only outfielder who failed to hit .300 in 1924 (.289) and in 1927 (.297).

* * *

Eddie Goostree, a top scout, had 21 prospects make the big leagues, including such Tiger favorites as Schoolboy Rowe, Hub and Gee Walker, Tommy Bridges, Rudy York, Virgil Trucks, and Dizzy Trout. That man sure could pick 'em!

* * *

Tiger Tales (continued)

The 1940 pennant has long been credited to manager Del Baker's decision to move slugger Hank Greenberg to left field and give Rudy York first base. But the real key in making the move a success was the work Tiger coach Bing Miller put into making Greenberg an acceptable leftfielder. A .312 lifetime hitter, Miller was a star outfielder for Connie Mack's championship Athletics of the late twenties and early thirties.

* * *

According to his nephew, former Tiger hurler Bob Troy should receive credit for inventing the forkball instead of Bullet Joe Bush. Troy appeared in only one game for the Bengals in 1912, pitching 6 2/3 innings, yielding nine hits, and losing in his only big league start. Sadly enough, Troy was killed in World War I, dying in Meuse, France on October 7, 1918.

* * *

Don Demeter's 266-game errorless streak came to an end when a dog ran onto the field, distracting him into making a wild throw after cleanly fielding the ball.

* * *

Although Ty Cobb never led the Tigers to a pennant as manager, he did have a marked impact on the team's batting performance. He lifted the team batting average from .270 in 1920 to .316 during his first year as manager in 1921. During Cobb's tenure, from 1921 to 1926, the team averaged .302. His greatest protege was outfielder Harry Heilmann, who won four batting titles and compiled a lofty .342 lifetime average. But Cobb never could live down giving minor league pitcher Carl Hubbell his release!

* * *

The Tigers could field an awesome mythical all-time team of .300 hitters. Imagine a lineup with these lifetime averages:

First Base — Hank Greenberg, .313
Second Base — Charlie Gehringer, .320
Third Base — George Kell, .306
Shortstop — Harvey Kuenn, .303
Left Field — Sam Crawford, .309
Center Field — Ty Cobb, .367
Right Field — Harry Heilmann, .342
Catcher — Mickey Cochrane, .324

* * *

The Tigers paid for their 1905 spring training rent in Augusta, Georgia by giving the local team a young pitcher, Eddie Cicotte. Cicotte won 210 games during his Major League career, but he is best known for his infamous involvement in the 1919 Black Sox scandal.

* * *

Former pitcher Ed Rakow was quite an athlete. At one time, he was a good football player in the Pittsburgh area. Rakow played quarterback for the semi-pro Bloomfield Rams, but he lost his job in 1956 to an up-and-coming signal caller named Johnny Unitas.

* * *

The 1921 Tigers compiled an incredible team batting average of .316 — and still managed to finish in sixth place, 26½ games behind the Yankees. Rightfielder Harry Heilmann led the league with a .394 average, closely followed by playing manager and centerfielder Ty Cobb at .389. The other regulars in the lineup had these averages: leftfielder Bobby Veach, .338; first baseman Lu Blue, .308; catcher Johnny Bassler, .307; shortstop Ira Flagstead, .305; third baseman Ducky Jones, .303; and second baseman Pep Young, .299.

* * *

Where did the "Tiger" nickname originate? It appears that an unidentified headline writer at the *Free Press* coined it in 1895 when Detroit had a team in the Western League, a forerunner of the American League.

* * *

One day in the early 1900s, a strapping young pitcher showed up at Bennett Field seeking a tryout. He was so big that the team could only provide him with a shirt for the tryout instead of a complete uniform.

After hitting Germany Schaefer in the neck with a fast ball and cracking Charley O'Leary's ribs with a pitch, he was sent packing.

The youngster with poor control managed to tame his wildness. Big Jeff Tesreau wound up winning 118 games in seven seasons with the New York Giants, including 20-game winning seasons in 1913 and 1914.

* * *

Dizzy Trout's career with the Tigers almost never got off the ground, thanks to a run-in with Mickey Cochrane. At the 1937 training camp, after several poor showings in exhibitions, Trout borrowed a police motorcycle and made a couple of trips around the field.

Passing Cochrane, Trout asked his manager, "How am I doin', Mike?"

"Just fine," replied the fiery skipper. "You can keep riding that thing to Toledo, because that's where you'll be this year."

Trout spent the next two seasons at Toledo.

* * *

Aaron Robinson is remembered for more than just being what the Tigers received when they traded southpaw Billy Pierce to the White Sox.

In the stretch drive of September, 1950, Robinson was the goat on a play that seriously hurt the Bengals' bid for first.

The Indians had the bases loaded with one out in the 10th when Luke Easter grounded to first baseman Don Kolloway. Kolloway touched first and threw home to Robinson. Unaware that the forceout situation was gone, Robinson stepped on the plate and did not tag Bob Lemon who slid home for a 2-1 Indian win.

Asked about the play, Robinson explained that he never saw Kolloway step on first.

The Tigers eventually finished 3 games in back of the league-leading Yankees.

* * *

Babe Ruth was Frank Navin's first choice to succeed Bucky Harris as manager in 1934. The Yankees were eager to find a way to ease Ruth out gracefully, and a deal to the Tigers as a playing manager seemed ideal.

Navin asked Ruth to come to Detroit to meet with him, but the Babe had scheduled a trip to Hawaii with his family and said he would see Navin upon his return.

The rebuff annoyed Navin, who then made the celebrated deal to obtain Mickey Cochrane from the Philadelphia Athletics.

* * *

The infield of the 1934 American League champion Tigers drove in an incredible 462 runs among them. Leading the way was first baseman Hank Greenberg with 139 RBIs, followed by second baseman Charlie Gehringer (127), shortstop Billy Rogell (100), and third baseman Marv Owen (96).

14. TOP TIGER PERFORMANCES

INDIVIDUAL BATTING

Highest average season	.420	Ty Cobb	1911
Most times at bat, season	679	Harvey Kuenn	1953
	642	Rusty Staub (LH)	1978
Most runs scored, season	147	Ty Cobb	1911
Most hits, season	248	Ty Cobb	1911
*Most hits in succession	12	Walt Dropo	1952
Most pinch hits in succession	5	Vic Wertz	1962
Most singles, season	169	Ty Cobb	1911
	167	Harvey Kuenn (RH)	1953

135

Individual Batting (continued)

+Most cons. hits in game (12 inn.)	7	Cesar Gutierrez	.... June 21, 1970
Most hits in game (22 inn.)	7	Rocky Colavito	.... June 24, 1962
Most two-base hits, season	63	Hank Greenberg	 1934
§Most three-base hits, season	26	Sam Crawford	 1914
Most home runs, season	58	Hank Greenberg	 1938
	41	Norm Cash (LH)	 1961
*Most home runs, home park (season)	39	Hank Greenberg	 1938
*Most home runs, one month	18	Rudy York	 1937
Most home runs, first season	35	Rudy York	 1937
Most runs batted in, season	183	Hank Greenberg	 1937
*Most total bases, inning	8	Al Kaline	 1955
§Most total bases, 9-inn. game	16	Ty Cobb	 1925
Most total bases, season	397	Hank Greenberg	 1937
Most bases on balls, season	137	Roy Cullenbine	 1947
*Most strikeouts, 9-inn. game	5	Chet Laabs	 1938
Most strikeouts, season	141	Jake Wood	 1961
Fewest strikeouts, season	13	Charley Gehringer	 1936
		Harvey Kuenn	 1954
&Most hit by pitcher, season	24	Bill Freehan	 1968
Most cons. games hit safely	40	Ty Cobb	 1911

MISC. INDIVIDUAL BATTING

&Most stolen bases, season	96	Ty Cobb	 1915
+Most caught stealing, season	38	Ty Cobb	 1915
&Most consecutive stolen bases	27	Ron LeFlore	 1978
*Most intentional walks, 9-inn. game	3	Bill Freehan	.... June 2, 1971
*Most times hit into DP, game	4	Goose Goslin	 1934
Most times hit into DP, season	29	Jimmy Bloodworth	 1943
*Fewest times hit into DP, season	0	Dick McAuliffe (151G)	 1968
Most RBI in game	8	Jim Northrup	.... June 24, 1968
			July 11, 1973
Three successive homers, inning		Cullenbine, Wakefield, Evers	 1947
		Kuenn, Torgeson, Maxwell	 1956
		Cash, Boros, Brown	 1961
		Northrup, Cash, Horton	 1971
		Rodriguez, Kaline, Horton	 1972
		Kaline, Freehan, Stanley	 1974
Three home runs in game		Cobb 1925, Higgins 1940, York, 1941, Mullin 1949, Kaline, 1955, Maxwell 1959, Colavito 1961, + '62, Boros 1962, Horton 1970, Freehan 1971	
*Most home runs in inning	2	Al Kaline	 1955
*Most home runs, cons. app., 2 games	4	Greenberg 1938, Maxwell 1959	
*Most home runs in double-header	4	Maxwell 1959, Colavito 1961	

136

*Most home runs, two cons. games	5	Ty Cobb	1925
Most home runs, bases filled, season	4	Rudy York 1938, Ray Boone 1953, Jim Northrup 1968	

TEAM FIELDING LEADERS

First basemen	.997	Norm Cash	1964
Second basemen	.987	Frank Bolling	1959
		Dick McAuliffe	1971
Third basemen	.987	Aurelio Rodriguez	1978
+Shortstops	.990	Ed Brinkman	1972
*Outfielders	1.000	Mickey Stanley	1968 & 1970
		Al Kaline	1971
Catchers	.997	Bill Freehan	1970
Team fielding season	.984		1972
§Most games by shortstop, season	162	Ed Brinkman	1973
+Most cons. games, no errors by shortstop	72	Ed Brinkman	1972
+Fewest errors, season, by shortstop	7	Ed Brinkman	1972
+Most cons. games, no errors by outfielder (AL only)	242	Al Kaline	1969–1972
+Most cons. games, no errors by outfielder (140–NL, 126–AL)	266	Don Demeter	1962–1965
*Most putouts by leftfielder, game	11	Willie Horton	1969
§Most putouts by centerfielder, game	11	Mickey Stanley	1973
Highest fielding avg. by OF, career	.991	Mickey Stanley	1964–1978
Most chances acc. by catcher, game	19	Bill Freehan	1969
+Most chances acc. by catcher, career	10,662	Bill Freehan	1961–1976
+Most putouts by catcher, career	9,941	Bill Freehan	1961–1976
+Highest field avg. by catcher, career	.993	Bill Freehan	1961–1976

INDIVIDUAL PITCHING

Most victories, season	31	Denny McLain	1968
	29	Hal Newhouser (LH)	1944
Highest season percentage	.862	Bill Donovan (25–4)	1907
Lowest earned run avg.	1.81	Hal Newhouser	1945
Most games, season	69	Fred Scherman	1971
Most games started, season	45	Mickey Lolich	1971
Most games finished, season	60	John Hiller	1973

Individual Pitching (continued)

Most complete games, season	42	George Mullin	1904
&Most victories by pitcher in relief, season	17	John Hiller	1974
*Most defeats by pitcher in relief, season	14	John Hiller	1974
+Most saves, season	38	John Hiller	1973
Most defeats, season	23	George Mullin	1904
Most innings pitched, season	381	George Mullin	1904
Most shutouts pitched, season	9	Denny McLain	1969
Most bases on balls, season	158	Joe Coleman	1974
Most strikeouts, game	16	Mickey Lolich (twice)	1969
Most strikeouts, season	308	Mickey Lolich	1971
	280	Denny McLain (RH)	1968
Most cons. strikeouts, game	7	Denny McLain	1965
		John Hiller	1970
*Most cons. strikeouts, start of game	6	John Hiller	1968
+Most cons. strikeouts in relief	7	Denny McLain	1965
§Most cons. victories, one season	16	Schoolboy Rowe	1934
Most home run pitches, season	42	Denny McLain	1966
*Most hit batsmen, game	4	Earl Whitehill	1924
		Frank Lary	1960
Most hit batsmen, season	23	Howard Ehmke	1922
*Most wild pitches, game	5	Charles Wheatley	1912
Most wild pitches, season	16	Jean Dubuc	1912

TEAM RECORDS

&Team batting, season	.316		1921
Most runs scored, inning	13	vs. New York	June 17, 1925
Most runs scored, game	21	vs. Cleveland	Sept. 15, 1901
		Philadelphia	July 17, 1908
		St. Louis	July 25, 1920
		Chicago	July 1, 1936
&Most runs scored, doubleheader	36	vs. St. Louis	Aug. 14, 1937
&Most runs yielded, inning	17	to Boston	June 18, 1953
Most runs yielded, game	24	to Philadelphia	May 18, 1912
Most hits, game	28	vs. New York	Sept. 29, 1928
&Most hits, season	1724		1921
&Most hits yielded, inning	14	to Boston	June 18, 1953
Most hits yielded, game	27	to Boston	June 18, 1953
*Most sacrifice hits, innings	3	vs. Baltimore	July 12 (1), 1970
&Most doubles, game	11	vs. New York	July 14, 1934
§Most triples, game	6	vs. New York	June 17, 1922
Most home runs, inning	4	Trout, Priddy, Wertz, Evers vs. New York	June 23, 1950
		Kaline, Freehan, Stanley, Brinkman at Cleveland	July 29, 1974

138

Most home runs, game	6	vs. St. Louis	Aug. 14, 1937
		Philadelphia	June 11, 1954
		Kansas City	July 20, 1962
		California	July 4, 1968
		Oakland	Aug. 17, 1969
		Boston	Aug. 9, 1971
Most home runs, season	209		1962
*Most bases on balls, 9-inn. game	18	vs. Philadelphia	May 9, 1916
Most strikeouts, 9-inn. game	18	vs. Cleveland	Oct. 1, 1938
Most strikeouts, extra-inn. game (10)	21	vs. Cleveland	Sept. 18, 1966
Most strikeouts by pitchers, season	1069		1965
*Most pinch hitters used, inn.	6	vs. NY (7th inn.)	Sept. 5, 1971
&Most pinch hits, game	4	vs. Chicago	April 22, 1953
Most pinch hit home runs, season	8		1971
Most cons. games won	14		1909 & 1934
Most cons. games lost	19		1975
Most victories, season	103		1968
Fewest victories, season	50		1952
§Longest game by innings	24	vs. Phila. (1-1 tie)	July 21, 1945
&Longest 9-inn. game in time	3:54	vs. Kansas City	July 23 (2), 1961
&Longest extra-inn. game in time	7:00	vs. NY (22 inn.)	June 24, 1962
+Most tie games played	10		1904
Most one-run games played	65		1971
+Most cons. errorless games	12		1963
+Fewest errors, season, by club	96		1972
Most errorless games, season, by club	84		1973
*Fewest balks, season by club	0		1972
&Most games, league, club	12,435		1901–present

TOP TIGER PERFORMANCES

(Records prior 1961 in 154-game schedule, 162 in 1961 and later except 156 in 1972)

American League Record
§American League Record Tied

+Major League Record
*Major League Record Tied

TIGER ALL-STAR GAME SELECTIONS

1933
Charlie Gehringer*

1934
Tommy Bridges
Mickey Cochrane
Charlie Gehringer*

1935
Tommy Bridges
Mickey Cochrane
Charlie Gehringer*
Schoolboy Rowe

1936
Tommy Bridges
Charlie Gehringer*
Leon Goslin
Schoolboy Rowe

1937
Tommy Bridges
Charlie Gehringer*
Hank Greenberg
Gerald Walker

1938
Charlie Gehringer*
Hank Greenberg
Vern Kennedy
Rudy York

1939
Tommy Bridges*
Hank Greenberg*
Bobo Newsom

1940
Tommy Bridges
Hank Greenberg*
Bobo Newsom

1941
Al Benton
Birdie Tebbetts*
Rudy York*

1942
Al Benton
Hal Newhouser
Birdie Tebbetts*
Rudy York*

1943
Hal Newhouser
Dick Wakefield*
Rudy York

1944
Pinky Higgins
Hal Newhouser
Dizzy Trout
Rudy York

1945
No game

1946
Hal Newhouser

1947
George Kell*
Pat Mullin
Hal Newhouser*
Dizzy Trout

1948
Hoot Evers*
George Kell*
Pat Mullin*
Hal Newhouser

1949
George Kell*
Virgil Trucks
Vic Wertz

1950
Hoot Evers*
Ted Gray
Art Houtteman
George Kell*

1951
Fred Hutchinson
George Kell*
Vic Wertz*

1952
Vic Wertz

1953
Harvey Kuenn

1954
Ray Boone*
Harvey Kuenn

1955
Bill Hoeft
Al Kaline*
Harvey Kuenn*

1956
Ray Boone
Al Kaline*
Harvey Kuenn*
Charley Maxwell

1957
Jim Bunning*
Al Kaline*
Harvey Kuenn*
Charley Maxwell

1958
Al Kaline
Harvey Kuenn

1959
Jim Bunning
Al Kaline+
Harvey Kuenn+

1960
Al Kaline+
Frank Lary+

1961
Jim Bunning+
Norm Cash*+
Rocky Colavito+
Al Kaline+
Frank Lary

1962
Hank Aguirre+
Jim Bunning+
Rocky Colavito+
Al Kaline

1963
Jim Bunning
Al Kaline*

1964
Bill Freehan
Al Kaline
Jerry Lumpe

1965
Bill Freehan
Willie Horton*
Al Kaline
Dick McAuliffe*

1966
Norm Cash
Bill Freehan*
Al Kaline
Dick McAuliffe*
Denny McLain*

1967
Bill Freehan*
Al Kaline*
Dick McAuliffe

1968
Bill Freehan*
Willie Horton*
Denny McLain
Don Wert

1969
Bill Freehan*
Mickey Lolich
Denny McLain

1970
Bill Freehan*
Willie Horton

1971
Norm Cash
Bill Freehan*
Al Kaline
Mickey Lolich

1972
Norm Cash
Bill Freehan*
Mickey Lolich

1973
Ed Brinkman
Bill Freehan
Willie Horton

1974
John Hiller
Al Kaline

1975
Bill Freehan

1976
Mark Fidrych*
Ron LeFlore*
Rusty Staub*

1977
Mark Fidrych#
Jason Thompson

1978
Jason Thompson

Tiger All-Star Game Selections (continued)

1979
Steve Kemp

1980
Lance Parrish
Alan Trammell

*Voted starter or started
#Selected but unable to play
+Two games 1959–62

15. TIGERS TO REMEMBER
VARIOUS AWARDS

Tiger of the Year
(Selected by Detroit Baseball Writers Assn.)

1965 — Don Wert	1971 — Mickey Lolich	1977 — Ron LeFlore
1966 — Denny McLain	1972 — Ed Brinkman	1978 — Ron LeFlore
1967 — Bill Freehan	1973 — John Hiller	1979 — Steve Kemp
1968 — Denny McLain	1974 — Al Kaline	1980 — Alan Trammell
1969 — Denny McLain	1975 — Willie Horton	
1970 — Tom Timmerman	1976 — Mark Fidrych	

Rookie of the Year
(Selected by Detroit Sports Broadcasters Assn.)

1969 — Mike Kilkenny	1973 — Dick Sharon	1977 — Dave Rozema
1970 — Elliott Maddox	1974 — Ron LeFlore	1978 — Lou Whitaker
1971 — None eligible	1975 — Vern Ruhle	1979 — Lynn Jones
1972 — Chuck Seelbach	1976 — Mark Fidrych	1980 — Rick Peters

King Tiger
(Congeniality Award by Tiger Fan Clubs)

1961 — Steve Boros	1968 — Bill Freehan	1975 — Bill Freehan
1962 — Mike Roarke	1969 — Norm Cash	1976 — Mickey Stanley
1963 — Bill Freehan	1970 — Al Kaline	1977 — Mickey Stanley
1964 — Hank Aguirre	1971 — Fred Scherman	1978 — Lance Parrish
1965 — Don Wert	1972 — Fred Scherman	1979 — Steve Kemp
1966 — Dick McAuliffe	1973 — John Hiller	1980 — Alan Trammell
1967 — Bill Freehan	1974 — Mickey Lolich	

The Sporting News Awards

Most Valuable Player (AL) — Hank Greenberg 1935, 1940
 Charlie Gehringer 1937
 Eddie Mayo 1945
Player of the Year (AL) — Al Kaline 1955, 1963
Pitcher of the Year (AL) — Denny McLain 1968, 1969
Player of the Year (ML) — Hal Newhouser 1945
 Denny McLain 1969
Fireman of the Year (AL) — John Hiller 1973
Rookie of the Year (AL) — Harvey Kuenn 1953

Rookie Pitcher of the Year (AL) — Mark Fidrych 1976
Dave Rozema 1977
Manager of the Year (ML) — Red Rolfe 1950
Mayo Smith 1968
Executive of the Year (ML) — W. O. Briggs, Sr. 1940
James A. Campbell 1968

Gold Glove Awards

1957 Al Kaline, OF	A! Kaline, OF
1958 Frank Bolling, 2B	1967 Bill Freehan, C
Al Kaline, OF	Al Kaline, OF
1959 Al Kaline, OF	1968 Bill Freehan, C
1961 Al Kaline, OF	Mickey Stanley, OF
Frank Lary, P	1969 Bill Freehan, C
1962 Al Kaline, OF	Mickey Stanley, OF
1963 Al Kaline, OF	1970 Mickey Stanley, OF
1964 Al Kaline, OF	1972 Ed Brinkman, SS
1965 Bill Freehan, C	1973 Mickey Stanley, OF
Al Kaline, OF	1976 Aurelio Rodriguez, 3B
1966 Bill Freehan, C	1980 Alan Trammell, SS

Silver Bat Award

1980 Lance Parrish, c

Batting Champions

Ty Cobb: 1907 1909 1911 1913 1915 1918
1908 1910 1912 1914 1917 1919
Harry Heilmann: 1921 1925
1923 1927
Heinie Manush: 1926
Al Kaline: 1955
Charlie Gehringer: 1937
Harvey Kuenn: 1959
George Kell: 1949
Norm Cash: 1961

Home Run Champions

Sam Crawford: 1908
1914 (tie)
Ty Cobb: 1909
Hank Greenberg: 1935 (tie)
1938 1940 1946
Rudy York: 1943

RBI Champions

Ty Cobb: 1909
Hank Greenberg: 1935 1937
1940 1946
Rudy York: 1943
Ray Boone: 1955

Triple Crown Winner

Ty Cobb: 1909 (.377 batting average, 9 home runs, 115 runs batted in)

Baseball Writers Assn. Awards

Chalmers Award (AL) — Ty Cobb 1911
Most Valuable Player (AL) — Mickey Cochrane 1934
Hank Greenberg 1935, 1940
Charlie Gehringer 1937
Hal Newhouser 1944, 1945
Denny McLain 1968
Cy Young Award (AL) — Denny McLain 1968 (unanimous) 1969 (tied)
Rookie of the Year (AL) — Harvey Kuenn 1953
Mark Fidrych 1976
Lou Whitaker 1978

Other Awards

Roberto Clemente Award — Al Kaline 1973
Joseph E. Cronin Trophy — Al Kaline 1974
Lou Gehrig Trophy — Al Kaline 1970
The Hutch Award — Al Kaline 1970
John Hiller 1973
Comeback Player of the Year (AL) — Norm Cash 1965, 1971
John Hiller 1973
World Series Most Valuable Player — Mickey Lolich 1968
Designated Hitter of the Year (AL) — Willie Horton 1975
Rusty Staub 1978
American League Player of the Month — Al Kaline, September, 1974
Willie Horton, April, 1976
Ron LeFlore, May, 1976
Mark Fidrych, June, 1976
American League Player of the Week — Willie Horton, Aug. 3, 1975; April 25, 1976
Ron LeFlore, May 9, 1976
Ben Oglivie, June 6, 1976
Jason Thompson, June 25, 1978
Lance Parrish, May 29, 1979
Alan Trammell, May 12, 1980
Tom Brookens, August 18, 1980
Steve Kemp, September 14, 1980

Greatest Tigers Ever
(Selected by fans in 1969)

Ty Cobb, OF
Mickey Cochrane, C
Charlie Gehringer, 2B

Hank Greenberg, 1B
Harry Heilmann, OF
Al Kaline, OF
George Kell, 3B

Denny McLain, RHP
Hal Newhouser, 1HP
Bill Rogell, SS

MICHIGAN SPORTS HALL OF FAME

NAME	SELECTED	NAME	SELECTED
Bridges, Tommy	1963	Jennings, Hughie	1958
Briggs, Walter O. Sr.	1969	Kaline, Al	1978
Cobb, Ty	1955	Kell, George	1969
Cochrane, Mickey	1957	Manush, Heinie	1964
Crawford, Sam	1958	Mullin, George	1962
Egan, Wish	1960	Navin, Frank	1976
Gehringer, Charlie	1956	Newhouser, Hal	1962
Goslin, Goose	1955	Rogell, Billy	1970
Greenberg, Hank	1958	Rowe, Schoolboy	1961
Heilmann, Harry	1956	York, Rudy	1972

NATIONAL BASEBALL HALL OF FAME

	POS.	YEAR SELECTED	YEARS AT DETROIT	PLAYING CAREER
Averill, Earl	OF	1975	1939–40	1929–41
Barrow, Edward G.	MGR	1953	1903–04	
Cobb, Ty	OF–MGR	1936	1905–26	1905–28
Cochrane, Mickey	C–MGR	1947	1934–38	1925–37
Crawford, Sam	OF	1957	1903–17	1899–17
Evans, Billy	GEN MGR	1973	1947–51	
Gehringer, Charlie	IF	1949	1924–42	1924–42
Goslin, Goose	OF	1968	1934–37	1921–38
Greenberg, Hank	1B–OF	1956	1930–46	1930–47
Harris, Bucky	IF–MGR	1975	1929–33 1955–56	1919–31
Heilmann, Harry	OF–1B	1952	1914–29	1914–32
Hoyt, Waite	P	1969	1930–31	1918–38
Jennings, Hughie	SS–MGR	1945	1907–20	1891–18
Kaline, Al	OF	1980	1953–74	1953–74
Manush, Heinie	OF	1964	1923–27	1923–39
Mathews, Eddie	3B–1B	1978	1967–68	1952–68
Simmons, Al	OF	1953	1936	1924–44
Thompson, Sam	OF	1974	1885–88* 1906	1885–06

*Detroit in the National League

145

DENNY McLAIN

He was an enigma wrapped in mystery; an athlete of unquestioned skill, a pitching star who burst upon the baseball firmament destined for Cooperstown. And yet, at age 28 he was washed up, his brilliant career dashed upon the rocks of high living, financial mismanagement, and too much fame too soon.

Dennis Dale McLain is described by those who know him well as a "great guy, a friendly guy," and as "the most complex personality I've ever known."

It serves no purpose to repeat in detail what everyone already knows about him: his incredible 31-win 1968 season that led the Tigers to a pennant; his 1970 suspension for involvement with bookmakers; and his swift downward spiral that carried him to Washington, Oakland, Atlanta, and finally to Shreveport, Louisiana, in search of his once-awesome skills.

People have a hard time imagining that even today Denny McLain could be pitching in the majors at age 37, along with such contemporaries as Tommy John, Gaylord Perry, and Ferguson Jenkins.

In his 10-year career he fashioned some pretty spectacular statistics. In just the brief span between 1966 and 1969, he won 92 games, or 25 percent of the team wins in that period, struck out 814 batters (19 percent of the team total), completed 75 games (38 percent of the team total), and threw 22 shutouts (an even third of the team total).

McLain's Career Record

Year	Team	Wins	Losses	ERA	G	GS	CG	IP	H	BB	SO	ShO
1963	Detroit	2	1	4.29	3	3	2	21	20	16	22	0
1964	Detroit	4	5	4.05	19	16	3	100	84	37	70	0
1965	Detroit	16	6	2.61	33	29	13	220.1	174	62	192	4
1966	Detroit	20	14	3.92	38	38	14	264.1	205	104	192	4
1967	Detroit	17	16	3.79	37	37	10	235	209	73	161	3
1968	Detroit	31*	6	1.96	41	41*	28*	336*	241	63	280	6
1969	Detroit	24*	9	2.80	42	41*	23	325*	288*	67	181	9*
1970	Detroit	3	5	4.65	14	14	1	91	100	28	52	0
1971	Wash.	10	22*	4.27	33	32	9	217	233	72	103	3
1972	Oakland	1	2	6.14	5	5	0	22	32	8	8	0
	Atlanta	3	5	6.50	15	8	2	54	60	18	21	0
10 years		131	91	3.39	280	264	105	1885.2	1646	548	1282	29

WORLD SERIES

Year	Team	Wins	Losses	ERA	G	GS	CG	IP	H	BB	SO	ShO
1968	Detroit	1	2	3.24	3	3	1	16.2	18	4	13	0

*League leader

TY COBB

The plaque in front of the office entrance at Tiger Stadium says it all: "The greatest Tiger of them all."

Certainly no ballplayer ever burned with a more competitive zeal. Baseball's greatest hitter and base runner compiled a phenomenal record that is still unequaled: a .367 lifetime average; twelve league batting titles, including nine in succession; the only player to exceed 4,000 career hits. Cobb hit .400 or better three times, including .420 in 1911, and stole an incredible 892 bases during his 24-year career, which included 22 years in Detroit.

"The Georgia Peach" stood 6 feet high and weighed 175 pounds. A left-hand hitter, Cobb led the Tigers to three consecutive pennants in 1907–09, but failed to duplicate that success as a playing manager from 1921–26.

It is to his ultimate credit that he was the first player elected for the new Baseball Hall of Fame in 1936. As the years passed, Cobb enjoyed his annual visits to Cooperstown, where he could reflect on the good old days and swap stories with his old adversaries.

He died in 1961, a wealthy man thanks to successful investments in Coca-Cola. He had few, if any, close friends, and never seemed to recover from the shock of his father's accidental death from a gunshot wound from his mother while Cobb was starting his big league career.

Cobb's Career Record

Year	Team	G	AB	R	H	2B	3B	HR	RBI	Avg.	SB
1905	Detroit	41	150	19	36	6	0	1	15	.240	2
1906	Detroit	97	350	44	112	13	7	1	41	.320	23
1907	Detroit	150	605	97	212*	29	15	5	116*	.350	49*
1908	Detroit	150	581	88	188*	36*	20*	4	101*	.324*	39
1909	Detroit	156	573	116*	216*	33	10	9*	115*	.377*	76*
1910	Detroit	140	509	106*	196	36	13	8	88	.385*	65
1911	Detroit	146	591	147*	248*	47*	24*	8	144*	.420*	83*
1912	Detroit	140	553	119	227*	30	23	7	90	.410*	61
1913	Detroit	122	428	70	167	18	16	4	67	.390*	52
1914	Detroit	97	345	69	127	22	11	2	57	.368*	35
1915	Detroit	156	563	144*	208*	31	13	3	99	.369*	96*
1916	Detroit	145	542	113*	201	31	10	5	68	.371	68*
1917	Detroit	152	588*	107	225*	44*	23*	7	102	.383*	55*
1918	Detroit	111	421	83	161	19	14*	3	64	.382*	34
1919	Detroit	124	497	92	191*	36	13	1	70	.384*	28
1920	Detroit	112	428	86	143	28	8	2	63	.334	14
1921	Detroit	128	507	124	197	37	16	12	101	.389	22
1922	Detroit	137	526	99	211	42	16	4	99	.401	9
1923	Detroit	145	556	103	189	40	7	6	88	.340	9
1924	Detroit	155	625	115	211	38	10	4	74	.338	23
1925	Detroit	121	415	97	157	31	12	12	102	.378	13
1926	Detroit	79	233	48	79	18	5	4	62	.339	9
1927	Phila.	134	490	104	175	32	7	5	93	.357	22
1928	Phila.	95	353	54	114	27	4	1	40	.323	5
24 Years		3033	11429	2244	4191	724	297	118	1959	.367	892

WORLD SERIES

3 years		17	65	7	17	4	1	0	11	.262	4

*Led League

MICKEY COCHRANE

Mickey Cochrane's incredible competitive spirit was the ingredient needed to lead the Tigers to a pennant, which he did as playing manager in 1934 and 1935. But this same fierce desire proved his undoing, as he suffered a nervous breakdown in 1936 and then was fired in 1938 following a stormy series of disagreements with Walter O. Briggs, the owner.

He remains a beloved figure in Tiger lore. "Black Mike" was not only a potent batsman but also a top-notch catcher. Cochrane made his mark with Connie Mack's Athletics in the late twenties and early thirties before being obtained in December, 1933 for catcher Johnny Pasek and cash.

Named to the Hall of Fame in 1947, Cochrane caught in 100 games or more for 11 consecutive seasons, a testament to his durability. He compiled a lifetime batting average of .320 and was named Most Valuable Player in 1928 while with the Athletics.

His career as a player came to an abrupt halt on May 25, 1937 when he suffered a fractured skull after being beaned by a pitch from Bump Hadley of the Yankees.

Cochrane's Career Record

Year	Team	G	AB	R	H	2B	3B	HR	RBI	Avg.
1925	Phila.	134	420	69	139	21	5	6	55	.331
1926	Phila.	120	370	50	101	8	9	8	47	.273
1927	Phila.	126	432	80	146	20	6	12	80	.338
1928	Phila.	131	468	92	137	26	12	10	57	.293
1929	Phila.	135	514	113	170	37	8	7	95	.331
1930	Phila.	130	487	110	174	42	5	10	85	.357
1931	Phila.	122	459	87	160	31	6	17	89	.349
1932	Phila.	139	518	118	152	35	4	23	112	.293
1933	Phila.	130	429	104	138	30	4	15	60	.322
1934	Detroit	129	437	74	140	32	1	2	76	.320
1935	Detroit	115	411	93	131	33	3	5	47	.319
1936	Detroit	44	126	24	34	8	0	2	17	.270
1937	Detroit	27	98	27	30	10	1	2	12	.306
13 years		1428	5169	1041	1652	333	64	119	832	.320
WORLD SERIES	31	110	17	27	4	0	2	6	.245	

HANK GREENBERG

One of the game's great right-handed sluggers, Hammerin' Hank Greenberg might have gone on to even greater heights had he not suffered a broken wrist in 1936 and missed four seasons because of World War II.

Greenberg had a knack for the dramatic, as evidenced by his return from the War in 1945 in time to lead the Tigers to a pennant. On the last day of the season, his grandslam against the Browns nailed down the flag for Detroit.

Combined with Gehringer and Goslin, he helped make the "G" men a formidable force during the 1930s. He spent most of his career as a first baseman, but was shifted to left field in 1940 to make room at first for up-and-coming Rudy York, a move that paid off in a Tiger pennant.

Greenberg led the league in home runs four times, including 1938 when he slugged 58 homers to set an American League record for the most home runs in a season by a right-handed batter. That same year, he hit two or more homers in a game 11 times, a Major League record. Named Most Valuable Player in 1935 and 1940, he led the league in homers and RBIs both those seasons.

As he began to slow up in the field, the Tigers decided to sell Greenberg to Pittsburgh before the 1947 season. He played just one year for the Pirates under a contract that made him the game's first $100,000 player. He then became a front-office executive with Cleveland and later with the White Sox. He was named to the Hall of Fame in 1956.

Greenberg's Career Record

Year	Team	G	AB	R	H	2B	3B	HR	RBI	Avg.
1930	Detroit	1	1	0	0	0	0	0	0	.000
1933	Detroit	117	449	59	135	33	3	12	87	.301
1934	Detroit	153	593	118	201	63*	7	26	139	.339
1935	Detroit	152	619	121	203	46	16	36*	170*	.328
1936	Detroit	12	46	10	16	6	2	1	16	.348
1937	Detroit	154	594	137	200	49	14	40	183*	.337
1938	Detroit	155	556	144*	175	23	4	58*	146	.315
1939	Detroit	138	500	112	156	42	7	33	112	.312
1940	Detroit	148	573	129	195	50*	8	41*	150*	.340
1941	Detroit	19	67	12	18	5	1	2	12	.269
1942-43-44	IN MILITARY SERVICE									
1945	Detroit	78	270	47	84	20	2	13	60	.311
1946	Detroit	142	523	91	145	29	5	44*	127*	.277
1947	Pittsburgh	125	402	71	100	13	2	25	74	.249
13 years		1394	5193	1051	1628	379	71	331	1276	.313
WORLD SERIES	23	85	17	27	7	2	5	22	.318	

*Led League

CHARLIE GEHRINGER

No second baseman ever brought more smoothness, grace, and efficiency to his position than Charlie Gehringer—the "Mechanical Man."

Gehringer made even the most difficult plays look routine. More important, he was a major offensive cog in the Tiger machine of the mid-1930s, one of the heralded "G" men with Hank Greenberg and Goose Goslin.

When he first joined the Tigers in late 1924, manager Ty Cobb felt Gehringer's lack of fieriness might keep him from making the grade. But the taciturn Gehringer made up for his shortcomings as a "holler" guy with his dependable glove and picture-perfect swing.

He hit .300 or better in 13 out of 14 seasons during one stretch of his career, with his biggest year coming in 1937 when he won the league's Most Valuable Player Award while garnering the batting title with a .371 average.

Gehringer finished his career as a player in 1942 after 19 seasons, racking up a career average of .320. He came back to baseball as general manager of the Tigers from 1951 to 1953. He was elected to the Hall of Fame in 1949 and is a regular attendee of the annual induction ceremonies.

Gehringer's Career Record

Year	G	AB	R	H	2B	3B	HR	RBI	Avg.	SB	Fielding
1924	5	11	2	6	0	0	0	1	.545	1	.966
1925	8	18	3	3	0	0	0	0	.167	0	1.000
1926	123	459	62	127	19	17	1	48	.277	9	.973
1927	133	508	110	161	29	11	4	61	.317	17	.965
1928	154	603	108	193	29	16	6	74	.320	15	.962
1929	155*	634	131*	215*	45*	19*	13	106	.339	28*	.975*
1930	154*	610	143	201	47	15	16	98	.330	19	.979*
1931	101	383	67	119	24	5	4	53	.311	13	.979
1932	152	618	112	184	44	11	19	107	.298	9	.967
1933	155*	628	103	204	42	6	12	105	.325	5	.981*
1934	154*	601	134*	214*	50	7	11	127	.356	11	.981*
1935	150	610	123	201	32	8	19	108	.330	11	.985*
1936	154	641	144	227	60*	12	15	116	.354	4	.974
1937	144	564	133	209	40	1	14	96	.371*	11	.986*
1938	152	568	133	174	32	5	20	107	.306	14	.976
1939	118	406	86	132	29	6	16	86	.325	4	.977*
1940	139	515	108	161	33	3	10	81	.313	10	.972
1941	127	436	65	96	19	4	3	46	.220	1	.982*
1942	45	45	6	12	0	0	1	7	.267	0	1.000
19 years	2323	8858	1773	2839	574	146	184	1427	.320	182	.976

WORLD SERIES

	20	81	12	26	4	0	1	7	.321	2	.976

AL KALINE

"There is only one Al Kaline. Players like Kaline come along just once in a lifetime." So said superscout Ed Katalinas, justifiably proud of his greatest find's election to Baseball's Hall of Fame. Kaline joined just nine other Hall of Famers in being elected in the first year of eligibility—Banks, Feller, Koufax, Mantle, Mays, Musial, Jackie Robinson, Spahn, and Williams. Yet during his heyday with the Tigers, Kaline always seemed overshadowed by the stars in bigger media centers—Mays and Mantle.

No matter. Tiger fans know where the Baltimore native ranks in their hearts. Al Kaline is a rarity—one of a handful who went right from high school to the major leagues and then never played a day in the minors. During his 22-year career, Kaline played in more games and hit more home runs than any Tiger in team history. He finished second to the great Ty Cobb in at bats, hits, extra-base hits, total bases, and runs batted in. Only Charlie Gehringer and Cobb topped him in runs scored and doubles.

Al Kaline (continued)

What makes his career even more remarkable is that he played all those years with a childhood foot deformity that was never entirely corrected, even with surgery. He suffered numerous injuries with his all-out style of play, which caused him to miss the equivalent of a full season of action. But he endured to make his mark among baseball's greatest stars.

Among his accomplishments were: Ten Gold Gloves for defensive skill in the outfield; selection on the American League All-Star team for 15 years, 7 as a starter and 13 years in a row; and playing at least 100 games for 19 straight seasons.

Kaline signed for a reported $30,000 salary and bonus with the Tigers in 1953 and joined the club upon graduation from Southern High School in Baltimore. He became a regular in 1954, following an injury to Steve Souchock, and became the youngest batting champion in American League history in 1955 with a .340 average at age 20, beating the record of Ty Cobb by a few months.

His finest moment on the playing field came during the 1968 World Series, as he led the Bengals to a comeback win over the Cardinals, hitting .379 with 2 homers and 8 RBIs.

He called his election to Cooperstown in 1980 the greatest honor in his life, and was swiftly saluted by the ball club two weeks later by being the first Tiger player ever to have his number retired.

"Al Kaline was the type of player whose enthusiasm for the game and loyalty to his team were unequalled," said John Fetzer. "We in Detroit were very fortunate to have had this fine player and man from the beginning of his career throughout. On and off the field, Al Kaline symbolizes class and excellence."

Amen.

Kaline's Career Record

Year	G	AB	R	H	2B	3B	HR	RBI	Avg.	E	Field.
1953	30	28	9	7	0	0	1	2	.250	0	1.000
1954	138	504	42	139	18	3	4	43	.276	9	.971
1955	152	588	121	200*	24	8	27	102	.340*	7	.979
1956	153	617	96	194	32	10	27	128	.314	6	.984
1957	149	577	83	170	29	4	23	90	.295	5	.985
1958	146	543	84	170	34	7	16	85	.313	2	.994
1959	136	511	86	167	19	2	27	94	.327	4	.989
1960	147	551	77	153	29	4	15	68	.278	5	.987
1961	153	586	116	190	41*	7	19	82	.324	4	.990
1962	100	398	78	121	16	6	29	94	.304	4	.983
1963	145	551	89	172	24	3	27	101	.312	2	.992
1964	146	525	77	154	31	5	17	68	.293	3	.990
1965	125	399	72	112	18	2	18	72	.281	3	.985
1966	142	479	85	138	29	1	29	88	.288	2	.993*
1967	131	458	94	141	28	2	25	78	.308	4	.983
1968	102	327	49	94	14	1	10	53	.287	7	.977
1969	131	456	74	124	17	0	21	69	.272	7	.974
1970	131	467	64	130	24	4	16	71	.278	6	.989
1971	133	405	69	119	19	2	15	54	.294	0	1.000*
1972	106	278	46	87	11	2	10	32	.313	1	.994
1973	91	310	40	79	13	0	10	45	.255	1	.997
1974	147	558	71	146	28	2	13	64	.262	0	.000
22 years	2834	10116	1622	3007	498	75	399	1583	.297	82	.987

WORLD SERIES RECORD

1968	7	29	6	11	2	0	2	8	.379	0	1.000

All-Star Game Record

	16	37	7	12	1	0	2	5	.324	0	1.000

*Led League

150

HALL OF FAME PROFILES

EARL AVERILL . . . This stellar outfielder spent his best seasons with Cleveland, compiling a solid .318 average for his career. Though only 5 feet 9 inches and 170 pounds, he had considerable power, breaking the 30-homer mark three times in his career. He came to Detroit in the twilight of his major league days in June, 1939 and stayed through the championship 1940 season before going to the Boston Braves. He proved a key pinch hitter in 1940, with 12 hits in 38 at bats. He was voted into the Hall of Fame in 1975.

ED BARROW . . . Elected to the Hall of Fame in 1953, this executive is best known for his 24-year tenure as business manager of the Yankees. He spent a season and a half as manager of the Tigers (1903–04), leading the club to a fifth place finish in his only full season, 1903. He is credited with converting Babe Ruth from a pitcher into an outfielder while managing Boston in 1918.

SAM CRAWFORD . . . "Wahoo Sam" spent 15 seasons in Detroit after beginning his career with Cincinnati. He was a feared batsman, noted for his power in a dead-ball era. He is the only player to top both leagues in home runs, hitting 16 in the National League in 1901 and leading the American League with 7 in 1908 and 8 in 1914. He ended his career with a .309 average. He was a skilled base stealer as well, with 367 career steals. With the Tigers, he led the league in RBIs three times and triples five times. He joined his teammate Ty Cobb in the Hall of Fame in 1957.

BILLY EVANS . . . A noted umpire who became a front-office executive, Evans served as the Tiger general manager from 1947 to 1951. He is recognized as the foremost umpire in American League history, serving from 1906 to 1927. He was voted into the Hall of Fame posthumously in 1973.

LEON (GOOSE) GOSLIN . . . One of the fabled "G" men of the 1930s, Goslin was a great clutch hitter who helped the Senators win three pennants and proved invaluable in the 1934–35 championship seasons for Detroit. A .316 career hitter, Goose enjoyed his best year in Detroit in 1936, when he hit .315, slugged 24 homers, and batted in 125 runs. He drove in the winning run in the deciding game of the 1935 World Series. He made Cooperstown in 1958.

BUCKY HARRIS . . . Harris is the only man to serve as Tiger manager twice, with his first stint coming from 1929–33 and the second from 1955–56. While not enjoying any notable successes in Detroit, Harris won two flags as the "Boy Wonder" manager of the Washington Senators in 1924–25. He joined Earl Averill's entrance into the Hall of the Fame in 1975.

HARRY HEILMANN . . . Joining the Tigers in 1914 and filling in for an injured Ty Cobb, Heilmann didn't really hit his form until 1921, when playing manager Cobb suggested he close up his batting stance. The result was a league-leading .394. Heilmann went on to win three more batting titles, including breaking the .400 barrier with a .403 average in 1923. He finished with a .342 average for his 17-year career and was enshrined at Cooperstown in 1952.

WAITE HOYT . . . He is best known for his great clutch pitching as the mainstay of the Yankee pitching staff during the 1920s. He pitched parts of two seasons for the Tigers (1930–31), compiling a mediocre 12–16 record before moving on to the Athletics. He ended his 21-year career with 237 wins, and was voted into the Hall of Fame in 1969.

HUGHIE JENNINGS . . . A standout shortstop for the old Baltimore Orioles, Jennings made his mark in Detroit history as the manager who led the team to three consecutive pennants in his first three years as manager. The colorful redhead made his managerial trademark the yell, "E-yah!" Hughie managed the Bengals for 14 seasons, longer than any other man in Tiger history. He was fired after leading the club to a seventh place finish in 1920, and was replaced by Ty Cobb. He once said his greatest disappointment was winning 100 games with Detroit in 1915 and finishing second to Boston's league-leading 101 wins. He was enshrined at Cooperstown in 1945, 17 years after his death.

HEINIE MANUSH... The Tuscumbia Thumper, named after his Alabama birthplace, broke in as a Tiger rookie in 1923 with a .334 average. He put together five standout seasons for Detroit, including a league-leading .378 season in 1926 before being traded to the St. Louis Browns in December, 1927. A career .330 hitter, Manush put in 18 seasons with six big league clubs. He joined the Hall of Fame in 1964.

EDDIE MATHEWS... An all-time great third baseman with the National League Braves, Ed finished his big-league career on a up-beat note with the World Championship 1968 Tigers. Although he was well past his prime as a player, Mathews contributed greatly to the title effort with his leadership and ability to inspire others. He slugged 512 homers in his career and was a top-notch third baseman. He entered the Hall of Fame in 1978.

AL SIMMONS... "Bucketfoot Al" would never have made the Hall of Fame on his form alone. He spent just one season in Detroit (1936), batting a creditable .327. But his best years came as a member of the Philadelphia Athletics during their glory years of the early 1930s, winning the league batting title in 1930 (.381) and 1931 (.390). He ended his 20-year career in 1944 with a .334 average and joined Cooperstown in 1953.

SAM THOMPSON... Big Sam made his greatest contributions with the old National League Detroit club in the 1880s and the Phillies in the rest of the century. He returned to the big leagues in 1906 after a 7-year absence at age 46 when he joined the injury-riddled Tigers for a brief 8-game stay. He had a .331 career average and was voted into the Hall of Fame in 1974.

16. TIGER CAREER BATTING LEADERS

(Detroit records only, not including Post Season)

GAMES		DOUBLES		RBI	
Kaline	2,834	Cobb	665	Cobb	1,826
Cobb	2,804	Gehringer	574	Kaline	1,583
Gehringer	2,323	Kaline	498	Heilmann	1,454
Crawford	2,114	Heilmann	497	Gehringer	1,427
Cash	2,018	Crawford	403	Crawford	1,264
Heilmann	1,989	Greenberg	366	Greenberg	1,202
Bush	1,872	Veach	345	Cash	1,087
Freehan	1,774	Kuenn	244	Veach	1,042
McAuliffe	1,656	Cash	241	York	936
Veach	1,605	Freehan	241	Horton	886

AT BATS		TRIPLES		EXTRA-BASE HITS	
Cobb	10,586	Cobb	286	Cobb	1,063
Kaline	10,116	Crawford	250	Kaline	972
Gehringer	8,860	Gehringer	146	Gehringer	904
Crawford	7,993	Heilmann	145	Heilmann	806
Heilmann	7,297	Veach	136	Greenberg	741
Bush	6,970	Kaline	75	Crawford	723
Cash	6,593	Bush	73	Cash	654
Freehan	6,073	McAuliffe	70	Veach	540
Veach	5,982	Greenberg	69	York	517
McAuliffe	5,898	Blue	66	Horton	504

RUNS		HOME RUNS		TOTAL BASES	
Cobb	2,086	Kaline	399	Cobb	5,475
Gehringer	1,774	Cash	373	Kaline	4,852
Kaline	1,622	Greenberg	306	Gehringer	4,257
Bush	1,242	Horton	262	Heilmann	3,778
Heilmann	1,209	York	239	Crawford	3,579
Crawford	1,115	Freehan	200	Cash	3,233
Cash	1,028	McAuliffe	192	Greenberg	2,950
Greenberg	980	Gehringer	184	Veach	2,654
Veach	860	Heilmann	164	Horton	2,549
McAuliffe	856	Northrup	145	Freehan	2,502

HITS		BATTING		STOLEN BASES	
Cobb	3,902	Cobb	367	Cobb	865
Kaline	3,007	Heilmann	342	Bush	400
Gehringer	2,839	Fothergill	337	Crawford	317
Heilmann	2,499	Kell	325	LeFlore	294
Crawford	2,466	Manush	321	Moriarty	190
Veach	1,860	Gehringer	320	Veach	189
Cash	1,793	Greenberg	319	Gehringer	182
Bush	1,745	G. Walker	317	Jones	140
Freehan	1,591	Kuenn	314	Kaline	137
Greenberg	1,528	McCosky	312	Walker	132
		Veach	311	Schaefer	123
		Crawford	309	Heilmann	110
		Kaline	297		

BATTING LEADERS BY YEARS
(Hits, HR, RBI, Ave.)

Year	Leader In	Hits	Leader In	HR	Leader In	RBI	Leader In	Ave.
1901	Barrett	159	Barrett	4	Elberfeld	76	Elberfeld	.308
			Holmes	4				
1902	Barrett	154	Casey	3	Elberfeld	64	Barrett	.303
1903	Crawford	184	Crawford	4	Crawford	89	Crawford	.335
1904	Barrett	167	Crawford	2	Crawford	73	Barrett	.268
			Hickman	2				
			McIntyre	2				
1905	Crawford	171	Crawford	6	Crawford	75	Crawford	.297
1906	Crawford	166	Coughlin	2	Crawford	72	Crawford	.295
			Crawford	2				
			O'Leary	2				
			Schaefer	2				
1907	Cobb	212*	Cobb	5	Cobb	116*	Cobb	.350*
1908	Cobb	188*	Crawford	7*	Cobb	101*	Cobb	.324*
1909	Cobb	216*	Cobb	9*	Cobb	115*	Cobb	.377*
1910	Cobb	196	Cobb	8	Crawford	120*	Cobb	.385*
1911	Cobb	248*	Cobb	8	Cobb	144*	Cobb	.420*
1912	Cobb	227*	Cobb	7	Crawford	109	Cobb	.410*
1913	Crawford	193	Crawford	9	Crawford	83	Cobb	.390*
1914	Crawford	183	Crawford	8#	Crawford	104*	Cobb	.368*
1915	Cobb	208*	Burns	5	Crawford	112#	Cobb	.369*
					Veach	112#		

Batting Leaders by Years (continued)

Year	Leader In	Hits	Leader In	HR	Leader In	RBI	Leader In	Ave.
1916	Cobb	201	Cobb	5	Veach	91	Cobb	.371
1917	Cobb	225*	Veach	8	Veach	103*	Cobb	.383*
1918	Cobb	161	Heilmann	5	Veach	78*	Cobb	.382*
1919	Cobb	191#	Heilmann	8	Veach	101	Cobb	.384*
	Veach	191#						
1920	Veach	188	Veach	11	Veach	113	Cobb	.334
1921	Heilmann	237*	Heilmann	19	Heilmann	139	Heilmann	.394*
1922	Cobb	211	Heilmann	21	Veach	126	Cobb	.401
1923	Heilmann	211	Heilmann	18	Heilmann	115	Heilmann	.403*
1924	Cobb	211	Heilmann	10	Heilmann	113	Heilmann	.346
1925	Heilmann	225	Heilmann	13	Heilmann	133	Heilmann	.393*
1926	Manush	188	Manush	14	Heilmann	103	Manush	.378*
1927	Heilmann	201	Heilmann	14	Heilmann	120	Heilmann	.398*
1928	Gehringer	193	Heilmann	14	Heilmann	107	Heilmann	.328
1929	Alexander	215#	Alexander	25	Alexander	137	Heilmann	.344
	Gehringer	215#						
1930	Gehringer	201	Alexander	20	Alexander	135	Gehringer	.330
1931	Stone	191	Stone	10	Alexander	87	Stone	.327
1932	Gehringer	184	Gehringer	19	Stone	108	Walker	.323
1933	Gehringer	204	Gehringer	12	Gehringer	105	Gehringer	.325
			Greenberg	12				
1934	Gehringer	214*	Greenberg	26	Greenberg	139	Gehringer	.356
1935	Greenberg	203	Greenberg	36#	Greenberg	170*	Gehringer	.330
1936	Gehringer	227	Goslin	24	Goslin	125	Gehringer	.354
1937	Walker	213	Greenberg	40	Greenberg	183*	Gehringer	.371*
1938	Fox	186	Greenberg	58*	Greenberg	146	Greenberg	.315
1939	McCosky	190	Greenberg	33	Greenberg	112	Gehringer	.325
1940	McCosky	200#	Greenberg	41*	Greenberg	150*	Greenberg	.340
							McCosky	.340
1941	Higgins	161	York	27	York	111	McCosky	.324
1942	McCosky	176	York	21	York	90	McCosky	.293
1943	Wakefield	200*	York	34*	York	118*	Wakefield	.316
1944	Cramer	169	York	18	York	98	Higgins	.297
1945	York	157	Cullenbine	18	Cullenbine	93	Mayo	.285
			York	18				
1946	Lake	149	Greenberg	44*	Greenberg	127*	Kell	.327
1947	Kell	188	Cullenbine	24	Kell	93	Kell	.320
1948	Evers	169	Mullin	23	Evers	103	Evers	.314
1949	Wertz	185	Wertz	20	Wertz	113	Kell	.343*
1950	Kell	218*	Wertz	27	Wertz	123	Kell	.340
1951	Kell	191*	Wertz	27	Wertz	94	Kell	.319
1952	Groth	149	Dropo	23	Dropo	70	Groth	.284
1953	Kuenn	208*	Boone	22	Dropo	96	Kuenn	.308
1954	Kuenn	201#	Boone	20	Boone	85	Kuenn	.306
1955	Kaline	200*	Kaline	27	Boone	116#	Kaline	.340*
1956	Kuenn	196*	Maxwell	28	Kaline	128	Kuenn	.332
1957	Kuenn	173	Maxwell	24	Kaline	90	Kaline	.295
1958	Kuenn	179	Harris	20	Kaline	85	Kuenn	.319
1959	Kuenn	198*	Maxwell	31	Maxwell	95	Kuenn	.353*
1960	Kaline	153	Colavito	35	Colavito	87	Kaline	.278
1961	Cash	193*	Colavito	45	Colavito	140	Cash	.361*
1962	Colavito	164	Cash	39	Colavito	112	Bruton	.278

Year	Leader In	Hits	Leader In	HR	Leader In	RBI	Leader In	Ave.
1963	Kaline	172	Kaline	27	Kaline	101	Kaline	.312
1964	Lumpe	160	McAuliffe	24	Cash	83	Freehan	.300
1965	Wert	159	Cash	30	Horton	104	Horton	.273
1966	Cash	168	Cash	32	Horton	100	Kaline	.288
1967	Freehan	146	Kaline	25	Kaline	78	Kaline	.308
1968	Northrup	153	Horton	36	Northrup	90	Horton	.285
1969	Northrup	160	Horton	28	Horton	91	Northrup	.295
1970	Stanley	143	Northrup	24	Northrup	80	Kaline	.278
1971	Rodriguez	153	Cash	32	Cash	91	Kaline	.294
1972	Rodriguez	142	Cash	22	Cash	61	Northrup	.261
1973	Stanley	147	Cash	19	Rodriguez	58	Horton	.316
1974	Sutherland	157	Freehan	18	Kaline	64	Freehan	.297
1975	Horton	169	Horton	25	Horton	92	Horton	.275
1976	Staub	176	Thompson	17	Staub	96	LeFlore	.316
1977	LeFlore	212	Thompson	31	Thompson	105	LeFlore	.325
1978	LeFlore	198	Thompson	26	Staub	121	LeFlore	.297
1979	LeFlore	180	Kemp	26	Kemp	105	Kemp	.318
1980	Trammell	168	Parrish	24	Kemp	101	Trammell	.300

*Led League   #Tied for league lead

BATTING LEADERS BY YEARS
(Runs, 2B, 3B, SB)

Year	Leader In	Runs	Leader In	2B	Leader In	3B	Leader In	SB
1901	Casey	105	Holmes	28	Gleason	12	Holmes	35
1902	Barrett	93	Barrett	19	Harley	8	Barrett	24
1903	Barrett	95	Crawford Carr	23	Crawford	25*	Barrett	27
1904	Barrett	83	Crawford	21	Crawford	17	Crawford	20
1905	Crawford	73	Crawford	40	Crawford	10	Crawford	22
1906	Crawford	65	Crawford	23	Crawford	16	Schaefer Coughlin	31
1907	Crawford	102*	Crawford	34	Crawford	17	Cobb	49*
1908	McIntyre	105*	Cobb	36*	Cobb	20*	Schaefer	40
1909	Cobb	116*	Crawford	35*	Crawford	14	Cobb	76*
1910	Cobb	106*	Cobb	36	Crawford	19*	Cobb	65
1911	Cobb	147*	Cobb	47*	Cobb	24*	Cobb	83*
1912	Cobb	119	Cobb Crawford	30	Cobb	23	Cobb	61
1913	Bush	98	Crawford	32	Crawford	23*	Cobb	52
1914	Bush	97	Cobb Crawford Burns	22	Crawford	26*	Cobb Bush	35
1915	Cobb	144*	Veach	40*	Crawford	19*	Cobb	96*
1916	Cobb	113*	Veach	33	Veach	15	Cobb	68*
1917	Bush	112*	Cobb	44*	Cobb	23*	Cobb	55*
1918	Cobb	83	Veach	21	Cobb	14*	Cobb	34
1919	Cobb	92	Veach	45*	Veach	17*	Cobb	28
1920	Veach	92	Veach	39	Veach	15	Bush	15
1921	Cobb	124	Veach Heilmann	43	Cobb	16	Cobb	22
1922	Blue	131	Cobb	42	Cobb	16	Rigney	17
1923	Heilmann	121	Heilmann	44	Heilmann	11	Haney	12
1924	Cobb	115	Heilmann	45*	Heilmann	16	Cobb	23

155

Batting Leaders by Years (continued)

Year	Leader In	Runs	Leader In	2B	Leader In	3B	Leader In	SB
1925	Wingo	104	Heilmann O'Rourke	40	Cobb	12	Blue	19
1926	Manush	95	Heilmann	41	Gehringer	17	Blue	13
1927	Gehringer	110	Heilmann	50	Manush	18	Neun	22
1928	Gehringer	108	Heilmann	38	Gehringer	16	Rice	20
1929	Gehringer	131*	Gehringer Johnson	45*	Gehringer	19*	Gehringer	27*
1930	Gehringer	144	Gehringer	47	Gehringer	15	McManus	23*
1931	Johnson	107	Alexander	47	Johnson	19*	Johnson	33
1932	Gehringer	112	Gehringer	44	Davis	13	Walker	30
1933	Gehringer	103	Gehringer Rogell	42	Fox	13	Walker	26
1934	Gehringer	134*	Greenberg	63*	Owen	9	White	28
1935	Gehringer	123	Greenberg	46	Greenberg	16	White	19
1936	Gehringer	144	Gehringer	60*	Gehringer	12	Walker	17
1937	Greenberg	137	Greenberg	49	Greenberg	14	Walker	23
1938	Greenberg	144*	Fox	35	Fox	10	Fox	16
1939	McCosky	120	Greenberg	42	McCosky	14	Fox	23
1940	Greenberg	129	Greenberg	50*	McCosky	19*	McCosky	13
1941	York	91	York	29	Campbell	10	McCosky	8
1942	York	81	Higgins	34	McCosky	11	McCosky	11
1943	Wakefield	91	Wakefield	38*	York	11	Hoover Harris	6
1944	Higgins	79	Higgins	32	Cramer	9	Mayo	9
1945	Cullenbine	80	Cullenbine	27	Cramer	8	Webb	8
1946	Lake	105	Greenberg	29	Kell	9	Lake	15
1947	Lake	96	Kell	29	Lake Mullin	6	Lake	11
1948	Mullin	91	Evers	33	Mullin	11	Lipon	4
1949	Kell	97	Kell	38	Kell	9	Kell Kolloway	7
1950	Kell	114	Kell	56*	Evers	11*	Lipon	9
1951	Kell	92	Kell	36*	Priddy Mullin	6	Kell	10
1952	Groth Dropo	56	Priddy	23	Mullin	5	Mullin	4
1953	Kuenn	94	Kuenn	33	Kuenn	7	Kuenn	6
1954	Kuenn	81	Kuenn	28	Tuttle	11	Kaline Kuenn	9
1955	Kaline	121	Kuenn	38*	Kaline	8	Torgeson	9
1956	Kaline Kuenn Maxwell	96	Kaline Kuenn	32	Kaline	10	Kuenn	9
1957	Kaline	83	Kuenn	30	Kuenn Bolling	6	Kaline	11
1958	Bolling	91	Kuenn	39*	Harris	8	Wilson	10
1959	Yost	115*	Kuenn	42*	Kuenn	7	Kaline	10
1960	Yost	78	Kaline	29	Yost	5	Kaline	19
1961	Colavito	129	Kaline	41*	Wood	14*	Wood	30
1962	Cash	94	Colavito	30	Kaline	6	Wood	24
1963	Colavito	91	Colavito	29	Bruton	8	Wood	18
1964	McAuliffe	85	Kaline	31	Freehan	8	Bruton	14

Year	Leader In	Runs	Leader In	2B	Leader In	3B	Leader In	SB
1965	Wert	81	Cash	23	McAuliffe	6	Lumpe	7
1966	Cash	98	Kaline	29	McAuliffe	8	Wert	6
1967	Kaline	94	Kaline	28	McAuliffe	7	Stanley	9
1968	McAuliffe	95*	Northrup	29	McAuliffe	10	McAuliffe	8
1969	Cash	81	Northrup	31	McAuliffe Northrup	5	Stanley	8
1970	Stanley	83	Kaline	24	Stanley	11	Stanley	10
1971	Cash Northrup	72	Rodriguez	30	Rodriguez	7	Northrup	7
1972	Rodriguez	65	Rodriguez	23	Stanley	6	Taylor	5
1973	Stanley	81	Rodriguez	27	Northrup	7	Taylor	9
1974	Kaline	71	Kaline	28	Freehan Rodriguez	5	LeFlore	23
1975	LeFlore	66	Rodriguez	20	Rodriguez LeFlore	6	LeFlore	28
1976	LeFlore	93	Staub	28	LeFlore	8	LeFlore	58
1977	LeFlore	100	Staub	34	LeFlore Fuentes	10	LeFlore	39
1978	LeFlore	126*	Staub LeFlore	30	Whitaker	7	LeFlore	68*
1979	LeFlore	110	Kemp Parrish	26	LeFlore	10	LeFlore	78
1980	Trammell	107	Parrish	34	Brookens	9	Brookens Peters	13

*League leader

17. TIGERS HITTING 20 HOME RUNS

1922 — Harry Heilmann 21
1929 — Dale Alexander 25
1930 — Dale Alexander 20
1934 — Hank Greenberg 26
1935 — Hank Greenberg 36
1936 — Goose Goslin 24
1937 — Hank Greenberg 40
       Rudy York 35
1938 — Hank Greenberg 58
       Rudy York 33
       Charlie Gehringer 20
1939 — Hank Greenberg 33
       Rudy York 20
1940 — Hank Greenberg 41
       Rudy York 33
1941 — Rudy York 27
1942 — Rudy York 21
1943 — Rudy York 34
1946 — Hank Greenberg 44
1947 — Roy Cullenbine 24
1948 — Pat Mullin 23
1949 — Vic Wertz 20
1950 — Vic Wertz 27
       Hoot Evers 21
1951 — Vic Wertz 27
1952 — Walt Dropo 23*

1953 — Ray Boone 22**
1954 — Ray Boone 20
1955 — Al Kaline 27
       Ray Boone 20
1956 — Charlie Maxwell 28
       Al Kaline 27
       Ray Boone 25
1957 — Charley Maxwell 24
       Al Kaline .... , 23
1958 — Gail Harris 20
1959 — Charley Maxwell 31
       Al Kaline 27
       Eddie Yost 21
1960 — Rocky Colavito 35
       Charley Maxwell 24
1961 — Rocky Colavito 45
       Norm Cash 41
1962 — Norm Cash 39
       Rocky Colavito 37
       Al Kaline 29
       Chico Fernandez 20
1963 — Al Kaline 27
       Norm Cash 26
       Rocky Colavito 22
1964 — Dick McAuliffe 24
       Norm Cash 23

Tigers Hitting 20 Home Runs (continued)

	Don Demeter	22		Al Kaline	21
1965 —	Norm Cash	30	1970 —	Jim Northrup	24
	Willie Horton	29	1971 —	Norm Cash	32
1966 —	Norm Cash	32		Willie Horton	22
	Al Kaline	29		Bill Freehan	21
	Willie Horton	27	1972 —	Norm Cash	22
	Dick McAuliffe	23	1975 —	Willie Horton	25
1967 —	Al Kaline	25	1977 —	Jason Thompson	31
	Norm Cash	22		Rusty Staub	22
	Dick McAuliffe	22		Ben Oglivie	21
	Bill Freehan	20	1978 —	Jason Thompson	26
1968 —	Willie Horton	36		Rusty Staub	24
	Norm Cash	25	1979 —	Steve Kemp	26
	Bill Freehan	25		Champ Summers	20
	Jim Northrup	21		Jason Thompson	20
1969 —	Willie Horton	28	1980 —	Lance Parrish	24
	Jim Northrup	25		Steve Kemp	21
	Norm Cash	22			

*Also hit 6 HR at Boston
**Also hit 4 HR at Cleveland

18. TIGERS WITH 100 RBIs

1907 — Ty Cobb	116		Charlie Gehringer	106
1908 — Ty Cobb	101	1930 — Dale Alexander	135
1909 — Ty Cobb	115	1932 — John Stone	108
1910 — Sam Crawford	120		Charlie Gehringer	107
1911 — Ty Cobb	144	1933 — Charlie Gehringer	105
	Sam Crawford	115	1934 — Hank Greenberg	139
1912 — Sam Crawford	109		Charlie Gehringer	127
1914 — Sam Crawford	104		Billy Rogell	100
1915 — Sam Crawford	112		Goose Goslin	100
	Bobby Veach	112	1935 — Hank Greenberg	170
1917 — Bobby Veach	103		Goose Goslin	109
	Ty Cobb	102		Charlie Gehringer	108
1919 — Bobby Veach	101	1936 — Goose Goslin	125
1920 — Bobby Veach	113		Charlie Gehringer	116
1921 — Harry Heilmann	139		Al Simmons	112
	Bobby Veach	128		Marv Owen	105
	Ty Cobb	101	1937 — Hank Greenberg	183
1922 — Bobby Veach	126		Gee Walker	113
1923 — Harry Heilmann	115		Rudy York	103
1924 — Harry Heilmann	113	1938 — Hank Greenberg	146
1925 — Harry Heilmann	133		Rudy York	127
	Ty Cobb	102		Charlie Gehringer	107
1926 — Harry Heilmann	103	1939 — Hank Greenberg	112
1927 — Harry Heilmann	120	1940 — Hank Greenberg	150
	Bob Fothergill	114		Rudy York	134
1928 — Harry Heilmann	107	1941 — Rudy York	111
1929 — Dale Alexander	137	1943 — Rudy York	118
	Harry Heilmann	120	1946 — Hank Greenberg	127

1948 — Hoot Evers 103
1949 — Vic Wertz 133
1950 — Vic Wertz 123
      Hoot Evers 103
      George Kell 101
1955 — Ray Boone 116
      Al Kaline 102
1956 — Al Kaline 128
1961 — Rocky Colavito 140
      Norm Cash 132

1962 — Rocky Colavito 112
1963 — Al Kaline 101
1965 — Willie Horton 104
1966 — Willie Horton 100
1977 — Jason Thompson 105
      Rusty Staub 101
1978 — Rusty Staub 121
1979 — Steve Kemp 105
1980 — Steve Kemp 101

19. TIGERS STEALING 20 BASES

1901 — Ducky Holmes 35
      Doc Casey 34
      Kid Gleason 32
      Jimmy Barrett 26
      Kid Elberfeld 23
1902 — Jimmy Barrett 24
      Doc Casey 22
      Dick Harley 20
1903 — Jimmy Barrett 27
1904 — Sam Crawford 20
1905 — Sam Crawford 22
1906 — Germany Schaefer 31
      Bill Coughlin 31
      Matty McIntyre 29
      Sam Crawford 24
      Ty Cobb 23
      Davy Jones 21
1907 — Ty Cobb 49
      Davy Jones 30
      Germany Schaefer 21
      Claude Rossman 20
1908 — Germany Schaefer 40
      Ty Cobb 39
      Matty McIntyre 20
1909 — Ty Cobb 76
      Donie Bush 53
      George Moriarty 34
      Sam Crawford 30
1910 — Ty Cobb 83
      Donie Bush 49
      George Moriarty 33
      Davy Jones 25
      Tom Jones 22
      Sam Crawford 20
1911 — Ty Cobb 83
      Donie Bush 40
      Sam Crawford 37
      George Moriarty 28
      Davy Jones 25
      Delos Drake 20
1912 — Ty Cobb 61

      Sam Crawford 41
      Donie Bush 35
      Baldy Louden 28
      George Moriarty 27
1913 — Ty Cobb 52
      Donie Bush 44
      George Moriarty 33
      Bobby Veach 22
1914 — Ty Cobb 35
      Donie Bush 35
      George Moriarty 34
      Sam Crawford 25
      George Burns 23
      Bobby Veach 20
1915 — Ty Cobb 96
      Donie Bush 35
      Oscar Vitt 26
      Sam Crawford 24
1916 — Ty Cobb 68
      Bobby Veach 24
      Ralph Young 20
1917 — Ty Cobb 55
      Donie Bush 34
      Bobby Veach 21
1918 — Ty Cobb 34
      Bobby Veach 21
1919 — Ty Cobb 28
      Donie Bush 22
1921 — Ty Cobb 22
1924 — Ty Cobb 23
1927 — Johnny Neun 22
      Jack Tavener 20
1928 — Harry Rice 20
1929 — Charlie Gehringer 27
      Roy Johnson 20
1930 — Marty McManus 23
1931 — Roy Johnson 33
1932 — Gee Walker 30
1933 — Gee Walker 26
1934 — Jo Jo White 28
      Pete Fox 25

Tigers Stealing 20 Bases (continued)

	Gee Walker 20	1974 — Ron LeFlore 23	
1937 — Gee Walker 23		1975 — Ron LeFlore 28	
1939 — Pete Fox 23		1976 — Ron LeFlore 58	
	Barney McCosky 20	1977 — Ron LeFlore 39	
1961 — Jake Wood 30		1978 — Ron LeFlore 68	
1962 — Jake Wood 24		1979 — Ron LeFlore 78	
1974 — Ron LeFlore 23			Lou Whitaker 20

TIGERS' LONGEST HITTING STREAKS

Games	Player	Season
40	Ty Cobb, OF	1911
35	Ty Cobb, OF	1917
34	Jonathan Stone, OF	1930
30	Goose Goslin, OF	1934
30	Ron LeFlore, OF	1976*

*Start of season (April 17-May 27)

CONSECUTIVE GAMES PLAYED BY TIGERS

511 — Charlie Gehringer, Sept. 3, 1927 — May 7, 1931.
504 — Charlie Gehringer, June 25, 1932 — Aug. 11, 1935.
458 — Rocky Colavito, June 21, 1960 — May 21, 1963.
434 — Ed Brinkman, Sept. 26, 1971 — Aug. 9, 1974*.

*Regular season only, missed all but one game of 1972 playoff.

20. HITTING FOR THE CYCLE

Tigers Hitting for the Cycle

Date	Player	Opponent
Sept. 17, 1920	Bobby Veach	vs. Boston (12 innings)
Sept. 26, 1926	Bob Fothergill	vs. Boston
April 20, 1937	Gee Walker	vs. Cleveland
May 27, 1939	Charlie Gehringer	vs. St. Louis
Sept. 14, 1947	Vic Wertz	at Washington (1st game)
June 2, 1950	George Kell	at Philadelphia (2nd game)
Sept. 7, 1950	Hoot Evers	vs. Cleveland (10 innings)

Opponents Hitting for the Cycle at Detroit

Aug. 13, 1921	George Sisler	St. Louis (10 innings)
June 27, 1922	Ray Schalk	Chicago
July 26, 1928	Bob Meusel	New York
Aug. 2, 1940	Joe Cronin	Boston
Sept. 3, 1976	Mike Hegan	Milwaukee

21. TIGER CAREER PITCHING LEADERS

(Detroit records only, regular season)

Games

Hiller	545
Dauss	538
Lolich	508
Trout	493
Newhouser	460
Mullin	435
Bridges	424
Aguirre	334
Whitehill	325
Trucks	316

Games Started

Lolich	459
Mullin	395
Dauss	388
Newhouser	373
Bridges	362
Trout	305
Whitehill	287
Lary	274
Bunning	251
Donovan	242

Games Won

Dauss	223
Mullin	208
Lolich	207
Newhouser	200
Bridges	194
Trout	161
Donovan	142
Whitehill	133
Lary	123
Bunning	118

Games Lost

Dauss	182
Mullin	180
Lolich	175
Trout	153
Newhouser	148
Bridges	138
Whitehill	119
Lary	110
Sorrell	101
Trucks	96

Innings Pitched

Mullin	3,394
Dauss	3,391
Lolich	3,363
Newhouser	2,944
Bridges	2,826
Trout	2,592
Whitehill	2,172
Donovan	2,139
Lary	2,009
Bunning	1,867

Complete Games

Mullin	336
Dauss	245
Donovan	213
Newhouser	212
Bridges	207
Lolich	190
Trout	156
Whitehill	148
Killian	142
Lary	123
Willett	123

Strikeouts

Lolich	2,679
Newhouser	1,770
Bridges	1,674
Bunning	1,406
Mullin	1,380
Dauss	1,201
Trout	1,199
McLain	1,150
Donovan	1,079
Trucks	1,046

Shutouts

Lolich	39
Mulin	33
Newhouser	33
Bridges	32
Donovan	29
Trout	28
McLain	26
Dauss	21
Lary	20
Trucks	20

Tiger Career Pitching Leaders (continued)

Saves

Hiller	125
Fox	55
Benton	45
Lopez	42
Dauss	39
Sherry	37
Scherman	34
Trout	34
Gladding	33
Timmerman	33
Aguirre	27

20-Win Seasons

Mullin	5
Newhouser	4
Bridges	3
Coveleski	3
Dauss	3
McLain	3
Coleman	2
Killian	2
Lary	2
Lolich	2
Trout	2

PITCHING LEADERS BY YEARS
(Wins, Losses, IP, ERA)

Year	Leader In	Wins	Leader In	Losses	Leader In	IP	Leader In	ERA
1901	Miller	23	Cronin Siever	15	Miller	332	Yeager	2.61
1902	Mercer	15	Mercer	18	Mercer	282	Siever	1.91*
1903	Mullin	19	Donovan Kitson	16	Mullin	321	Mullin	2.25
1904	Donovan Mullin	17	Mullin	23	Mullin	382	Mullin	2.40
1905	Killian	22	Mullin	21	Mullin	348*	Killian	2.27
1906	Mullin	21	Mullin	18	Mullin	330	Siever	2.71
1907	Donovan Killian	25	Mullin	20	Mullin	357	Killian	1.78
1908	Summers	24	Mullin	12	Summers	301	Summers	1.64
1909	Mullin	29*	Summers	12	Mullin	304	Killian	1.71
1910	Mullin	21	Mullin Summers	12	Mullin	289	Donovan	2.42
1911	Mullin	18	Willett	14	Mullin	234	Mullin	3.07
1912	Dubuc Willett	17	Mullin	17	Willett	284	Dubuc	2.77
1913	Dubuc	16	Dubuc Willett	14	Dubuc	243	Dauss	2.68
1914	Coveleski	21	Dauss	15	Coveleski	303	Dauss	2.86
1915	Dauss	24	Coveleski Dauss	13	Coveleski	313	Coveleski	2.45
1916	Coveleski	22	Dauss James	12	Coveleski	324	Coveleski	1.97
1917	Dauss	17	Ehmke	15	Dauss	271	James	2.09
1918	Boland	13	Dauss	16	Dauss	250	Boland	2.65
1919	Dauss	21	Boland	16	Dauss	256	Leonard	2.77
1920	Ehmke	15	Dauss	21	Dauss	270	Ehmke	3.29
1921	Ehmke	13	Dauss	15	Leonard	245	Leonard	3.75
1922	Pillette	19	Ehmke	17	Ehmke	280	Pillette	2.85
1923	Dauss	21	Pillette	19#	Dauss	316	Dauss	3.62
1924	Whitehill	17	Dauss Stoner	11	Whitehill	233	Collins	3.21

Year	Leader In	Wins	Leader In	Losses	Leader In	IP	Leader In	ERA
1925	Dauss	16	Collins, Dauss, Whitehill	11	Whitehill	239	Dauss	3.16
1926	Whitehill	16	Whitehill	13	Whitehill	252	Gibson	3.48
1927	Whitehill	16	Whitehill	14	Whitehill	236	Whitehill	3.36
1928	Carroll	16	Whitehill	16	Carroll	231	Carroll	3.27
1929	Uhle	15	Sorrell, Whitehill	15	Uhle	249	Uhle	4.08
1930	Whitehill	17	Whitehill	13	Uhle	239	Uhle	3.65
1931	Sorrell, Whitehill	13	Bridges, Whitehill	16	Whitehill	272	Uhle	3.50
1932	Whitehill	16	Sorrell	14	Whitehill	244	Bridges	3.36
1933	Marberry	16	Fisher, Sorrell	15	Marberry	238	Bridges	3.09
1934	Rowe	24	Bridges	11	Bridges	275	Auker	3.42
1935	Bridges	21	Rowe	13	Rowe	276	Bridges	3.51
1936	Bridges	23*	Auker	16	Bridges	295	Bridges	3.60
1937	Lawson	18	Bridges	12	Auker	253	Auker	3.88
1938	Bridges	13	Auker	10	Kennedy	190	Gill	4.12
1939	Bridges	17	Rowe	12	Newsom	246	Newsom	3.37
1940	Newsom	21	Benton	10	Newsom	264	Newsom	2.83
1941	Benton	15	Newsom	20*	Newsom	250	Benton	2.97
1942	Trucks	14	Trout	18	Benton	227	Newhouser	2.45
1943	Trout	20#	Newhouser	17	Trout	247	Bridges	2.39
1944	Newhouser	29*	Gentry, Gorsica, Trout	14	Trout	352*	Trout	2.12*
1945	Newhouser	25*	Trout	15	Newhouser	313	Newhouser	1.81*
1946	Newhouser	26#	Trout	13	Newhouser	293	Newhouser	1.94*
1947	Hutchinson	18	Newhouser	17*	Newhouser	285	Newhouser	2.87
1948	Newhouser	21*	Houtteman	16	Newhouser	272	Newhouser	3.01
1949	Trucks	19	Newhouser, Trucks	11	Newhouser	292	Trucks	2.81
1950	Houtteman	19	Newhouser	13	Houtteman	275	Houtteman	3.54
1951	Trucks	13	Gray, Trout	14#	Gray	197	Hutchinson	3.68
1952	Gray	12	Houtteman	20*	Gray	224	Newhouser	3.74
1953	Garver	11	Gray	15	Garver, Hoeft	198	Garver	4.45
1954	Gromek	18	Gromek	16	Gromek	253	Gromek	2.74
1955	Hoeft	16	Garver	16	Lary	235	Hoeft	2.99
1956	Lary	21*	Hoeft	14	Lary	294*	Lary	3.15
1957	Bunning	20#	Lary	16	Bunning	267*	Bunning	2.69
1958	Lary	16	Lary	15	Lary	260*	Lary	2.90
1959	Bunning, Lary, Mossi	17	Foytack	14	Bunning	250	Mossi	3.36
1960	Lary	15	Lary	15	Lary	274*	Bunning	2.79
1961	Lary	23	Bunning	11	Lary	275	Mossi	2.96
1962	Bunning	19	Mossi	13	Bunning	258	Aguirre	2.21*
1963	Regan	15	Aguirre	15	Bunning	248	Aguirre	3.67
1964	Wickersham	19	Wickersham	12	Wickersham	254	Lolich	3.26

Pitching Leaders by Years (continued)

Year	Leader In	Wins	Leader In	Losses	Leader In	IP	Leader In	ERA
1965	McLain	16	Wickersham	14	Lolich	244	McLain	2.61
1966	McLain	20	Lolich McLain	14	McLain	264	Wilson	2.59
1967	Wilson	22#	McLain	16	Wilson	264	Lolich	3.04
1968	McLain	31*	Wilson	12	McLain	336*	McLain	1.96
1969	McLain	24*	Lolich	11	McLain	325*	McLain	2.80
1970	Lolich	14	Lolich	19*	Lolich	273	Lolich	3.79
1971	Lolich	25*	Lolich	14	Lolich	376*	Lolich	2.92
1972	Lolich	22	Coleman Lolich	14	Lolich	327	Lolich	2.50
1973	Coleman	23	Coleman Lolich	15	Lolich	309	Coleman	3.53
1974	Hiller	17	Lolich	21*	Lolich	308	Lolich	4.15
1975	Lolich	12	Coleman Lolich	18	Lolich	241	Lolich	3.78
1976	Fidrych	19	Roberts	17	Roberts	252	Fidrych	2.34*
1977	Rozema	15	Arroyo	18	Rozema	218	Rozema	3.09
1978	Slaton	17	Rozema Wilcox	12	Slaton	234	Rozema	3.14
1979	Morris	17	Wilcox	10	Morris	198	Morris	3.28
1980	Morris	16	Morris	15	Morris	250	Underwood	3.59

*Led League   #Tied for league lead

PITCHING LEADERS BY YEARS
(Games, CG, SO, Saves)

Year	Leader in Games		Leader in CG		Leader in SO		Leader in Saves	
1901	Miller Siever	38	Miller	35	Siever	85	Miller Yeager Cronin	1
1902	Mercer Mullin	35	Mercer	28	Mullin	78	Mercer Siever Miller McCarthy	1
1903	Mullin	41	Donovan	34*	Donovan	187	Mullin	3
1904	Mullin	45	Mullin	42	Mullin	161	Mullin Killian Kitson	1
1905	Mullin	44	Mullin	35*	Mullin	168	Killian Kitson	1
1906	Mullin	40	Mullin	35	Mullin	123	Eubank Killian	2
1907	Mullin	46	Mullin	35	Mullin	146	Mullin	3
1908	Summers	40	Mullin	26	Donovan	141	Summers Mullin Willett Killian Winter Suggs	1
1909	Willett	41	Mullin	29	Mullin	124	Works	3
1910	Mullin	38	Mullin	27	Donovan	107	Browning	2

Year	Leader in Games		Leader in CG		Leader in SO		Leader in Saves	
1911	Willett	38	Mullin	25	Mullin	87	Willett	2
							Summers	
1912	Willett	37	Willett	24	Dubuc	97	Dubuc	3
	Dubuc							
1913	Dubuc	36	Dubuc	22	Dauss	107	Dauss	1
			Dauss				Lake	
							Comstock	
							Zamloch	
							Williams	
1914	Dauss	45	Coveleski	23	Dauss	150	Dauss	4*
1915	Coveleski	50*	Dauss	27	Coveleski	150	Coveleski	4
							Steen	
							Oldham	
1916	Boland	46	Coveleski	22	Coveleski	108	Dauss	4
1917	Cunningham	44	Dauss	22	Dauss	102	Boland	6
1918	Dauss	33	Dauss	21	Dauss	73	Dauss	3
1919	Boland	35	Dauss	22	Leonard	102	Love	2
1920	Ayers	46	Ehmke	23	Ayers	103	Ehmke	3
1921	Oldham	40	Leonard	16	Leonard	120	Middleton	7*
			Dauss					
1922	Ehmke	45	Pillette	18	Ehmke	108	Dauss	4
1923	Cole	52	Dauss	22	Dauss	105	Cole	5
1924	Holloway	49	Whitehill	16	Collins	75	Dauss	6
1925	Doyle	45	Dauss	16	Whitehill	83	Doyle	8
1926	Whitehill	36	Gibson	16	Whitehill	109	Dauss	9
	Wells							
	Holloway							
1927	Whitehill	41	Whitehill	17	Whitehill	95	Holloway	6
1928	Smith	39	Carroll	19	Whitehill	93	Vangilder	5
1929	Whitehill	38	Uhle	23	Whitehill	103	Stoner	4
1930	Sullivan	40	Uhle	18	Uhle	117	Sullivan	5
1931	Sorrell	35	Whitehill	22	Bridges	105	Uhle	2
	Bridges						Hogsett	
	Herring							
1932	Hogsett	47	Whitehill	17	Bridges	108	Hogsett	7
1933	Hogsett	45	Bridges	17	Bridges	120	Hogsett	9
1934	Rowe	45	Bridges	23	Bridges	151	Hogsett	3
							Marberry	
1935	Rowe	42	Bridges	23	Bridges	163*	Hogsett	5
1936	Rowe	41	Bridges	26	Bridges	175*	Lawson	3
	Lawson						Rowe	
							Sorrell	
							Kimsey	
1937	Auker	39	Auker	19	Bridges	138	Russell	4
1938	Coffman	39	Bridges	13	Bridges	101	Eisenstat	4
			Gill					
1939	Benton	37	Newsom	21	Newsom	164	Benton	5
1940	Benton	42	Newsom	20	Newsom	164	Benton	17*
1941	Newsom	43	Newsom	12	Newsom	175	Benton	7
1942	Newhouser	38	Trout	13	Benton	110	Newhouser	5
1943	Trout	44	Trout	18	Newhouser	144	Trout	6
1944	Trout	49	Trout	33*	Newhouser	187*	Gorsica	4
1945	Trout	41	Newhouser	29*	Newhouser	212*	Overmire	4
1946	Trout	38	Newhouser	29	Newhouser	275	Caster	4

Year	Leader in Games		Leader in CG		Leader in SO		Leader in Saves	
1947	Newhouser	40	Newhouser	24*	Newhouser	176	Benton	7
1948	Trucks	43	Newhouser	19	Newhouser	143	Houtteman	10
	Houtteman							
1949	Trucks	41	Newhouser	22	Trucks	153*	Trucks	4
1950	White	42	Houtteman	21	Gray	102	Calvert	4
							Trout	
							Houtteman	
1951	Trout	42	Hutchinson	9	Gray	131	Trout	5
			Gray					
1952	White	41	Gray	13	Gray	138	White	5
1953	Herbert	43	Garver	13	Gray	115	Herbert	6
1954	Herbert	42	Gromek	17	Hoeft	114	Zuverink	4
1955	Aber	39	Hoeft	17	Hoeft	133	Aber	3
							Birrer	
							Coleman	
1956	Foytack	43	Lary	20	Foytack	184	Aber	7
1957	Bunning	45	Bunning	14	Bunning	182	Maas	6
	Maas							
1958	Aguirre	44	Lary	19*	Bunning	177	Aguirre	5
1959	Morgan	46	Mossi	15	Bunning	201*	Morgan	9
1960	Sisler	41	Lary	15*	Bunning	201*	Aguirre	10
1961	Aguirre	45	Lary	22*	Bunning	194	Fox	12
1962	Nischwitz	48	Bunning	12	Bunning	184	Fox	16
1963	Fox	46	Aguirre	14	Bunning	196	Fox	11
1964	Lolich	44	Lolich	12	Lolich	192	Sherry	11
1965	Gladding	46	McLain	13	Lolich	226	Fox	10
1966	Sherry	55	McLain	14	McLain	192	Sherry	20
1967	Gladding	42	Wilson	12	Wilson	184	Gladding	12
1968	Dobson	47	McLain	28*	McLain	280	Dobson	7
							Patterson	
1969	Dobson	49	McLain	23	Lolich	271	McMahon	11
1970	Timmerman	61	Lolich	13	Lolich	230	Timmerman	27
1971	Scherman	69	Lolich	29*	Lolich	308*	Scherman	20
1972	Seelbach	61	Lolich	23	Lolich	250	Seelbach	14
1973	Hiller	65*	Lolich	17	Lolich	214	Hiller	38*
1974	Hiller	59	Lolich	27	Lolich	202	Hiller	13
1975	Hiller	36	Lolich	19	Lolich	139	Hiller	14
	Walker							
1976	Hiller	56	Fidrych	24*	Hiller	117	Hiller	13
1977	Hiller	45	Rozema	16	Hiller	115	Foucault	13
1978	Hiller	51	Wilcox	16	Wilcox	132	Hiller	15
1979	Lopez	61	Morris	9	Morris	113	Lopez	21
1980	Lopez	67	Wilcox	13	Morris	112	Lopez	21

*League leader

22. TIGERS' 20-GAME WINNERS

```
1906 — George Mullin ............................................... 21–18
1907 — Bill Donovan ............................................... 25–4
         Ed Killian ................................................ 25–13
         George Mullin ............................................. 20–20
1908 — Oren Summers .............................................. 24–12
1909 — George Mullin ............................................. 29–9
         Edgar Willett ............................................. 22–9
1910 — George Mullin ............................................. 21–12
1914 — Harry Coveleski ........................................... 22–12
1915 — George Dauss .............................................. 23–13
         Harry Coveleski ........................................... 23–13
1916 — Harry Coveleski ........................................... 23–10
1919 — George Dauss .............................................. 21–9
1923 — George Dauss .............................................. 21–13
1934 — Schoolboy Rowe ............................................ 24–8
         Tommy Bridges ............................................ 22–11
1935 — Tommy Bridges ............................................. 21–10
1936 — Tommy Bridges ............................................. 23–11
1940 — Bobo Newsom ............................................... 21–5
1943 — Dizzy Trout ............................................... 20–12
1944 — Hal Newhouser ............................................. 29–9
         Dizzy Trout .............................................. 27–14
1945 — Hal Newhouser ............................................. 25–9
1946 — Hal Newhouser ............................................. 26–9
1948 — Hal Newhouser ............................................. 21–12
1956 — Frank Lary ................................................ 21–13
         Billy Hoeft .............................................. 20–14
1957 — Jim Bunning ............................................... 20–8
1961 — Frank Lary ................................................ 23–9
1966 — Denny McLain .............................................. 20–14
1967 — Earl Wilson ............................................... 22–11
1968 — Denny McLain .............................................. 31–6
1969 — Denny McLain .............................................. 24–9
1971 — Mickey Lolich ............................................. 25–14
         Joe Coleman .............................................. 20–9
1972 — Mickey Lolich ............................................. 22–14
1973 — Joe Coleman ............................................... 23–15
```

23. NO-HIT GAMES BY TIGER PITCHERS

```
1912 — George Mullin vs. St. Louis, July 4 (at Detroit) .................... 7–0
1952 — Virgil Trucks vs. Washington, May 15 (at Detroit) ................. 1–0
         Virgil Trucks vs. New York, Aug. 25 (at New York) ................ 1–0
1958 — Jim Bunning vs. Boston, July 20 (at Boston) ....................... 3–0
```

No-Hit Games Vs. Tigers

```
1902 — Jim Callahan, Chicago, Sept. 20 (at Chicago) ..................... 3–0
1905 — Frank Smith, Chicago, Sept. 6 (at Detroit) ....................... 15–0
1912 — Earl Hamilton, St. Louis, Aug. 30 (at Detroit) ................... 5–1
1918 — Hub Leonard, Boston, June 3 (at Detroit) ......................... 5–0
1922 — Charley Robertson, Chicago, April 30 (at Detroit) ................ 2–0*
1948 — Bob Lemon, Cleveland, June 30 (at Detroit) ....................... 2–0
```

1951 — Bob Feller, Cleveland, July 1 (at Cleveland) 2–1
1967 — Steve Barber-Stu Miller, Baltimore, April 30 (at Baltimore) 2–0*
       Joe Horlen, Chicago, Sept. 10 (at Chicago) 6–0
1973 — Steve Busby, Kansas City, April 27 (at Detroit) 3–0
       Nolan Ryan, California, July 15 (at Detroit) 6–0

---

*Perfect game
+Tiger victory

24. WORLD SERIES AND PLAYOFFS

1907 WORLD SERIES

The 1907 World Series matched two vastly different ball clubs. The National League champion Cubs were easy winners over the second-place Pirates, while the Tigers fought tooth and nail through September with Philadelphia, Chicago, and Cleveland.

For the Cubs, it marked the second straight appearance in the fall classic. The Tigers, on the other hand, had risen from a sixth-place finish the year before to the top under the tutelage of first-year manager Hughie Jennings. A key to Detroit's success was 20-year-old Ty Cobb, the American League batting champion with a .350 average.

Game 1 at Chicago — October 8					24,377			
Detroit	0 0 0	0 0 0	0 3 0	0 0 0 — 3	9 3	Game called due
Chicago	0 0 0	1 0 0	0 0 2	0 0 0 — 3	10 5	to darkness

A passed ball in the ninth inning by catcher Boss Schmidt allowed the Cubs to tie the score at 3 and cause the eventual stalemate at the end of twelve because of darkness.

Tiger ace Wild Bill Donovan entered the ninth with a 3–1 lead, just three outs from victory. But Frank Chance led off with a single, and Donovan hit Harry Steinfeldt with a pitch to put the tying runs on. After one out, an error by third baseman Bill Coughlin loaded the bases. Chance scored on a grounder to cut the lead to one run, and a passed ball by Schmidt allowed the tying run to score.

Game 2 at Chicago — October 9				21,901		
Detroit	0 1 0	0 0 0	0 0 0 — 1 9 1	LP Mullin
Chicago	0 1 0	2 0 0	0 0 x — 3 9 1	WP Pfiester

Cub southpaw Jack Pfiester went the distance in a nine-hit, 3–1 victory, as the Cubs stole four more bases to go with the seven stolen the day before. Cub centerfielder Jimmy Slagle drove in the go-ahead run with a single in the fourth, scoring shortstop Joe Tinker.

Game 3 at Chicago — October 10				13,114		
Detroit	0 0 0	0 0 1	0 0 0 — 1 6 1	LP Siever
Chicago	0 1 0	3 1 0	0 0 x — 5 10 1	WP Reulbach

The Tiger offense again failed to produce, as Cub pitcher Ed Reulbach scattered six hits to win 5–1. Cub second sacker Johnny Evers was the offensive star with three hits, including two doubles.

Game 4 at Detroit — October 11				11,306		
Chicago	0 0 0	0 2 0	3 0 1 — 6 7 2	WP Overall
Detroit	0 0 0	1 0 0	0 0 0 — 1 5 2	LP Donovan

A disappointing crowd of 11,306 turned out in rainy weather, perhaps indicating the city's realization that their team was outmatched. Cub righty Orvie Overall limited the Bengals, who were fast turning into kitties, to only five hits. The bitterest pill to swallow came in the seventh inning when the Cubs scored three times without hitting the ball out of the infield, thanks to two stolen bases.

Game 5 at Detroit — October 12						7,370	
Chicago	1 1 0	0 0 0	0 0 0—2	7 1	WP Brown
Detroit	0 0 0	0 0 0	0 0 0—0	7 2	LP Mullin

Mordecai (Three-Finger) Brown displayed his Hall of Fame form with a seven-hit, 2–0 shutout to win the World Series for the Cubs, 4 games to none. Four stolen bases by the Cubs in this game gave them a record 18 for the Series. But the real secret of the Cubs' success was their pitching, which held the Tigers to a puny .209 batting average. Ty Cobb was held in check with a .200 average, while Sam Crawford contributed a measly .238.

Top Tiger Hitter — First baseman Claude Rossman, 8 for 20, .400
Top Tiger Pitcher — Wild Bill Donovan, two complete games, 1.71 ERA
Top Cub Hitter — Third baseman Harry Steinfeldt, 8 for 17, .471
Top Cub Pitcher — Orvie Overall, 18 innings pitched, 1.00 ERA
Total Attendance: 78,068
Winning Player's Share: $2,143
Losing Player's Share: $1,946

1908 WORLD SERIES

The Tigers and Cubs had a return engagement in the 1908 World Series, with the Bengals looking to avenge their poor showing of the year before.

Unfortunately, the result was pretty much the same: too much Cub pitching. But what most people remember about the 1908 season is not the Series, but the famous mistake that enabled the Cubs to snatch the pennant away from John McGraw's New York Giants.

Young Fred Merkle, a substitute first baseman for the Giants, made a critical base running error by failing to touch second after the Giants had apparently scored the winning run in a September 23 showdown with the Cubs. The alert Cubs picked up his mistake, made a force out at second, and turned a victory into a tie. In the rematch scheduled for October 8, the Cubs easily beat the Giants 4–2 to win the flag.

Game 1 at Detroit — October 10						10,812	
Chicago	0 0 4	0 0 0	1 0 5—10	14 2	WP Brown
Detroit	1 0 0	0 0 0	3 2 0— 6	10 4	LP Summers

The 1908 Series opened on a rainy Saturday in Detroit. The Cubs jumped out to a quick lead by knocking Tiger starter Ed Killian out of the box with four runs in the third.

Trailing 5–1 after six-and-a-half innings, the Tigers rallied for five runs in the seventh and eighth and had victory in their grasp. But knuckleballer Ed Summers, who had won 24 games in the regular season, faltered in relief in the ninth when the Cubs got six straight hits and five runs to win 10–6.

Game 2 at Chicago — October 11						17,760	
Detroit	0 0 0	0 0 0	0 0 1—1	4 1	LP Donovan
Chicago	0 0 0	0 0 0	0 6 x—6	7 1	WP Overall

With the second game shifted to Chicago, Tiger hurler Wild Bill Donovan and Cub pitcher Orvie Overall hooked up in a classic pitchers' duel, with neither team scoring through the first seven innings. The Cubs broke the deadlock when shortstop Joe Tinker hit a wind-blown home run to right field with Solly Hofman aboard. The Cubbies then scored four more times before Donovan could retire the side, and the game was out of reach.

```
Game 3 at Chicago — October 12                    14,543
Detroit          1 0 0   0 0 5   0 2 0 — 8 11 4   WP  Mullin
Chicago          0 0 0 . 3 0 0   0 0 0 — 3  7 2   LP  Pfeister
```

The Cubs got out to a quick 3–1 lead after four innings, and it looked like the Tigers faced elimination. But the Tigers rallied for five runs in the sixth and Mullin held the lead for the Bengals' first World Series victory. Ty Cobb paced the Tiger attack with four hits, two RBIs, and two stolen bases.

```
Game 4 at Detroit — October 13                    12,907
Chicago          0 0 2   0 0 0   0 0 1 — 3 10 0   WP  Brown
Detroit          0 0 0   0 0 0   0 0 0 — 0  4 1   LP  Summers
```

Cub ace Three-Finger Brown handcuffed the Tigers in game four with a masterful four-hit, 3–0 shutout to give the Bruins a commanding 3–1 Series lead. Back–to–back scoring singles by Harry Steinfeldt and Solly Hofman were all the Cubs needed to beat the Tigers before a disappointed home crowd.

```
Game 5 at Detroit — October 14                    6,210
Chicago          1 0 0   0 1 0   0 0 0 — 2 10 0   WP  Overall
Detroit          0 0 0   0 0 0   0 0 0 — 0  3 0   LP  Donovan
```

Not to be outdone by his teammate Brown, Cub hurler Orvie Overall shut out the Tigers on three hits to win a second straight World Championship for the Cubs. Only 6,210 Tiger fans showed up in chilly weather for the last game, an all-time record low crowd for the World Series. Overall recorded 10 strikeouts in his shutout as the Tigers watched helplessly.

Top Tiger Hitter — Center fielder Ty Cobb, 7 for 16, .368
Top Tiger Pitcher — George Mullin, 1 complete game victory, 1.00 ERA
Top Cub Hitter — First baseman Frank Chance, 8 for 19, .421
Top Cub Pitcher — Orvie Overall, 2 wins, 15 strikeouts, 0.98 ERA
Total Attendance: 62,232
Winning Player's Share: $1,318
Losing Player's Share: $870

1909 WORLD SERIES

The 1909 World Series promised a matchup of the two reigning superstars of the day — Pittsburgh's Honus Wagner and the Tigers' Ty Cobb. Each man had won his respective league batting and RBI titles, while Cobb had garnered the Triple Crown.

Oddly enough, a 27–year old unknown Pirate pitcher named Babe Adams would prove the hero of the Series, which went the full seven games.

Game 1 at Pittsburgh — October 8   29,264
Detroit   1 0 0   0 0 0   0 0 0 — 1 6 4   LP Mullin
Pittsburgh   0 0 0   1 2 1   0 0 x — 4 5 0   WP Adams

The first game opened in the Pirates' new stadium, Forbes Field, with a surprise Pittsburgh starter — Babe Adams. Manager Fred Clarke's choice proved wise as Adams held the Tigers to six hits and one run. The Pirates scored four runs off 29-game winner George Mullin to grab the lead after six innings.

With two men on and two out in the seventh, Ty Cobb hit a long drive to center field. Pirate centerfielder Tommy Leach made a superb running catch to preserve the lead and end the Tiger threat.

Game 2 at Pittsburgh — October 9   30,915
Detroit   0 2 3   0 2 0   0 0 0 — 7 9 3   WP Donovan
Pittsburgh   2 0 0   0 0 0   0 0 0 — 2 5 1   LP Camnitz

Ty Cobb's daring steal of home in the third inning sparked the Tigers to three runs and helped break the game open against Pirate 25-game winner Howie Camnitz. Wild Bill Donovan held the Bucs to five hits in winning his first Series victory.

Game 3 at Detroit — October 11   18,277
Pittsburgh   5 1 0   0 0 0   0 0 2 — 8 10 3   WP Maddox
Detroit   0 0 0   0 0 0   4 0 2 — 6 10 5   LP Summers

The Pirates pounded Tiger starter Ed Summers for five runs in the first inning and managed to hold off a late Tiger rally to win game three. Honus Wagner literally stole the show in this game with three hits, three RBIs, and three stolen bases.

Game 4 at Detroit — October 12   17,036
Pittsburgh   0 0 0   0 0 0   0 0 0 — 0 5 6   LP Leifield
Detroit   0 2 0   3 0 0   0 0 x — 5 8 0   WP Mullin

George Mullin and the Tigers evened the Series at two games each with a five-hit shutout of the Pirates, striking out 10. Ty Cobb and catcher Oscar Stanage each contributed two RBIs to this win.

Game 5 at Pittsburgh — October 13   21,706
Detroit   1 0 0   0 0 2   0 1 0 — 4 6 1   LP Summers
Pittsburgh   1 1 1   0 0 0   4 1 x — 8 10 2   WP Adams

Returning to Pittsburgh, the Pirates started first-game winner Babe Adams, who managed to handle the Tigers once more. Player-manager Fred Clarke belted a two-run homer in the seventh to break a 3–3 tie and lead the Bucs to their third triumph. Home runs by Davy Jones and Sam Crawford were wasted in defeat.

Game 6 at Detroit — October 14   10,535
Pittsburgh   3 0 0   0 0 0   0 0 1 — 4 7 3   LP Willis
Detroit   1 0 0   2 1 1   0 0 x — 5 10 3   WP Mullin

Unlike the 1907 and 1908 teams, this year's Tigers refused to give up without a fight. Surviving a three-run first inning, George Mullin managed to keep the Pirates in check and win. The win set the stage for a showdown two days later for the championship.

Game 7 at Detroit — October 16   17,562
Pittsburgh   0 2 0   2 0 3   0 1 0 — 8 7 0   WP Adams
Detroit   0 0 0   0 0 0   0 0 0 — 0 6 3   LP Donovan

Babe Adams made the win look surprisingly easy, scattering six hits as he pitched the Pirates to an 8–0 win and the world title. Honus Wagner and second sacker Dots Miller each got two RBIs to pace the Pirate attack against Wild Bill Donovan and George Mullin. For the third time in a row, the Tigers were denied baseball's ultimate prize. The anticipated Cobb–Wagner confrontation proved a mismatch, as Cobb managed a feeble .231, while Wagner hit .333 and drove in six runs. Detroit's weak catching proved costly once more, as the Pirates stole a record-tying 18 bases.

Top Tiger Hitter — Second baseman Jim Delahanty, 4 doubles, .346
Top Tiger Pitcher — George Mullin, 2 wins, 3 complete games, 2.25 ERA
Top Pirate Hitter — Centerfielder Tommy Leach, 9 hits, 8 runs, .360
Top Pirate Pitcher — Babe Adams, 3 wins, 3 complete games, 1.33 ERA
Total Attendance: 145,807
Winning Player's Share: $1,825
Losing Player's Share: $1,275

1934 WORLD SERIES

The 1934 season saw the rise of two new baseball powers — the free-spirited St. Louis Cardinals and the Detroit Tigers under the leadership of Mickey Cochrane.

The acquisition of Cochrane from Philadelphia the previous winter gave the Bengals just what they needed — a great catcher and a fiery leader. He played a key role in a murderous offense that included Hank Greenberg, Charlie Gehringer, and Goose Goslin. The Tigers boasted two 20-game winners in Schoolboy Rowe and Tommy Bridges.

But the Tigers would run up against a two-edged sword — the Dean brothers, Dizzy and Paul. Dizzy had won 30 games in the regular season, while brother Paul, also known as Daffy, contributed 19 wins. The '34 Series quickly became their stage to show their stuff.

```
Game 1 at Detroit — October 3                    42,505
St. Louis       0 2 1  0 1 4  0 0 0 — 8 13 2  WP Dizzy Dean
Detroit         0 0 1  0 0 1  0 1 0 — 3  8 5  LP Crowder
```

The combination of thirteen Cardinal hits and five Tiger infield errors proved disastrous in game one, as Dizzy Dean scattered eight hits to win, 8–3. Outfielder Joe Medwick paced the Cardinal attack with four hits, including a home run.

```
Game 2 at Detroit — October 4                    43,451
St. Louis    0 1 1  0 0 0  0 0 0  0 0 0 — 2 7 3  LP  Walker
Detroit      0 0 0  1 0 0  0 0 1  0 0 1 — 3 7 0  WP  Rowe
```

Trailing 2–1 into the bottom of the ninth, the Tigers rallied to tie the game on a pinch-single by Gee Walker. The Tigers won in the 12th when Gehringer and Greenberg walked and Goslin singled to center field to score Gehringer with the winning run. Schoolboy Rowe scattered seven hits for the win, going the distance.

```
Game 3 at St. Louis — October 5                   34,073
Detroit       0 0 0  0 0 0  0 0 1 — 1 8 2  LP  Bridges
St. Louis     1 1 0  0 2 0  0 0 x — 4 9 1  WP  Paul Dean
```

Back on their home turf, the Redbirds went one game up on the Tigers on the strength of Paul Dean's eight-hit, 4-1 win. The Tigers left 13 men on base against Dean, who walked five batters. The offensive star was third baseman Pepper Martin, who had a double and triple, and scored two runs.

```
Game 4 at St. Louis — October 6              37,492
Detroit           0 0 3  1 0 0  1 5 0 — 10 13 1  WP Auker
St. Louis         0 1 1  2 0 0  0 0 0 —  4 10 5  LP Walker
```

Detroit broke a 4-4 tie in the late innings to even the Series at two games each, as Hank Greenberg had four hits and three RBIs, and shortstop Billy Rogell added four RBIs to pace the Tiger attack. Eldon Auker scattered 10 hits to go the distance for the win.

The Cardinals had a close call in the fourth when they used Dizzy Dean as a pinch-runner. He failed to slide into second and caught a Billy Rogell throw right on the head. He was carried off the field on a stretcher, but as a local paper reported, "They x-rayed Dizzy's head and found nothing."

```
Game 5 at St. Louis — October 7              38,536
Detroit           0 1 0  0 0 2  0 0 0 — 3 7 0  WP Bridges
St. Louis         0 0 0  0 0 0  1 0 0 — 1 7 1  LP Dizzy Dean
```

With just one day's rest, Tommy Bridges subdued the Redbirds and Dizzy Dean, 3-1, with a seven-hitter. Charlie Gehringer's home run in the sixth provided the winning margin. It was a leadoff homer that hit the right field pavilion roof.

```
Game 6 at Detroit — October 8               44,551
St. Louis         1 0 0  0 2 0  1 0 0 — 4 10 2  WP Paul Dean
Detroit           0 0 1  0 0 2  0 0 0 — 3  7 1  LP Rowe
```

Despite returning home with a one-game lead, the Tigers couldn't handle Paul Dean, who had beaten them in game three. Dean helped his own cause in the seventh by singling in the winning run and setting the stage for a climatic seventh game.

```
Game 7 at Detroit — October 9               40,902
St. Louis         0 0 7  0 0 2  2 0 0 — 11 17 1  WP Dizzy Dean
Detroit           0 0 0  0 0 0  0 0 0 —  0  6 3  LP Auker
```

A seven-run, third-inning barrage, led by Frankie Frisch's bases-loaded double, gave Dizzy Dean a comfortable margin to win. But all he really needed was just the first run, as he shut out the Tigers to lead St. Louis to the World Championship.

In the sixth inning, outfielder Joe Medwick tripled and slid hard into Tiger third baseman Marv Owen, touching off a brief scuffle. When Medwick took his left field position in the bottom of the inning, the frustrated Tiger fans began pelting him with garbage. Three times he tried to take the field and three times he retreated, before Commissioner Landis took action to avoid a riot. With the Cardinals ahead 9-0, Landis ordered Medwick removed from the game so play could continue.

Top Tiger Hitter — Second sacker Charlie Gehringer, 11 for 29, .379
Top Tiger Pitcher — Schoolboy Rowe, 2 complete games, 1 win, 2.95 ERA
Top Cardinal Hitter — Leftfielder Joe Medwick, 11 hits, 5 RBIs, .379
Top Cardinal Pitcher — Paul Dean, 2 wins, 2 complete games, 1.00 ERA
Total Attendance: 281,510
Winning Player's Share: $5,390
Losing Player's Share: $3,355

First baseman Rudy York hit 33 homers and drove in 134 runs in the 1940 pennant chase.

Bobo Newsom led the pitching staff with a 21-5 record in 1940.

Al Benton became one of the Tigers first relief aces, leading the 1940 champs with 17 saves.

As a sophomore in 1940, Dizzy Trout had yet to display the 20-game win form that would surface in 1943-44.

Smooth fielding second sacker Eddie Mayo hurdles sliding Athletic Ford Garrison while completing a double play started by shortstop Joe Hoover. (AP wirephoto, courtesy of Gene Elston)

Shortstop Joe Hoover slides safely into home, beating the tag by Senator catcher Fermin Guerra, who got the ball wide on a throw from right fielder Roberto Ortiz. (AP wirephoto, courtesy of Gene Elston)

FIFTIES' FAVORITES

Right-hander Virgil Trucks threw two no-hitters for Detroit in 1952.

Fred Hutchinson won 92 games for the Tigers before becoming a full-time manager in 1952.

George Kell hit .340 for the Tigers in 1950 as their pennant chase fell three games short.

Outfielder Hoot Evers patrolled left field in the late Forties and early Fifties for the Bengals.

Al Kaline was the youngest batting champion in history, hitting, .340 at age 20 in 1955.

Ozzie Virgil was the first black to play for the Bengals, obtained from the Giants for the 1958 season.

Outfielder Harvey Kuenn won the batting title in 1959 with a .353 average. He then was traded to Cleveland for Rocky Colavito.

Hank Aguirre was a dependable starter and reliever for the Tigers, but one of the worst hitters in baseball history.

THE TIGERS IN THE SIXTIES

Al Kaline was the heart and soul of the ball club during the Sixties, leading the club to the 1968 World Championship.

Southpaw Mickey Lolich won 102 games for the Tigers during the decade of the Sixties.

Catcher Bill Freehan holds virtually every major club record for catching. He enjoyed a .300 season in 1964.

Relief ace Terry Fox gave the Tigers five solid seasons in the bullpen during the Sixties.

The first black starting player for
Detroit was second baseman Jake
Wood, who led the league in triples
with 14 in his debut year, 1961.

Obtained for popular Harvey Kuenn,
Rocky Colavito won the fans
immediately with 35 homers in 1960.

In 1963, Phil Regan led the pitching
staff in wins with 15. He later became
a star reliever in the National League.

"The Yankee Killer," Frank Lary led
the American League in wins with 21
in 1956. He won 23 games in 1961.

FOUR 1968 CHAMPIONS

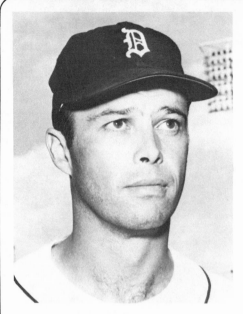

Eddie Mathews contributed a key role in 1968 as a team leader and inspiration to younger players.

Hurler Earl Wilson won 13 games in the 1968 pennant drive.

Third baseman Don Wert was a steady fielder, but suffered from a subpar .200 season in 1968.

Second sacker Dick McAuliffe scored a league-leading 95 runs during the 1968 season.

The team held a Recognition Day on September 14, 1975, to honor veterans of the 1968 world and 1972 divisional champs. From left are: Mickey Stanley, Gates Brown, Mickey Lolich, Willie Horton and Bill Freehan.

Norm Cash put in 15 seasons with Detroit, slugging 373 home runs and winning a batting title in 1961 with a .361 average.

Frank Howard ended his career in Detroit hitting 12 homers as a designated hitter in 1973.

TIGER BRAINTRUST

Bob Scheffing
(1961-63)

Bill Norman
(1958-59)

Ralph Houk
(1974-78)

Chuck Dressen
(1963-66)

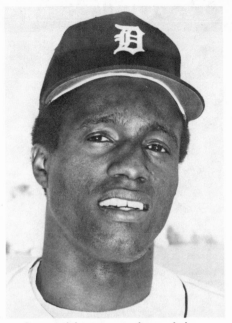

In one of the worse trades made by the Tigers, outfielder Ben Oglivie was sent to Milwaukee for pitcher Jim Slaton. Oglivie has blossomed into one of the top sluggers in the league.

Given up for finished in 1977, Will Horton bounced back as a designated hitter for the Seattle Mariners.

A controversial former Tiger, Ron LeFlore has carried a rep as a mediocre fielder and prima donna who refuses to bunt to the National League.

Rusty Staub spent three productive seasons as the Bengals' designated hitter before a salary dispute sent him packing.

CURRENT TIGER FAVORITES

Tom Brookens (3B)

Richie Hebner (1B)

Rick Peters (CF)

Dan Petry (P)

Dan Schatzeder (P)

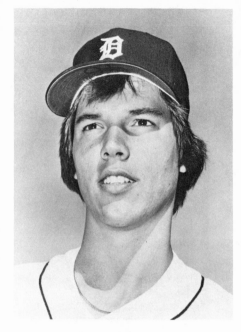

Pat Underwood (P)

Milt Wilcox (P)

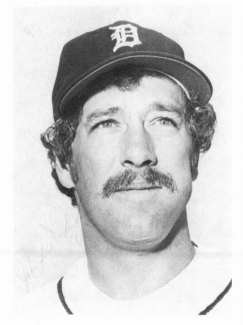

John Wockenfuss (UT)

Sparky Anderson has vowed to make
the Tigers a contender by the 1982
season. The team's progress indicates
his plan is on track. Anderson's
competitive fire met some resistance
initially with the team, but he has now
taken firm control and has the team
headed in the right direction.

Champ Summers immediately won
the allegiance of Tiger fans upon his
arrival in 1979. He credits the
atmosphere at Tiger Stadium for his
success and vows he will never wear
any other uniform.

Sparky Anderson has called Jack
Morris the best right-hander in the
league. He has been the Tiger ace for
the past two seasons and obviously is
a key to the Tigers' bid to become a
contender.

Lance Parrish has established himself
as the best catcher in the American
League. In addition to perfecting his
catching skills, Parrish has become a
leading power hitter.

Left fielder Steve Kemp has driven in 100 runs or more in each of the past two seasons.

Hampered by injuries in 1980, Lynn Jones hopes to contribute more in the Tiger lineup this year.

Many scouts rate Alan Trammell as the best all-around Tiger player today, as well as the top shortstop in the American League.

Sweet Lou Whitaker was the Rookie of the Year in 1978. He combines with Trammell to form a top double-play duo.

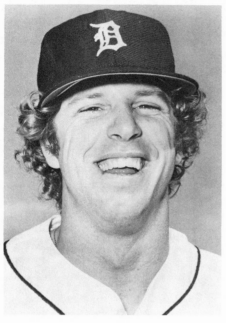

The Tigers are hoping "the Bird,"
Mark Fidrych, will return to the
sensational form he displayed in
winning 19 games in 1976.

The all-time best Tiger reliever is
southpaw John Hiller, who retired in
1980 as the Tiger's liftime appearance
leader with 545 games.

The current ace of the Tiger bull-pen
is Aurelio Lopez, better known as
"Senor Smoke."

Another pitcher looking to return to
form is Dave Rozema, a 15-game
winner in 1977.

AFTERMATH OF A TRADE

At the author's request, Jason Thompson signed this photo as follows: "Best of luck to the Tigers, the fans and the city of Detroit and thanks for some great memories."

New right fielder Al Cowens takes his first batting practice cuts as a Tiger. (Photo by author)

Tiger broadcaster Ernie Harwell (center) interviews Jason Thompson (r) and Al Cowens for their reactions to the trade for his pre-game radio show. (Photo by author)

Batting coach Gates Brown imparts a few pearls of wisdom to Al Cowens. (Photo by author)

Al Kaline accepts his induction
plaque as Charlie Gehringer (seated
to the right of the podium) looks on.
(Photo by author)

The Kaline family, wife Louise and sons Mark and Mike, beam with pride as
Al Kaline is inducted into the Hall of Fame. (Photo by author)

Flanked by Duke Snider (left) and Ted
Williams, Al Kaline awaits induction
into the Hall of Fame. In the lower left
foreground is a teammate from his
rookie year, pitcher Ralph Branca.
(Photo by author)

1935 WORLD SERIES

After four unsuccessful appearances in the World Series, the Tigers had every right to wonder if they would ever win the championship.

The 1935 season produced a new opponent for Mickey Cochrane's Bengals — the Chicago Cubs, led by their catcher, Gabby Hartnett. This matchup gave the Tigers the chance to avenge their '07 and '08 Series losses to the Cubs. The Cubs brought a strong pitching staff into the Series, but the Tiger attack of Greenberg, Gehringer, Cochrane, and Goslin proved equal to the challenge.

```
Game 1 at Detroit — October 2                              47,391
Chicago        2 0 0   0 0 0   0 0 1 — 3 7 0   WP Warneke
Detroit        0 0 0   0 0 0   0 0 0 — 0 4 3   LP Rowe
```

The Cubs pitching lived up to advance notice as Lon Warneke shut out the Tigers on four hits in the Series opener, 3–0. The Bruins struck early in the first with two runs on a double by Augie Galan, a Schoolboy Rowe error, and a Gabby Hartnett single.

```
Game 2 at Detroit — October 3                              46,742
Chicago        0 0 0   0 1 0   2 0 0 — 3 6 1   LP Root
Detroit        4 0 0   3 0 0   1 0 x — 8 9 2   WP Bridges
```

The Tigers came right back with a strong effort by Tommy Bridges, who threw a six-hitter. The Bengals chased Cub starter Charlie Root in the first as Jo-Jo White singled, Cochrane doubled, Gehringer singled, and Hank Greenberg belted a two-run homer to left field. The win proved costly, however, as Greenberg suffered a broken wrist. The injury forced manager Cochrane to move Marv Owen from third to first for game three and replace Greenberg with Flea Clifton.

```
Game 3 at Chicago — October 4                              45,532
Detroit        0 0 0   0 0 1   0 4 0   0 1 — 6 12 2   WP Rowe
Chicago        0 2 0   0 1 0   0 0 2   0 0 — 5 10 3   LP French
```

The scene shifted to Chicago, where the Tigers squeaked out a 6–5 win in the 11th inning on Jo-Jo White's single with two men on base. In a rare relief role, Schoolboy Rowe pitched the last four innings to get the win.

```
Game 4 at Chicago — October 5                              49,350
Detroit        0 0 1   0 0 1   0 0 0 — 2 7 0   WP Crowder
Chicago        0 1 0   0 0 0   0 0 0 — 1 5 2   LP Carleton
```

The Tigers moved even closer to the title, beating the Cubs once more in Wrigley Field 2–1 behind the five-hit pitching of General Crowder. Two consecutive errors by leftfielder Augie Galan and shortstop Billy Jurges handed the Bengals the winning run in the sixth.

```
Game 5 at Chicago — October 6                              49,237
Detroit        0 0 0   0 0 0   0 0 1 — 1 7 1   LP Rowe
Chicago        0 0 2   0 0 0   1 0 x — 3 8 0   WP Warneke
```

A clutch relief performance by Bill Lee kept Chicago's hopes alive in game five. Lon Warneke held the 2–0 lead he had been given until he was forced to leave the game in the seventh with a shoulder injury. Lee pitched out of trouble in the ninth; he saved the victory when the Tigers got men on second and third with two out by getting Flea Clifton to foul out to first baseman Phil Cavaretta. Centerfielder Chuck Klein's two-run homer in the third proved to be the winning margin.

```
Game 6 at Detroit — October 7                    48,420
Chicago              0 0 1  0 2 0  0 0 0 — 3 12 0  LP  French
Detroit              1 0 0  1 0 1  0 0 1 — 4 12 1  WP  Bridges
```

After four frustrating tries, the Tigers finally won their first World's Championship before their own fans, setting off an impromptu celebration that brought 500,000 Detroiters out into the streets for a party until dawn.

With the score knotted at three after eight, the Cubs opened the ninth with a triple by third baseman Stan Hack. But Tommy Bridges hung tough and proceeded to strike out Billy Jurges, retire his mound opponent Larry French with a comebacker to the mound, and give up a fly ball to Augie Galan in left.

With one out in the bottom of the ninth, Mickey Cochrane singled and moved to second on Gehringer's grounder to first. Up to the plate stepped outfielder Goose Goslin, who rapped a single to right field to score Cochrane with the title-winning run.

Top Tiger Hitter — Right fielder Pete Fox, 10 for 26, .385
Top Tiger Pitcher — Tommy Bridges, 2 wins, 2 complete games, 2.50 ERA
Top Cub Hitter — Second baseman Billy Herman, 8 hits, 6 RBIs, .333
Top Cub Pitcher — Lon Warneke, 2 wins, 1 complete game, 0.54 ERA
Total Attendance: 286,672
Winning Player's Share: $6,545
Losing Player's Share: $4,199

1940 WORLD SERIES

A key change in position for Hank Greenberg spelled a 1940 pennant for the Tigers, ending a four-year Yankee reign at the top of the American League. Manager Del Baker shifted Greenberg from first base to left field and moved Rudy York to the gateway post. Aided by Bobo Newsom's 21 wins as the ace of the pitching staff, the Tigers entered the World Series against the Cincinnati Reds.

The Reds came in with a definite weakness at catcher. On August 2, reserve catcher Willard Hershberger shot himself in a tragic suicide. And in mid-September, Ernie Lombardi sprained his ankle, making it necessary for the Reds to activate coach Jimmy Wilson, a 40-year old who had been a one-time regular with the Phillies and Cardinals.

```
Game 1 at Cincinnati — October 2                 31,793
Detroit              0 5 0  0 2 0  0 0 0 — 7 10 1  WP  Newsom
Cincinnati           0 0 0  1 0 0  0 1 0 — 2  8 3  LP  Derringer
```

Two 20-game winners, the Tigers' Bobo Newsom and the Reds' Paul Derringer, squared off in game one, but a five-run Tiger second inning chased Derringer. Newsom scattered eight hits to win before a Reds' crowd that included his father, who tragically died of a heart attack the next day.

```
Game 2 at Cincinnati — October 3                 30,640
Detroit              2 0 0  0 0 1  0 0 0 — 3 3 1  LP  Rowe
Cincinnati           0 2 2  1 0 0  0 0 x — 5 9 0  WP  Walters
```

Bucky Walters threw a three-hitter to stop the Tigers in game two as outfielder Jimmy Ripple clubbed a two-run homer in the third to provide the winning margin.

```
Game 3 at Detroit — October 4                    52,877
Cincinnati           1 0 0  0 0 0  0 1 2 — 4 10 1  LP  Turner
Detroit              0 0 0  1 0 0  4 2 x — 7 13 1  WP  Bridges
```

In the third game at Briggs Stadium, Tommy Bridges hung on to beat the Reds 7–4 following a four-run outburst in the seventh and a two-run inning in the eighth by the Bengals. Two–run homers by Rudy York and third baseman Pinky Higgins in the seventh keyed the Tiger win.

Game 4 at Detroit — October 5					54,093	
Cincinnati	2 0 1	1 0 0	0 1 0—5	11 1	WP	Derringer
Detroit	0 0 1	0 0 1	0 0 0—2	5 1	LP	Trout

The Reds came back to even the Series at two each when Paul Derringer threw a complete game five-hit, 5–2 win over Dizzy Trout and the Tigers. The first four men in the Reds' lineup, third baseman Bill Werber, centerfielder Mike McCormick, rightfielder Ival Goodman, and first baseman Frank McCormick, each got two hits in this win.

Game 5 at Detroit — October 6					55,189	
Cincinnati	0 0 0	0 0 0	0 0 0—0	3 0	LP	Thompson
Detroit	0 0 3	4 0 0	0 1 x—8	13 0	WP	Newsom

The Tigers pounded Reds' pitching for 13 hits and eight runs to pace Bobo Newsom to an easy three-hit shutout. Leading the Tiger attack were a three-run homer by Hank Greenberg and two-hit games by shortstop Dick Bartell, centerfielder Barney McCosky, and second sacker Charlie Gehringer.

Game 6 at Cincinnati — October 7					30,481	
Detroit	0 0 0	0 0 0	0 0 0—0	5 0	LP	Rowe
Cincinnati	2 0 0	0 0 1	0 1 x—4	10 2	WP	Walters

With their backs to the wall, the Reds retaliated with a shutout of their own spun by Bucky Walters, who helped his own cause with a home run in the eighth.

Game 7 at Cincinnati — October 8					26,854	
Detroit	0 0 1	0 0 0	0 0 0—1	7 0	LP	Newsom
Cincinnati	0 0 0	0 0 0	2 0 0—2	7 1	WP	Derringer

The final game boiled down to a pitching duel between Paul Derringer and Bobo Newsom, who was pitching with one day's rest. The Tigers took the lead in the third when catcher Billy Sullivan singled, Newsom sacrificed him to second, and he scored on an error by Werber, who threw to first trying unsuccessfully to keep Gehringer from getting on with a single.

Newsom held the lead through six innings. But in the seventh, Frank McCormick doubled to left and scored on Jimmy Ripple's double to right. The Tigers had a play at the plate on the slow-footed McCormick, but shortstop Dick Bartell cut the ball off. Jimmie Wilson sacrificed Ripple to third, and he then scored on a sacrifice fly by shortstop Billy Myers. Derringer hung on to keep the Tigers at bay and preserve the Reds' World Championship.

Top Tiger Hitter — Leftfielder Hank Greenberg, 10 hits, 6 RBIs, .357
Top Tiger Pitcher — Bobo Newsom, 2 wins, 3 complete game, 1.38 ERA
Top Red Hitter — Third baseman Bill Werber, 10 hits, 4 doubles, .370
Top Red Pitcher — Bucky Walters, 2 wins, 2 complete games, 1.50 ERA
Total Attendance: 281,927
Winning Player's Share: $5,804
Losing Player's Share: $3,532

1945 WORLD SERIES

The effect of World War II on major league talent was never more vivid than the 1945 season, when two mediocre teams won their respective league titles. The Tigers edged out Washington on the last day of the season on a Hank Greenberg grand slam, to finish with 88 wins and a .575 winning percentage, lowest in league history. The Cubs were an aging team with a pitching staff that included three starters age 36 and older. This fourth World Series matchup between the Bengals and Bruins set the stage for Detroit to even the record between the two.

```
Game 1 at Detroit — October 3                 54,637
Chicago            4 0 3  0 0 0  2 0 0 — 9  13 0  WP Borowy
Detroit            0 0 0  0 0 0  0 0 0 — 0   6 0  LP Newhouser
```

In the series opener at Briggs Stadium, Tiger fans watched in horror as 25-game winner Hal Newhouser was shelled for seven runs in three innings. Hank Borowy, an 11-game winner for the Cubs after his acquisition in mid-year from the Yankees, threw a six-hit shutout to beat Detroit. Rightfielder Bill Nicholson paced the Cub attack with a triple and three RBIs.

```
Game 2 at Detroit — October 4                 53,636
Chicago            0 0 0  1 0 0  0 0 0 — 1   7 0  LP Wyse
Detroit            0 0 0  0 4 0  0 0 x — 4   7 0  WP Trucks
```

Less than a week after his discharge from the U.S. Navy, Detroit right hander Virgil Trucks scattered seven hits to beat the Cubs 4-1. Hank Greenberg's three-run homer in the fifth proved to be the big blow for the Tigers.

```
Game 3 at Detroit — October 5                 55,500
Chicago            0 0 0  2 0 0  1 0 0 — 3   8 0  WP Passeau
Detroit            0 0 0  0 0 0  0 0 0 — 0   1 2  LP Overmire
```

With a strong curve ball and tight control, Cub pitcher Claude Passeau pitched a near-flawless one-hitter to beat Detroit in game three. A single to Rudy York in the second and a walk to catcher Bob Swift in the sixth gave the Tigers their only baserunners. A Bill Nicholson single in the fourth scored leftfielder Peanuts Lowrey, who had doubled, for the deciding run.

```
Game 4 at Chicago — October 6                 42,923
Detroit            0 0 0  4 0 0  0 0 0 — 4   7 1  WP Trout
Chicago            0 0 0  0 0 1  0 0 0 — 1   5 1  LP Prim
```

The Tigers evened the Series as Dizzy Trout threw a five-hitter to stop the Cubs in Wrigley Field. Cub starter Ray Prim retired the first 10 Tiger batters, but gave up four runs in the fourth on singles by centerfielder Doc Cramer and first baseman Hank Greenberg, a Roy Cullenbine double, a walk, a forceout, and a single by catcher Paul Richards.

```
Game 5 at Chicago — October 7                 43,463
Detroit            0 0 1  0 0 4  1 0 2 — 8  11 0  WP Newhouser
Chicago            0 0 1  0 0 0  2 0 1 — 4   7 2  LP Borowy
```

The two teams repeated the first game matchup of Hal Newhouser and Hank Borowy, but this time three Hank Greenberg doubles paced Newhouser to an 8-4 win. Although giving up four runs, Newhouser went the distance and struck out nine Cub batters.

```
Game 6 at Chicago — October 8                    41,708
Detroit       0 1 0   0 0 0   2 4 0   0 0 0 — 7 13 1   LP  Trout
Chicago       0 0 0   0 4 1   2 0 0   0 0 1 — 8 15 3   WP  Borowy
```

The Cubs needed a win to stay alive and scrapped hard for a 12-inning 8-7 victory. They entered the seventh with a 5–3 lead, but starter Claude Passeau suffered a finger injury while knocking down a liner by Bengal third sacker Jimmy Outlaw. Relievers Hank Wyse and Ray Prim couldn't hold the lead and the Tigers tied the score in the eighth on a home run by Hank Greenberg. In the 12th, Cub third baseman Stan Hack hit a drive that bounced past leftfielder Greenberg to score pinch runner Bill Schuster and win the game for Hank Borowy, who had pitched four hitless innings in relief.

```
Game 7 at Chicago — October 10                   41,590
Detroit       5 1 0   0 0 0   1 2 0 — 9  9 1   WP  Newhouser
Chicago       1 0 0   1 0 0   0 1 0 — 3 10 0   LP  Borowy
```

The final showdown came after a one-day rest, with Cub manager Charlie Grimm gambling with Hank Borowy as the starter after his extensive use in games five and six. Borowy proved arm-weary as the Tigers chased him with three straight hits to open the game. Given an early five-run lead, Newhouser scattered 10 hits and struck out 10 to lead the Tigers to their second World Championship.

Top Tiger Hitter — Centerfielder Doc Cramer, 11 hits, .379
          Leftfielder Hank Greenberg, 2 homers, 7 RBIs, .304
Top Tiger Pitcher — Hal Newhouser, 2 wins, 2 complete games, 22 strikeouts, 6.10 ERA
Top Cub Hitter — First baseman Phil Caveretta, 11 hits, 5 RBIs, .423
Top Cub Pitcher — Hank Borowy, 2 wins, 1 complete game, 4.00 ERA
Total Attendance — 333,457
Winning Player's Share: $6,443
Losing Player's Share: $3,930

1968 WORLD SERIES

After missing the pennant by a gnat's eyelash in 1967, the Tigers returned determined to take it all in 1968 — and they did. The World Series boasted a confrontation between two super pitchers: the Tigers' 31-game winner Denny McLain and St. Louis' Bob Gibson, who won 22 and compiled a phenomenal 1.12 ERA. But the real star turned out to be southpaw Mickey Lolich, who gave the Tigers the lift they needed when their ace McLain let them down.

```
Game 1 at St. Louis — October 2                  54,692
Detroit       0 0 0   0 0 0   0 0 0 — 0  5 3   LP  McLain
St. Louis     0 0 0   3 0 0   1 0 0 — 4  6 0   WP  Gibson
```

The first game presented the battle of the superstars: McLain versus Gibson, with Gibson the clear victor. Gibson threw a five-hit shutout and struck out 17 Tigers, a Series record. McLain gave up three runs in the fourth to absorb the loss.

```
Game 2 at St. Louis — October 3                  54,692
Detroit       0 1 1   0 0 3   1 0 2 — 8 13 1   WP  Lolich
St. Louis     0 0 0   0 0 1   0 0 0 — 1  6 1   LP  Briles
```

Mickey Lolich evened the score for the Tigers in game two with a six-hitter. He aided his own cause in the third when he hit his first major league home run into the lower left field stands. First baseman Norm Cash and leftfielder Willie Horton also homered in the Tiger win.

```
Game 3 at Detroit — October 5                      53,634
St. Louis          0 0 0   0 4 0   3 0 0 — 7 13 0   WP Washburn
Detroit            0 0 2   0 1 0   0 0 0 — 3  4 0   LP Wilson
```

The Cardinals pounded the Tigers 7–3 in the first game in Detroit, as Tim McCarver and Orlando Cepeda blasted three-run homers and fleet Lou Brock stole three bases for the Redbirds. Homers by Al Kaline, with a man on, and Dick McAuliffe accounted for the Tiger runs.

```
Game 4 at Detroit — October 6                      53,634
St. Louis          2 0 2   2 0 0   0 4 0 — 10 13 0  WP Gibson
Detroit            0 0 0   1 0 0   0 0 0 —  1  5 4  LP McLain
```

On a rainy day in game four, Gibson and the Cardinals bested McLain once again as the St. Louis right-hander threw a five-hitter and struck out 10. Gibson helped himself with a home run to lead off the fourth. The Cardinals win gave them a 3–1 edge, placing the Tigers in the almost impossible position of having to win three straight.

```
Game 5 at Detroit — October 7                      53,634
St. Louis          3 0 0   0 0 0   0 0 0 — 3 9 0    LP Hoerner
Detroit            0 0 0   2 0 0   3 0 x — 5 9 1    WP Lolich
```

When Lolich yielded three runs to start off the game, the Tigers seemed all but dead. But he settled down and the Tigers began chipping away at the lead. A great throw by leftfielder Willie Horton to nail Lou Brock at the plate in the fifth fired the Bengals up. A three-run seventh, keyed by Al Kaline's two-run single, gave Lolich the runs he needed to win.

```
Game 6 at St. Louis — October 9                    54,692
Detroit            0 2 10  0 1 0   0 0 0 — 13 12 1  WP McLain
St. Louis          0 0 0   0 0 0   0 0 1 —  1  9 1  LP Washburn
```

After two discouraging defeats, Denny McLain was determined to keep the Tiger hopes burning. He rose to the occasion with a solid nine-hit performance, backed by a Tiger batting explosion that produced 10 runs in the third. Jim Northrup's grand slam was the major blow in the uprising and Kaline added four RBIs of his own with a homer and two singles.

```
Game 7 at St. Louis — October 10                   54,692
Detroit            0 0 0   0 0 0   3 0 1 — 4 8 1    WP Lolich
St. Louis          0 0 0   0 0 0   0 0 1 — 1 5 0    LP Gibson
```

Having come back off the deck, the Tigers entered game seven with their new ace Lolich against the almost invincible Gibson. The result was a classic pitching duel that found the game scoreless after six innings. With two out in the seventh, the Tigers broke the deadlock as Norm Cash and Willie Horton singled, and centerfielder Curt Flood misjudged Jim Northrup's liner for a bases-clearing triple. Catcher Bill Freehan then doubled home Northrup with another run.

Lolich pitched a fine three-hitter to win the Series for the Tigers. His three victories in the fall classic combined with his 17 regular season wins for the 20-game season he so dearly wanted.

Top Tiger Hitter — Rightfielder Al Kaline, 2 homers, 8 RBIs, .379
Top Tiger Pitcher — Mickey Lolich, 3 wins, 3 complete games, 1.67 ERA
Top Cardinal Hitter — Leftfielder Lou Brock, 13 hits, 7 stolen bases, .464
Top Cardinal Pitcher — Bob Gibson, 2 wins, 35 strikeouts, 1.67 ERA
Total Attendance: 379,670
Winning Player's Share: $10,937
Losing Player's Share: $7,079

1972 CHAMPIONSHIP SERIES

This fourth American League championship series matchup was a classic — the traditional, veteran Tigers against the upstart, mustached swinging A's.

Oakland had made the playoffs the year before but lost to Baltimore in three straight games. Detroit had narrowly nipped Boston for the Eastern Division title, and manager Billy Martin was looking to avenge a personal loss in the American League series, having had his '69 Twins fall to Baltimore in three straight.

For the first time, the American league championship series would go the distance — five hard-fought games coming down to a single-run verdict in the finale.

Game 1 at Oakland — October 7											29,536		
Detroit	0 1 0	0 0 0	0 0 0	0 1 —2	6 2	LP Lolich
Oakland	0 0 1	0 0 0	0 0 0	0 2 —3	10 1	WP Fingers

Tiger southpaw ace Mickey Lolich pitched great ball, carrying the Tigers into a 2–1 lead in the bottom of the 11th. But the A's came fighting back. The unlikely hero was pinch-hitter Gonzalo Marquez, a sub first baseman. With one out and two men on, he lashed a single off reliever Chuck Seelbach to drive in the tying run. On the same play, the relay throw from rightfielder Al Kaline eluded third baseman Aurelio Rodriguez, letting Gene Tenace score the winning run.

Kaline was charged with an error on the play, which tarnished his earlier heoics when he had blasted the Tigers into the lead with a homer in the top of the 11th off Rollie Fingers.

Game 2 at Oakland — October 8					31,088	
Detroit	0 0 0	0 0 0	0 0 0 —0	3 1	LP Fryman
Oakland	1 0 0	0 4 0	0 0 x —5	8 0	WP Odom

After the first-day cliffhanger, Oakland came roaring right back as the A's easily beat Detroit 5–0 behind Blue Moon Odom's three-hitter. The batting star of the game, shortstop Campy Campaneris, went three for three with three singles, two runs, and two stolen bases.

In the seventh inning, Campaneris caused an uproar when he threw his bat at Tiger reliever Lerrin LaGrow after being hit on the ankle with a pitch. Bengal manager Billy Martin led his players onto the field after Campaneris, but three umpires managed to keep Billy at bay and keep the brawl from getting out of hand. Both Campy and LaGrow were ejected, and league president Joe Cronin fined the Oakland shortstop $500 and banned him from the rest of the playoffs.

Game 3 at Detroit — October 10					41,156	
Oakland	0 0 0	0 0 0	0 0 0 —0	7 0	LP Holtzman
Detroit	0 0 0	2 0 0	0 1 x —3	8 1	WP Coleman

To stay alive in the series, the Tigers needed a big game from starter Joe Coleman — and he delivered. Coleman hurled a masterful seven-hit shutout and struck out 14 A's setting a new American League playoff record. Catcher Bill Freehan led the Tiger offense with a double, home run, and two runs scored.

Game 4 at Detroit — October 11											37,615		
Oakland	0 0 0	0 0 0	1 0 0	2 — 3	9 2	LP	Horlen
Detroit	0 0 1	0 0 0	0 0 0	3 — 4	10 1	WP	Hiller

The Tigers' staying power once more was clearly demonstrated as they came from behind dramatically in the 10th after Oakland scored twice in the top of the inning. Mickey Lolich had pitched nine strong innings, but his successor in the tenth, Chuck Seelbach, appeared to have lost the pennant when he yielded the go-ahead runs.

But the Tigers rallied with singles by Dick McAuliffe and Al Kaline, a wild pitch by Joel Horlen, and walk to pinch-hitter Gates Brown. With the bases loaded, second baseman Gene Tenace muffed a force-play attempt with a bad throw to let a run in. Relief pitcher Dave Hamilton forced in the tying run with a bases-loaded walk, and Jim Northrup singled to right field for the game-winner.

Game 5 at Detroit — October 12							50,276		
Oakland	0 1 0	1 0 0	0 0 0 — 2	4 0	WP	Odom
Detroit	1 0 0	0 0 0	0 0 0 — 1	5 2	LP	Fryman

With a chilly wind blowing, the Tigers watched their pennant dreams fade as Blue Moon Odom and Vida Blue combined on a five-hitter to win 2-1.

The A's scored their first run in the second when Reggie Jackson scored from third on a delayed double steal with Mike Epstein. Jackson suffered a pulled hamstring on the play, which would keep him out of the World Series.

The game-winner (and pennant-winner) was tallied in the fourth when Gene Tenace singled George Hendrick home from second base with two out. The hit was the only one in 17 at bats for Tenace during the playoffs.

Odom pitched brilliantly, but was relieved in the sixth after encountering difficulty breathing. Blue pitched superb relief under incredible conditions, as play was stopped several times while the field was cleared of debris thrown by raucous fans.

Top Tiger Hitter — Centerfielder Jim Northrup, 5 for 14, .357
Top Tiger Pitcher — Joe Coleman, 1 win, 1 complete game shutout, 0.00 ERA
Top A's Hitter — Rightfielder Matty Alou, 8 for 21, .381
Top A's Pitcher — Blue Moon Odom, 2 wins, 1 complete game, 0.00 ERA
Total Attendance: 189,671

25. A BASEBALL SENIOR STATESMAN

John E. Fetzer does not fit the mold of your modern sports owner. He isn't visibly active in his organization, he is not a headline-seeking egotist. Yet in his own quiet, behind-the-scenes style, he has done more to shape the destiny of baseball than any other owner in the past 20 years.

It was Fetzer who advocated, advanced, and won major network television contracts for major league baseball. The influx of the television money has changed the game forever and made possible the free agent revolution. Ironically, Fetzer's own team has disdained the free agent route to success in favor of the more traditional concept of building from a strong farm system.

Born in Decatur, Indiana, on March 25, 1901, John Earl Fetzer has been a Michigan resident most of his adult life. He made his mark in broadcasting, building a radio and television empire in the Midwest out of a single radio station in Kalamazoo. The broadcast concern has since developed into other areas, such as film production, oil production, Arizona land development, mining, manufacturing, and background music franchises.

But Fetzer's first love is baseball. He entered the Tiger organization as a part-owner in an 11-man syndicate in 1956 and gained full control four years later.

"The complexities of baseball are such . . . that a team should be run by one autonomous individual who has the authority to make decisions and expedite them," he once noted. He has carried out that belief by vesting total control of the daily operation of the Tigers in president and general manager Jim Campbell.

This move, made in 1978, has enabled Fetzer to devote more of his time to his service on baseball's Executive Committee and special projects assigned by the American League and Commissioner's offices.

In addition to his work in the television contract arena, Fetzer has been active in selecting league presidents, expansion, player pension plans, and league planning.

His distinguished service to major league baseball is indicative of his overall record of achievement as a businessman, broadcast pioneer, and government servant during World War II.

John Fetzer's commitment to Detroit and his fans kept the franchise strong and profitable during a time of great change and turmoil. His dedication to keeping the Tigers in a downtown stadium location came at a time when a beleaguered city needed a boost of confidence. Detroit owes a strong vote of thanks to this quiet, thoughtful man.

26.   A VISIT WITH THE BOSS

INTERVIEWS WITH JIM CAMPBELL AND SPARKY ANDERSON

At first glance, Jim Campbell strikes the casual observer as coming right out of Hollywood casting for the role of general manager. A seemingly gruff exterior, bald head, and ever-present cigar all contribute to the image of the ultimate sports executive. And that is just what Jim Campbell is—the ultimate sports executive.

He is entering his nineteenth year as general manager of the Detroit Tigers — longer than any other man in Detroit history who wasn't an owner as well. He has endured the "slings and arrows of outrageous fortune" thrown his way by the local press. He has been castigated for his reluctance to enter into the free agent market or disperse huge, multi-year contracts.

But it's hard to argue with success. And the Tigers are a success. They have won a World's Championship and divisional title during his tenure, and are building another contender now. Even though the team enjoys strong fan support, draws well, and the fans get their money's worth, the grumbling in Detroit remains. In their desire for a winner, some fans and sportwriters have adopted a short-range view that ignores the cyclical nature of the business.

So it was with some trepidation that the author ventured into an interview with Jim Campbell last May. Expecting to encounter a blunt, outspoken man with little time for serious questioning, imagine my delight upon meeting a man who is warm, witty, caring, and dedicated to the ball club and its fans. Jim Campbell is tough, but fair. He is a true gentleman struggling to cope with a world buffeted by shifting morals and standards. He is a man's man.

AUTHOR: I know from reading background information that you started back in 1949 right out of college. Why or how did you wind up with Detroit?

CAMPBELL: Well, I guess there are several reasons. Number one is that as a kid you grow up and become attached to a team. I happened to come from a small community in Ohio (Huron) right between Cleveland and Toledo. Anyway, as kids our little community was about split. Half of us were Cleveland or Detroit fans because right across the lake we could get the Detroit broadcast. Then there were teams back in the late 30s and 40s, Gehringer, Rogell, and that bunch. They had a great ball club up here so I always attached myself to Detroit. Then I decided I wanted to get into baseball as a career. When I was in college at Ohio State there was a gentlemen in my home town who was in the advertising end of *Fortune Magazine.* He had a summer home there and I used to mow his lawn and sometimes take care of his yard in the summer. He was a very close friend, both he and his wife, of Billy Evans, who was the general manager here in Detroit at that time. So Mr. Parker, Charlie Parker was his name, had always been a real nice guy. He died during my senior year in college, and Mrs. Parker, when I graduated, asked me if there was anything she could do for me that Charlie would have done had he been alive. And I said, well, I would like to get into baseball and it would be nice if I could talk to Billy Evans about a job. So she set up an appointment with me. Through that association, and also by way of my coach at Ohio State, Floyd Stahl, who was a very close friend of Detroit general manager George Troutman, I got a job with the Tigers down at Thomasville, Georgia in December or November of 1949. Then it was, you know . . .

AUTHOR: . . . working your way up through the system.

CAMPBELL: Up through Thomasville, Toledo, to Buffalo, then here to Detroit. I guess I have been general manager of the club for eighteen years. I think I have been general manager of the club now longer than anyone else. Frank Navin owned the club so he had an edge on me: he couldn't get fired. But it's been very interesting and we've had our ups and downs.

AUTHOR: Essentially all sport teams tend to go through cycles. Don't they?

CAMPBELL: Oh sure.

AUTHOR: You build up a team, the team gets a little older, you trade people off, and then start rebuilding again.

CAMPBELL: There's no one that stays up there forever.

AUTHOR: And you're in something of a rebuilding phase now?

CAMPBELL: Yes, we've been in it for three or four years. And it's tough too — especially as we try to go the route of developing our own players — but we've stayed with it. We did it before in the early sixties and developed a ball club that stayed right in contention for almost a decade really, from about 66–74.

AUTHOR: And that's essentially the same route you propose to follow?

CAMPBELL: That's what we're trying to do.

AUTHOR: Do you think that's preferable to going out like a Steinbrenner and trying to buy up free agents?

CAMPBELL: Well, each man has to make his own decision. My owner, Mr. Fetzer, whom I think is a tremendous man with a great influence on baseball, feels that the best way for the game or the industry to operate is to develop its own talent. But if we thought one player could tip us over we would reconsider that procedure. We signed one free agent, Tito Fuentes, when we really had no one to play second base. He did a good job for a year. But, as you know, the majority of clubs have not gotten into this free agent thing. Many people here in Detroit think that we are the only team in baseball that doesn't get involved in this, and that is far from the truth. There have been about eight or nine clubs that have gone into the free agent market in a big way.

A Visit With the Boss (continued)

AUTHOR: Seemingly with mixed success?

CAMPBELL: Yes — Cincinnati hasn't entered the market and neither have we.

AUTHOR: San Diego hasn't really panned out too much.

CAMPBELL: Baltimore hasn't either. No, you could point to a lot of clubs that haven't. Really, the Yankees are the only one that has made it what I would call a success. Boston has been in it deeply and they haven't won a pennant since the free-agent draft. The Yankees came within a hair of not being in it the two years they won the pennant. Bucky Dent's home run put them in that year. And the other year they pulled the last game out against Kansas City. So free-agency, or getting into the free-agent market, isn't a lock on a championship.

AUTHOR: You've got, I think you could argue historically, the oldest franchise in the American League.

CAMPBELL: The Tigers?

AUTHOR: You've played more games than any other team.

CAMPBELL: Is that right? I didn't know that. I know I always thought of the six originals — like Cleveland, Boston, and New York. Didn't they all start about the same time?

AUTHOR: I guess they did. I'm cheating a little bit. I'm going by the idea that you were established in the Western League, which then became the American League. It seems to me that over a period of time Detroit has had generations of fans develop.

CAMPBELL: Yes, it's all happened on the same site here too. That's interesting.

AUTHOR: What sort of factor did that play in deciding to stick with this location instead of going to a suburban, modern stadium? That idea had been kicked around I know.

CAMPBELL: When they built the Pontiac Stadium, or when the Pontiac Stadium was in the planning stage, the group in Pontiac who were putting this plan together came to Mr. Fetzer first. We all sat in Mr. Fetzer's office next door and they offered us the chance to go Pontiac. The concept was a domed stadium, right next to a football stadium, the Kansas City concept.

AUTHOR: In other words, two stadiums?

CAMPBELL: Two stadiums.

AUTHOR: Side by side.

CAMPBELL: But they would build the baseball stadium first. And knowing the history of the plan out there, if they'd built the baseball stadium first, there wouldn't have been a football stadium. Anyway, Mr. Fetzer turned it down and I always admired him for the stand he took. He said he felt baseball belonged to the City of Detroit, to the central hub of the city. He didn't believe in going to the suburbs, although he had nothing against them. But he felt baseball could be a catalyst to the rebirth of downtown Detroit in a new stadium here. That's what he was striving for, to get a new stadium either in this location or on the riverfront where it could act as a catalyst as it did in Cincinnati, Pittsburgh, and St. Louis. So he turned the Pontiac people down and naturally thanked them. The next step they tried was to build the stadium downtown. The bonds were sold, $154 million, and there was a three-day, seventy-two hour period after the bonds were sold in which the taxpayer could bring a class action suit. Three people joined together: a druggist from one of the suburbs, a young lawyer here in town, and the Mayor of Belleville, Michigan. They contested this bond issue, fought it all the way through

184

the State Supreme Court, and won on a split decision in Supreme Court. That killed the stadium downtown. So, the next thing was to renovate this stadium. That's what we're in the process of doing now.

AUTHOR: Has the stadium been sold to the city?

CAMPBELL: A sale/lease-back. We have complete control of the stadium, almost the same as owning it, but it was a vehicle to finance the renovation. By selling it to the city, this property qualified for $5 million in federal redevelopment funds. In addition to that $5 million, the balance of the money is paid and guaranteed by the Tigers, not the city or anyone else. It's all geared to our turnstiles and our rentals.

AUTHOR: Your attendance seems to be holding up very well despite the fact that there's a bad recession.

CAMPBELL: Yes, it's a funny thing, John. I've been through a couple of recessions here in the city — automobile strikes, things like that that lasted a long time — none of them have lasted for more than a year, and I hope this one won't either. But it's a funny thing, a recession evidently creates a lot of free time for people. We keep our ticket prices at an affordable level and they come to a ball game. It really hasn't hurt us too much. We have noticed a change in the location of our customers though: more will sit in the bleachers or general admission during a period like this. But they do come out to the ball park.

AUTHOR: They still keep coming?

CAMPBELL: Yes, Detroit is a great sports town. It's, I hate to say the best in the country, but certainly one of the best four or five sports town in this country. I don't think there's any question about that.

AUTHOR: I think the case could be made, given the fact that not all teams have enjoyed winning records.

CAMPBELL: No, that's right.

AUTHOR: And yet they still seem to enjoy fan support.

CAMPBELL: I know that right now we are in a down cycle here, but the last couple of years we've played ten or so games over .500. We haven't really been in contention, but I think the fans can see some progress, and they've taken to some of the young players we've had here. There has been tremendous fan support in this community.

AUTHOR: You mentioned the young players. With the retirement of John Hiller you've got what might be one of the youngest teams in the Major Leagues right now. Oakland might be another one.

CAMPBELL: Oakland might be and I think Minnesota is. We are sometimes criticized by the media about our total payroll being twenty-third or twenty-fourth out of the twenty-six clubs. My argument is that that's where it ought to be since we do have the youngest club. We're the twenty-fourth or twenty-fifth youngest club and we really haven't set the world on fire in terms of winning. So I think experience goes hand in hand with payroll progress: as our club gets another year older, our payroll this year will go up a half million dollars from last year.

AUTHOR: You're starting to put together what appears to be a pretty solid young nucleus with a catcher like Parrish, a double-play combination of Trammall and Whitaker, Gibson being groomed in centerfield, Kemp . . .

CAMPBELL: He really hit one last night, didn't he? God, he's strong!

AUTHOR: He sure did. What would you say is a realistic timetable before these guys would really comprise a contender?

CAMPBELL: You know I lay in bed at night . . .

AUTHOR: You probably ask yourself that question every night.

185

CAMPBELL: There'll be days you get so encouraged you think it's next year, or even this year. Then we'll hit a week like we had last week and you'll say my God, what's happened. Or two or three guys get hurt. I don't like to put my finger on timetables, but since you asked I'd have to say within a couple of years.

AUTHOR: When these fellows are hitting their late twenties, they're starting to hit their primes.

CAMPBELL: Well, even before their late twenties. Most of them are twenty-two, twenty-three. . . .

AUTHOR: Twenty-four?

CAMPBELL: Twenty-four years old, so I guess you would say late twenties. But it's very frustrating at times. When you have a fellow coming along and then he just levels off quicker than you thought he would. I'll tell you there's no secret formula. You can have a good ball club together and things happen. We should have won in 1967, but we had a couple of key injuries that were . . .

AUTHOR: Kaline broke his hand that year.

CAMPBELL: Kaline was injured, and McLain never won a game from the last week in August on. That's when the bear scared him and there was all this stuff about kicking the garbage pail. He had kicked a locker in the clubhouse. Anyway, things like that happen and it just throws the whole season out of kilter.

AUTHOR: I have noticed a good many of the players that have retired, Kaline, George Kell, Norm Cash, Bill Freehan, all seem to stay in this area after their careers are over.

CAMPBELL: Well, there are tremendous opportunities around Detroit for players and ex-players who want to exert themselves and try to do well. Vic Wertz has done very well, Charlie Gehringer is an outstanding example, and so is Al Kaline. Mickey Stanley is going to do well, so will Jim Northrup and Bill Freehan. It all goes back to what a tremendous sports community Detroit is. With the automobile industry here, and those people love baseball, these fellows make good contacts. If they work, they can do very well here. I think we probably have had more players play their entire careers with Detroit than has any club in baseball. Maybe to a fault. Maybe I kept some of these fellows too long when I could have gotten something at the end of their careers, but we have a kind of funny philosophy here. Take John Hiller last night — a year ago we could have traded John if he wanted to go, but we didn't. Kaline, Mickey Stanley, and Bill Freehan are the same way, they played out their careers here, and I think it's great.

AUTHOR: You mentioned Denny McLain a few minutes ago. What happened to Denny? At one point he looked like the greatest pitcher in modern history and then, all of a sudden, it was gone.

CAMPBELL: John, probably when I'm done with my baseball career I'll look back on it and I'll say that Denny was the most unusual guy I ever met. He was not a bad guy at all. A good guy really, but his makeup, his thinking, his approach to life is just one of the most unusual stories you could ever put together.

AUTHOR: You could probably write a book about that.

CAMPBELL: There have already been two or three books written about him. Mark Fidrych is another tremendous story, but Denny was . . . His life and his talents were so complex. He is just one of the most unusual men I ever

186

met in my life and still is a very good friend. Of course Mark is that way but in the years I have been general manager I've had so many . . . John Hiller is another example. He was coaching at Pompano Beach, helping Stubby Overmire look after our Lakeland club. This was after his heart attack and he was considering coming back. We had him examined by four or five of the very best cardiologists in the country, and they differed. About half of them would say go ahead and play ball, the other half said absolutely not: you can live a long life but don't test your luck. So we took the position that John had better retire. I went down to Pompano Beach and we went out in the right field bleachers. I told him, John, it's time for you to quit. He said I'm not going to quit. I said the hell you're not, you're gonna hang em up because you got a family, and all that. To make a long story short, I finally said I give up. I said if you're going to play, then you're going to play for us. But I could not talk him into quitting. The rest is history. He came back and established himself as one of the great players in Tiger history. And I thought, here's a guy I did my best to run out of baseball. So it shows you. . . . We had just had an incident here in Detroit that same fall, a Lion football player that died of a heart attack. That's in your mind, and I was thinking, God, what if something like that happened to John? But it shows you how wrong you can be in trying to run someone else's life.

AUTHOR: Obviously one of your prime responsibilities is player acquisition and moving players around. Obviously, the McLain trade was one of your better ones.

CAMPBELL: Yes.

AUTHOR: It gave you a solid nucleus.

CAMPBELL: That gave us the left side of an infield and a 20-game pitcher, Joe Coleman.

AUTHOR: What other trades do you look back on that you think were particularly good?

CAMPBELL: Well. There have been so many, I don't know. I have to refresh my memory.

AUTHOR: We could also turn it around and say do you have any you wish you didn't make?

CAMPBELL: Yes, there were a couple.

AUTHOR: A couple you wish you could take back?

CAMPBELL: Trading Ben Oglivie to Milwaukee backfired on us. We thought we could sign Slaton and we didn't. Bengie had become a very fine player. And the Nate Colbert trade also. We worked for a month or more putting a three-corner trade together: Eddie Brinkman went to St. Louis, I got Colbert, and Buzzie (Bavasi) got a pitcher from Bing (Devine). It was a three-corner deal and all three corners turned out badly. There wasn't one player who did well. We all thought it was a great deal — Colbert hit three home runs in the first weekend, and Buzzie was screaming and hollering. But Colbert didn't hit a foul ball after that. I finally sold him to Montreal about a month later.

AUTHOR: Thinking back to last night's game right now, Stan Papi makes you look like a genius.

CAMPBELL: Well . . .

AUTHOR: That was quite a debut for him before the Detroit fans.

CAMPBELL: I keep a book buried way down there with all the trades I made from my first one to. . . . Jerry Lumpe and Dave Wickersham was a good trade I thought. They both played well. Denny McLain — picking him up on waivers from Chicago had to be a good deal. So many deals you make

A Visit With the Boss (continued)

are really Mexican standoffs when you consider that the guy did what you needed.

AUTHOR: Ideally I guess that's what it should be all about. You fill a need and you help somebody else fill a need.

CAMPBELL: Sure. Many people think you make a deal to cheat the other guy but you really don't. Like this deal we just made with Cowens and . . .

AUTHOR: Thompson.

CAMPBELL: Everybody says we gave up on Jason. That's not the point at all. . . . We picked up Eddie Mathews. Although he played very little here, he probably contributed as much to our winning in 1968 as anything did. Just having him on the bench was great. Don McMahon helped us for Denny Ribant. You can go on and on: there's the Brinkman deal; Tony Taylor was a good pickup; Woody Fryman was a good pickup for us also.

AUTHOR: He's still going strong.

CAMPBELL: Yes. We thought he was done when we got rid of him. He went to Montreal and they thought he was done. They sent him to Cincinnati, and now they've got him back and he's probably pitching as well . . .

AUTHOR: As well as he ever did.

CAMPBELL: Yeah.

AUTHOR: I guess these days it's a little tougher to make trades because of the long-term contracts.

CAMPBELL: Oh, John. There's no comparison. . . . Rusty Staub for Mickey Lolich was a good trade for us. There are all kinds of them but . . .

AUTHOR: I was talking to Hal Middlesworth and he said the winter meeting used to be quite a flurry of activity. I guess it's getting tougher to put these deals together with the type of contracts you encounter. Does that take any of the fun out of it?

CAMPBELL: Yes, you can't sit down and talk to a club anymore about contracts unless you go back and almost research the contracts to see what the players' rights are. For example, if I trade for a contract, say a guy signed a four-year contract with the Chicago Cubs, or any club, and I take that contract over after one year, during those other three years he can demand a trade. I don't really have a four-year contract. I just have a one-year one.

AUTHOR: The rest is an option type of arrangement?

CAMPBELL: The theory was, I guess, that when they settled the contract he signed four years with the Cubs and not with Detroit. Now when he comes to Detroit he has a way to get out from under. It's just cut trading down to a bare minimum. Jerry Green did a piece I thought was really unfair the other day about trades since Sparky's been here. He criticized us for not getting anything for Jack Billingham and Aurelio Rodriguez. Well, the truth of the matter is that those are probably two of the best deals I made just to get something. I either get cash, and a pretty good piece of cash, or a player, because the player didn't have that kind of value. They think that because a guy has a name like Jack Billingham or Aurelio that you're going to go out and get a fine player for them. You're not. They're over the hill. At thirty-seven, or thirty-eight years old, you've had it in this business. And in this day and age, people are not going to give you a young player who's got six years control for a guy that is finished. Green said what lousy trades these two were. You know he just doesn't understand the business, unfortunately. There's no sense in arguing with him about it. The damage has been done.

188

AUTHOR: I noticed there was a story the other day that Sparky probably took a great deal of offense at about there being a list of about seven players that said they had been weeded out. I guess that's something you have to put up with in your business, guys looking for angles like that to get a story.

CAMPBELL: Overall, in the years I've been here the press has been pretty darn good compared to papers in some other cities. But you still get a small group that seems to enjoy being nasty. Some of them would rather, and believe me, I'm not talking about all of them, see you be unsuccessful. Not just our club, but others, because they love the negative approach. But, as I say, since I have been general manager, overall I think the media in Detroit has been very fair.

AUTHOR: Well, they certainly give you extensive coverage, three or four stories, plenty of statistics.

CAMPBELL: You have to take the bitter with the sweet, that's what you get paid for. It's like politics I guess.

AUTHOR: I imagine. Looking ahead to, say, another ten years, what innovations can we look for? Do you think we'll get to things like inter-league play?

CAMPBELL: No, I don't look for inter-league play, John, as much as I look for three divisional play. I think three-divisional play is on the horizon right now.

AUTHOR: Would you like some expansion included with it?

CAMPBELL: Not in our league. Possibly in the National.

AUTHOR: To get up to the same number?

CAMPBELL: I'm not even sure I can speak for the National League, but in our league, and even the National League, there is a real possibility of three divisions. It would help a little, maybe in transportation, to put some more teams in the playoff posture. It might have some merit if it can be worked out.

AUTHOR: How long do you think the two leagues can go on having a separate rule on the designated hitter?

CAMPBELL: Well, I think it's a shame it's gone this long. I think this should have been settled several years ago. I was very much opposed to the DH rule when it came in and, in fact, voted against it right up to the day it was accepted in our league. But I have to admit I was wrong. After it was in effect in our league for a week into the season, I forgot what it was even all about. It's just a part of baseball now, and I think a lot of my friends in the National League would find out as I did that it's good for the game.

AUTHOR: It certainly keeps some of the older players around a little longer.

CAMPBELL: It makes for more runs in a game. Their argument is that you lose the strategy of taking the pitcher out, and when to pinch hit for him. I think the offensive part of it is important — it puts more runs on the board for the fans. And, as you say, it kept Al Kaline in baseball another year. It was great for Al.

AUTHOR: And good for the fans when you keep an attachment to players like Rico Carty, Willie Horton, and others who have been around for some time.

CAMPBELL: I think the good points far outweigh the bad points.

AUTHOR: I've noticed that not only in Detroit but universally, in all the ballparks, there seems to be some problems with crowd control. What's going to have to happen there?

CAMPBELL: John, I don't know. We had a meeting here yesterday morning with the Detroit police officials. It's not the majority of fans in our case here. We have a little bit of a problem here in our bleachers brought about by a small group of younger people who just refuse to behave themselves. In

	order to get to it and stop it, we are certainly considering a lot of different things that we hope will be successful. But I think it's not only in the ball parks, but in our school systems as well. There are some rebellious young people that resist authority for some reason.
AUTHOR:	It's not just a matter of sports events but society in general.
CAMPBELL:	This chanting of profanities really started in intercollegiate basketball, and drifted into football and baseball. I'm open to suggestions if someone can tell me how to stop it.
AUTHOR:	You're for controlling it.
CAMPBELL:	It seems like the more announcements you make to try to stop it, the worse it gets.
AUTHOR:	Like throwing gasoline on the fire.
CAMPBELL:	Yes, but on the other hand, you can sit at home now and watch television in the evening hours and hear profanity, and read it in the newspapers also. It's unfortunate, but evidently it's becoming a recognized form of communication. I think that's a tragedy, but, nevertheless, probably no one swears more than I do.
AUTHOR:	But you do it in the right time and place. One last question because I know you are busy.
CAMPBELL:	No, I've got all the time you need.
AUTHOR:	You've worked for two basic owners, Mr. Briggs and Mr. Fetzer. Could you give me just a brief account of those two men and their unique characteristics?
CAMPBELL:	Well, I never really got to know Walter O. Briggs, Mr. Briggs, Sr., too well. I worked for him when I was out in the farm system and I didn't have any personal contact with him or Spike. I worked closely with Spike for a couple of years. But really, twenty-five years of my career have been involved with Mr. Fetzer, who I have the highest regard for. He's been — well, I've never had as much as one argument with the man. He's just been a tremendous influence on me and on this company. He is so well organized that he has the ability to look at a problem, dissect it, and in a very quiet way help resolve it with the input from people around him, which I think is the mark of a tremendous executive. He's meant so much to me; he has given me so much responsibility and has never second guessed me once. And I have made some mistakes. But we'll sit down and talk about things we should have done differently. He's just been a tremendous man to work for, and I think he's made a tremendous contribution to baseball as an industry.
AUTHOR:	He appears to be very influential and well respected within the higher levels of baseball.
CAMPBELL:	I've never known anybody that has been respected more than John Fetzer.
AUTHOR:	I gather his background in the television communications industry has played a large part in baseball's getting a much better overall set-up in television contracts.
CAMPBELL:	He helped. In fact, he was the guiding factor in bringing all of the clubs together for national television. He was the chairman of that league committee for years and without him I don't think that the television concept would have ever happened. He knew the television industry inside and out. In fact, he is one of the pioneers of television in this country. He's won all of its top awards for years. He's a heck of a guy.
AUTHOR:	He seems to be something of a dwindling breed in that he doesn't seem to call attention to himself. He doesn't seem to have to have any ego

190

needs in terms of ownership that are present with other owners. He doesn't seem to inject himself into the nitty gritty business things the way that a Finley, Steinbrenner, or Kroc does.

CAMPBELL: Well, no, he lets — put it this way, he lets me run this ball club along with the help of all of our guys here, and I'm responsible to him. And I have a close, very close, line of communication. I talk with him practically every day and keep him fully informed of what's going on. He never goes around me; he operates through a chain of command. He's just a beautiful guy to work for, and I can't say enough for him. Naturally, I'm prejudiced. I look at him as more than a boss — he's like family to me.

AUTHOR: Well, obviously, if you have had this long a business relationship you also develop a personal relationship.

CAMPBELL: That's right.

AUTHOR: And you probably also think along the same lines much of the time, I imagine.

CAMPBELL: He gave me the responsibility of running the ball club when I was about thirty-seven years old, and let me run it, make mistakes, and fight my way out of them. I don't know of any other owner that has ever done something like that. He really let me do what I felt was right.

After my session with Campbell, I came away with a firm impression about the Tiger operation. The ball club is deeply rooted in tradition and, in many respects, is a throwback to a simpler time.

The demands of the free agent era for instant success have not deterred the Tigers from adhering to the more traditional path — building a strong farm system. And with the young talent on the field today, much of it coming from Evansville, Montgomery and Lakeland, it's hard to quarrel with Campbell's approach.

The real test for the organization will come in keeping the Kemps, Trammells, and Parrishes contented and eager to stay in Detroit. The relaxed policy toward long-term contracts seems an admission that the club has decided to keep pace with the escalating salary demands of the 1980s without totally breaking the bank.

Hence, the decision to let a Ron LeFlore go elsewhere, while concentrating on keeping a Steve Kemp. The club is looking for players with durable, all-around skills that will stand the test of time, not just people who fill short-term needs.

I headed through the bowels of Tiger Stadium to the clubhouse for a rendezvous with Sparky Anderson, the man charged with taking this young team and giving it leadership.

The Tiger clubhouse, with its high ceilings and white tile walls, takes you back to the Cobb, Greenberg, and Kaline eras. But the youthful faces and blaring disco music are right out of the eighties. With this ever-present contrast of past and present in mind, I ventured into Anderson's office for the following exchange:

AUTHOR: When the opportunity came up here in Detroit last year, it obviously meant a change in leagues for you. What kind of adjustment period did you go through in having to get acquainted with the American League teams and personnel?

ANDERSON: It took a while to get to know the players and surroundings. But I did have one coach, Dick Tracewski, who had been here all the time, and he took care of all that for me. That made it pretty easy.

AUTHOR: So it wasn't that bad of a transition?

ANDERSON: No.

AUTHOR: In changing leagues, how do you feel about having to use a designated hitter or having the opportunity to use a designated hitter?

A Visit With the Boss (continued)

ANDERSON: I've never been a fan of the DH. I can't change now. I can see why the fans like it. But from a manager's standpoint, I don't like it. And I'll never change my views on that.

AUTHOR: But it doesn't stop you from going ahead and taking advantage of it. You seem to use it a little bit differently. You don't seem to have any one player who plays a 150-game season as a DH. You move it around and alter your lineup.

ANDERSON: I try to move it around, and I probably get that from George Bamberger. I watched Bamberger when I was in the National League and saw how the different clubs use things, and I thought Bamberger basically used it the best. I thought when I first got here that the idea of rotating the designated hitters and not using the same guy all the time was the best, using it to rest your people.

AUTHOR: You're in the middle of a rebuilding program here. Obviously you've got a lot of young ballplayers. Are you trying to mold them into a particular type of team? It doesn't appear to be like a Big Red Machine type of a team. How would you describe what you're trying to put together?

ANDERSON: Well, I think we're trying to put together a young ball club that will understand how to play the game of baseball. I think within two years we're going to have that, and that this can be a very good team. I don't think you're going to see many teams like the Cincinnati club of the 70s again, there isn't one in baseball now. And I don't think we're ever going to see another team of that magnitude with free-agency. I think Bob Howsam said that during that last year at the World Series.

AUTHOR: That was it. How do you compare the fans in the park here to what you've been used to in Cincinnati? Is it a different type of crowd?

ANDERSON: Fans in Cincinnati are very knowledgeable as are the fans from Detroit. I would say the biggest difference in Cincinnati was that the fans were much more conservative — they never threw things, and there was never anything but praise for the players. They never booed the players, the players were the key thing. They booed the manager a lot, which I thought was good because they booed the manager and loved their players. I think Detroit itself might be an all-around better baseball city in the sense that although they have been a fifth, sixth, and seventh-place club for so long, they'll still be able to draw a million and a half people each year. I don't know if Cincinnati could end up six years in a row from fourth on down and ever draw a million.

AUTHOR: In other words, it seems like the fans here are a little more involved and emotional?

ANDERSON: The fans are more emotionally involved. They really live and die with the Tigers, yet they are not afraid to let their feelings be known as far as booing and things like that. I don't think there's anything wrong with it, but that is the difference between the two teams' fans.

AUTHOR: How do you like this old ball park compared to the modern stadium you were used to in Cincinnati?

ANDERSON: I like this ball park. I think Cincinnati has the most beautiful ball park I ever played in as far as beauty is concerned. I don't think there is another ball park laid out like Riverfront Stadium in Cincinnati. But, from a fan's standpoint, I like this park much better because it has a great infield and outfield. The groundskeeper here should be proud of the fact that the stadium probably has got the best playing field in baseball. I don't know of any field in baseball that could compare to this one as far as the condition of the playing positions. And over there in Cincinnati, you've got astroturf. There's not a thing you can do on that astroturf except just watch the bullets fly.

AUTHOR: I know that some of the teams that come in here complain about the grass in the infield being too high. How do you respond to that?

ANDERSON: Well, I got a letter from the league president that I had to cut it. We cut it to his specifications and there was no problem. I'll cut it any way they want. That's not going to slow down play because I've got another trick that takes care of that. But as far as cutting the grass, I'll cut it to any length they want. That won't change the field.

AUTHOR: You're signed here through 1984. By the end of that season would you hope to be in a position where you've got a top contending team?

ANDERSON: Before then. I definitely want it by 1982. In my last four years I would like to be in the top three clubs. If we could do that, I'll be very pleased and satisfied. Then, if they want me to go, I'll go. In fact, I'll go anytime. Truthfully, anytime that Mr. Campbell or Mr. Fetzer are not satisfied I would go. Of course I'd be paid, but I'd go.

AUTHOR: You've got a pretty good nucleus being built up the middle — your catcher, your double-play combination, your centerfielder. Are there any other areas that you think need some work? In the corners, for instance?

ANDERSON: No, I think that now, finally — at least I believe — at this point we have a solidified ball club. We have a kid on third base now that I know can do it defensively — Brookens. But I do not know that he's going to hit them.

AUTHOR: He's pretty fast, pretty quick. He runs the bases well.

ANDERSON: He runs well. He's a very alert player. I don't know if he can play regularly. He's going to get the chance this year, and then we'll evaluate him. I think the only way to find out in this case is play him every day this year. If we think he can play well, then that would really help us. If we don't think he can, then we might have to go ahead and make a deal for a third baseman. Maybe even go to the free-agent market.

YEAR/FINISH	C	1B	2B	3B	SS	LF	CF	RF	DH/UT	SP	RP	MGR.
1901 3rd	Buelow Shaw	Dillon Crockett	Gleason	Casey	Elberfeld Lockhead*	Nance	Barrett	Holmes	McAllister	Miller Siever Yeager Cronin	Frisk Owen High	Stallings
1902 7th	McGuire Buelow	Dillon* Beck	Gleason O'Connell	Casey	Elberfeld	Harley Arndt* Mullin	Barrett Lepine	Holmes Yeager	McAllister	Mercer Mullin Siever Miller* Yeager	McCarthy Kisinger Cronin* Egan	Dwyer
1903 5th	McGuire Buelow	Carr	Smith Burns	Yeager Courtney	McAllister Elberfeld* Murphy	Lush Gessler*	Barrett	Crawford Mullin	Long	Mullin Donovan Kitson Kisinger Deering*	Eason Skopec Kane Jones Yeager	Barrow
1904 7th	Drill Wood Buelow*	Carr* Hickman Beville	Lowe Burns	Gremminger Coughlin	O'Leary	McIntyre Mullin	Barrett	Crawford Huelsman	Robinson	Donovan Mullin Killian Kitson	Stovall Jaeger Raymond Ferry	Barrow Lowe
1905 3rd	Drill Warner Doran	Lindsay	Schaefer	Coughlin	O'Leary	McIntyre Cobb	Cooley Barrett	Crawford Hickman*	Lowe	Mullin Killian Donovan Kitson Wiggs	Disch Ford Cicotte Eubank Jackson	Armour
1906 6th	Schmidt Warner* Payne	Lindsay	Schaefer Scheibeck	Coughlin Hetling	O'Leary	McIntyre Jones	Cobb	Crawford Thompson	Lowe	Mullin Siever Donahue Donovan Killian	Eubank Willett Wiggs Rowan	Armour
1907 1st	Schmidt Payne Archer	Rossman	Downs	Coughlin Lowe	O'Leary	Jones McIntyre	Crawford Killian	Cobb Mullin	Schaefer	Donovan Killian Mullin Siever	Eubank Willett E. Jones Malloy	Jennings

1908 1st	Schmidt Thomas Payne	Rossman	Downs Killefer	Coughlin Perry	Schaefer O'Leary Bush	McIntyre Jones	Crawford	Cobb		Summers Donovan Mullin Willett Killian	Siever Winter Suggs Malloy	Jennings
1909 1st	Schmidt Stanage Beckendorf	Rossman* Jones	Schaefer* Delahanty Killefer*	Moriarty	Bush	McIntyre Jones	Crawford	Cobb	O'Leary	Mullin Willett Summers Killian Donovan	Works Speer Suggs Lelivelt Lafitte	Jennings
1910 3rd	Stanage Schmidt Casey	Jones Simmons	Delahanty O'Leary Kirke	Moriarty Lathers	Bush	Jones McIntyre	Cobb	Crawford		Mullin Donovan Willett Summers Works	Stroud Browning Killian Pernoll Loudell	Jennings
1911 2nd	Stanage Schmidt Casey	Delahanty Gainor	O'Leary Baumann Lathers	Moriarty	Bush	Jones Drake	Cobb	Crawford Schaller		Mullin Willett Lafitte Summers Donovan	Works Covington Lively Mitchell Taylor	Jennings
1912 6th	Stanage J. Onslow	Moriarty Gainor E. Onslow	Louden Delahanty	Deal Corriden	Bush	Jones Veach	Cobb	Crawford	Vitt	Willett Dubuc Mullin Works* Covington	Lake Burns Wheatley Boehler Jensen	Jennings
1913 6th	Stanage McKee Gibson Rondeau	Gainor E. Onslow	Vitt Baumann	Moriarty	Bush	Veach	Cobb High	Crawford	Louden	Dubuc Willett Dauss Hall Lake	Zamloch House Comstock Klawitter L. Williams	Jennings

*traded during the season

Players By Position (continued)

YEAR/FINISH	C	1B	2B	3B	SS	LF	CF	RF	DH/UT	SP	RP	MGR.
1914 4th	Stanage Baker McKee	Burns	Kavanagh Baumann	Moriarty Purtell	Bush	Veach	Cobb High	Crawford Heilmann	Vitt	Coveleski Dauss Dubuc Cavet Main	Reynolds Hall Boehler Oldham J. Williams	Jennings
1915 2nd	Stanage Baker McKee Peters	Burns Jacobson*	Young Fuller	Vitt Moriarty	Bush	Veach	Cobb	Crawford	Kavanagh	Coveleski Dauss Dubuc Boland James	Steen Oldham Cavet Boehler Lowdermilk	Jennings
1916 3rd	Stanage Baker McKee Spencer	Burns	Young Fuller	Vitt	Bush Dyer	Veach Harper	Cobb Kavanagh*	Crawford	Heilmann	Coveleski Dauss Dubuc James Mitchell	Boland Cunningham Ehmke Erickson Boehler	Jennings
1917 4th	Stanage Spencer Yelle	Burns Crawford Ellison	Young Jones	Vitt	Bush Dyer	Veach	Cobb	Heilmann Harper		Dauss Boland James Mitchell Ehmke	Cunningham Jones Coveleski Couch	Jennings
1918 7th	Yelle Spencer Stanage	Heilmann Dressen Griggs Kavanagh	Young Coffey*	Vitt Jones	Bush	Veach	Cobb Walker	Harper		Boland Dauss Kallio Cunningham James	Jones Bailey Erickson Hall Finneran*	Jennings
1919 4th	Ainsmith Stanage Yelle	Heilmann	Young Ellison	Jones Dyer	Bush Dowd*	Veach	Cobb	Flagstead Shorten		Dauss Ehmke Leonard Boland Love	Ayers Cunningham Kallio Erickson* Mitchell	Jennings
1920 7th	Stanage Ainsmith Manion Woodall	Heilmann Ellison	Young	Pinelli Jones Hale	Bush	Veach	Cobb	Shorten Flagstead		Ehmke Dauss Leonard Oldham Ayers	Okrie Alten Baumgartner Glaiser Morrisette	Jennings

*traded during the season

196

Year												
1921 6th	Bassler, Woodall, Ainsmith*	Blue	Young, Barnes	Jones	Bush*, Flagstead, Meritt	Veach	Cobb	Heilmann, Shorten	Sargent	Ehmke, Leonard, Oldham, Dauss, Cole	Middleton, Holling, Sutherland, Parks, Perritt	Cobb
1922 3rd	Bassler, Woodall, Manion	Blue	Cutshaw, Clark	Jones, Haney	Rigney, Gagnon	Veach	Cobb, Fothergill	Heilmann, Flagstead		Pilette, Ehmke, Dauss, Oldham, Olsen	Johnson, Cole, Stoner, Moore, Holling	Cobb
1923 2nd	Bassler, Woodall, Manion	Blue	Haney, Pratt, Catshaw	Jones	Rigney, Kerr	Veach, Manush	Cobb, Fothergill	Heilmann		Dauss, Pilette, Holloway, Johnson, Collins	Cole, Francis, Olsen, Whitehill, Wells	Cobb
1924 3rd	Bassler, Woodall	Blue	Pratt, Burke, O'Rourke	Jones, Haney, Kerr	Rigney	Manush, Wingo	Cobb, Fothergill	Heilmann		Whitehill, Collins, Holloway, Stoner, Wells	Dauss, Johnson, Cole, Pilette, Leonard	Cobb
1925 4th	Bassler, Woodall	Blue, Neun	O'Rourke, Burke	Haney, Jones	Tavener, Rigney	Wingo, Manush	Cobb, Fothergill	Heilmann		Dauss, Holloway, Whitehill, Leonard, Collins	Doyle, Wells, Stoner, Cole*, Carroll	Cobb
1926 6th	Manion, Bassler, Woodall	Blue, Neun	Gehringer, Burke	Warner	Tavener	Fothergill, Wingo	Manush, Cobb	Heilmann	O'Rourke	Whitehill, Gibson, Wells, Collins, Stoner	Dauss, Holloway, Johns, Smith, Barfoot	Cobb
1927 4th	Woodall, Bassler, Shea	Blue, Neun	Gehringer	Warner	Tavener, DeViveiros	Fothergill, Wingo	Manush	Heilmann, Ruble	McManus	Whitehill, Collins, Holloway, Gibson, Stoner	Smith, Hankins, Carroll, Billings, Wells	Moriarty

*traded during the season

197

Players By Position (continued)

YEAR/FINISH	C	1B	2B	3B	SS	LF	CF	RF	DH/UT	SP	RP	MGR.
1928 6th	Hargrave Woodall	Sweeney Neun	Gehringer	McManus Warner	Tavener	Fothergill Wingo	Rice Stone	Heilmann Easterling	Galloway	Carroll Whitehill Sorrell Gibson Billings	Vangilder Stoner Smith Holloway Page	Moriarty
1929 6th	Phillips Hargrave Shea Hayworth	Alexander	Gehringer	McManus	Schuble Wuestling Akers	Johnson	Rice Stone	Heilmann Fothergill		Uhle Whitehill Sorrell Carroll Yde	Stoner Prudhomme Smith Graham Page	Harris
1930 5th	Hayworth Desautels Hargrave*	Alexander Shevlin	Gehringer	McManus	Koenig Rogell	Stone Fothergill* Easterling	Funk Doljack	Johnson Rice* Hughes	Akers	Whitehill Sorrell Uhle Hoyt Hogsett	Sullivan Wyatt Herring Cantrell Page	Harris
1931 7th	Hayworth Grabowski Schang	Alexander	Gehringer	McManus* Richardson	Rogell Akers	Stone G. Walker	H. Walker Doljack	Johnson	Koenig Owen	Sorrell Whitehill Uhle Bridges Herring	Sullivan Hogsett Hoyt* Wyatt Collier	Harris
1932 5th	Hayworth Ruel Desautels	Davis	Gehringer	Schuble Richardson	Rogell	Stone Lawrence	G. Walker White Doljack	Webb Johnson*	Rhiel	Whitehill Bridges Sorrell Wyatt Uhle	Hogsett Marrow Herring Goldstein Sewell	Harris
1933 5th	Hayworth Desautels Pasek	Greenberg Davis	Gehringer	Owen Schuble	Rogell	G. Walker Doljack	Fox White	Stone Rhiel		Marberry Bridges Sorrell Fischer Rowe	Hogsett Herring Auker Frasier Wyatt*	Harris Baker

*traded during the season

198

Year												
1934 1st	Cochrane Hayworth York	Greenberg	Gehringer	Owen Clifton	Rogell Schuble	Goslin	White G. Walker	Fox Doljack		Rowe Bridges Auker Sorrell Fischer	Marberry Hogsett Hamlin Phillips Frasier	Cochrane
1935 1st	Cochrane Hayworth Reiber	Greenberg	Gehringer	Owen Clifton Schuble	Rogell	Goslin Walker	White G. Walker	Fox Morgan		Bridges Rowe Auker Crowder Sullivan	Hogsett Lawson Sorrell Hatter Marberry	Cochrane
1936 2nd	Hayworth Cochrane Myatt Reiber	Burns Greenberg	Gehringer	Owen	Rogell Clifton	Goslin	Simmons White	G. Walker Fox		Bridges Rowe Auker Sorrell Wade	Lawson Kimsey Sullivan Phillips Crowder	Cochrane
1937 2nd	York Tebbetts Hayworth Cochrane	Greenberg	Gehringer English*	Owen Clifton	Rogell Gelbert	G. Walker Laabs	White	Fox Goslin		Lawson Auker Bridges Wade Gill	Russell Poffenberger Coffman Rowe McLaughlin	Cochrane
1938 4th	York Tebbetts	Greenberg	Gehringer McCoy	Ross Christman Piet	Rogell	D. Walker Laabs	Morgan White	Fox Cullenbine		Bridges Gill Kennedy Auker Lawson	Eisenstat Coffman Poffenberger Wade Benton	Cochrane Baker
1939 5th	Tebbetts	Greenberg	Gehringer McCoy	Higgins	Croucher Rogell Kress	Averill Cullenbine D. Walker*	McCosky Fleming	Fox Bell	York	Newsom Bridges Rowe Trout Hutchinson	Benton McKain Thomas Coffman Eisenstat*	Baker
1940 1st	Tebbetts Sullivan	York	Gehringer Meyer Metha	Higgins Kress	Bartell Croucher	Greenberg Averill	McCosky	Fox Campbell		Newsom Rowe Bridges Newhouser Gorsica	Benton Trout McKain Seats Hutchinson	Baker

*traded during the season

Players By Position (continued)

YEAR/FINISH	C	1B	2B	3B	SS	LF	CF	RF	DH/UT	SP	RP	MGR.
1941 4th (tie)	Tebbetts Sullivan	York	Gehringer Meyer	Higgins	Croucher Perry	Radcliff Mullin Greenberg	McCosky Stainback	Campbell Harris		Newsom Newhouser Gorsica Bridges Trout	Benton Thomas Rowe Giebell McKain	Baker
1942 5th	Tebbetts Parsons	York	Bloodworth Meyer Gehringer	Higgins	Hitchcock Franklin Lipon	McCosky Radcliff	Cramer	Harris	Ross	Trucks White Trout Bridges Benton	Newhouser Gorsica Henshaw Manders Fuchs	Baker
1943 5th	Richards Parsons Unser	York	Bloodworth Wood	Higgins	Hoover	Wakefield Radcliff	Cramer Metro	Harris Outlaw	Ross	Trout Trucks Bridges Newhouser White	Gorsica Henshaw Overmire Oana Orrell	O'Neill
1944 2nd	Richards Swift	York	Mayo Unser Borom	Higgins	Hoover Orengo	Wakefield Hostetler	Cramer Metro*	Outlaw Ross		Newhouser Trout Gentry Overmire Gorsica	Beck Mooty Orrell Eaton Henshaw	O'Neill
1945 1st	Swift Richards	York McHale	Mayo Borom	Maier	Webb Hoover	Outlaw Greenberg	Cramer Walker	Cullenbine Hostetler		Newhouser Trout Benton Overmire Mueller	Caster Wilson Eaton Tobin Orrell	O'Neill
1946 2nd	Tebbetts Richards Swift	Greenberg	Bloodworth Webb Mayo	Kell	Lake	Wakefield	Evers Cramer	Cullenbine Mullin	Outlaw	Newhouser Trout Trucks Hutchinson Benton	Caster Overmire Gorsica White Bridges	O'Neill

Year												
1947 2nd	Swift Wagner Tebbetts*	Cullenbine McHale	Mayo Webb	Kell	Lake	Wakefield Outlaw Mierkowicz	Evers Cramer	Mullin Wertz		Hutchinson Newhouser Trout Trucks Overmire	Benton White Gorsica Houtteman Gentry	O'Neill
1948 5th	Swift Wagner* Riebe	Vico Campbell	Mayo Lake	Kell Outlaw	Lipon Berry	Wertz Wakefield	Evers Groth	Mullin		Newhouser Trucks Hutchinson Trout Gray	Houtteman Overmire Benton White Pierce	O'Neill
1949 4th	Robinson Swift Riebe	Campbell Vico	Berry	Kell	Lipon Lake	Evers Wakefield	Groth	Wertz Mullin	Kolloway	Trucks Newhouser Houtteman Hutchinson Gray	Trout Grissom Kretlow Stuart White	Rolfe
1950 2nd	Robinson Swift Ginsberg	Kolloway Kryhoski	Priddy	Kell Lake	Lipon Berry	Evers Keller	Groth	Wertz Mullin		Houtteman Hutchinson Newhouser Trout Gray	Calvert White Stuart Rogovin Borowy	Rolfe
1951 5th	Ginsberg Swift House	Kryhoski Kolloway	Priddy	Kell	Lipon Berry	Evers Keller	Groth Souchock	Wertz Mullin		Trucks Cain Hutchinson Trout Gray	White Stuart Bearden Borowy Newhouser	Rolfe
1952 8th	Ginsberg Batts	Dropo Kolloway	Priddy Federoff	Hatfield	Berry Pesky	Mullin Lenhardt	Groth Mapes	Wertz* Souchock Hopp		Gray Houtteman Newhouser Trucks Wight	White Hoeft Stuart* Littlefield* Hutchinson	Rolfe Hutchinson
1953 6th	Batts Bucha	Dropo	Pesky Priddy Friend*	Boone Hitchcock	Kuenn	Nieman Mullin	Delsing Sullivan	Lund Souchock	Hatfield	Garver Gray Hoeft Gromek Branca	Herbert Marlowe Madison Erickson Miller	Hutchinson

*traded during the season

201

Players By Position (continued)

YEAR/FINISH	C	1B	2B	3B	SS	LF	CF	RF	DH/UT	SP	RP	MGR.
1954 5th	House Wilson	Dropo Belardi	Bolling Hatfield Bertoia	Boone	Kuenn	Delsing Nieman	Tuttle Lund	Kaline Evers		Gromek Garver Zuverink Hoeft Aber	Herbert Marlowe Miller Gray Branca*	Hutchinson
1955 5th	House Wilson Porter	Torgeson Fain* J. Phillips	Hatfield Malmberg	Boone Bertoia	Kuenn	Delsing Phillips	Tuttle	Kaline Maxwell		Hoeft Lary Gromek Garver Maas	Aber Birrer Foytack Coleman Bunning	Harris
1956 5th	House Wilson	Torgeson J. Phillips Belardi	Bolling Bertoia	Boone	Kuenn Brideweser	Maxwell Kennedy	Tuttle Small	Kaline		Lary Hoeft Foytack Gromek Trucks	Aber Masterson Maas Bunning Miller	Harris
1957 4th	House Wilson	Boone Philley	Bolling	Bertoia Finigan	Kuenn Samford	Maxwell Porter	Tuttle Groth	Kaline Small		Bunning Foytack Lary Maas Hoeft	Byrd Sleator Aber* Gromek Lee	Tighe
1958 5th	Wilson Hegan* Lau	Harris Boone*	Bolling	Bertoia Virgil	Martin Veal	Maxwell Zernial Hazle	Kuenn Groth	Kaline Francona		Lary Foytack Bunning Hoeft Moford	Aguirre Morgan Fischer Susce Cicotte	Tighe Norman
1959 4th	Berberet Wilson	Harris Osborne	Bolling	Yost	Bridges Veal	Maxwell Chrisley	Kuenn Groth	Kaline Zernial	Lepcio	Mossi Lary Bunning Foytack Narleski	Morgan Sisler Burnside Davie Schultz	Norman Dykes

*traded during the season

202

Year	C	1B	2B	3B	SS	OF	OF	OF		P	P	Mgr
1960 6th	Berberet Chiti Wilson*	Cash Biiko	Bolling Wise	Yost Virgil	Fernandez Veal	Maxwell Chrisley	Kaline	Colavito Amoros		Lary Bunning Mossi Burnside Bruce	Aguirre Sisler Foytack Fischer Semproch	Dykes Hitchcock Gordon
1961 2nd	Brown Roarke House	Cash Osborne	Wood	Boros Bertoia Virgil*	Fernandez	Colavito Maxwell	Bruton	Kaline Morton	McAuliffe	Lary Bunning Mossi Foytack Kline	Fox Aguirre Fischer* Regan Bruce	Scheffing
1962 4th	Brown Roarke	Cash Wertz	Wood	Boros Osborne	Fernandez Buddin	Colavito Goldy	Bruton	Kaline Morton		Bunning Aguirre Mossi Regan Foytack	Fox Nischwitz Kline Jones Lary	Scheffing
1963 5th	Triandos Freehan Roarke	Cash Herzog	Wood Smith	Phillips Wert	McAuliffe	Colavito G. Brown	Bruton	Kaline G. Thomas	McAuliffe	Regan Aguirre Bunning Mossi Lolich	Fox Gladding Anderson Sturdivant Faul	Scheffing Dressen
1964 4th	Freehan Roarke	Cash Wood	Lumpe	Wert Phillips	McAuliffe	G. Brown Demeter Horton	G. Thomas Bruton	Kaline Northrup		Wickersham Lolich Rakow Regan Aguirre	Sherry Gladding Fox Sparma Navarro	Dressen
1965 4th	Freehan Sullivan	Cash	Lumpe Wood	Wert	McAuliffe Oyler	Horton G. Brown	Demeter Northrup Stanley	Kaline G. Thomas		McLain Lolich Aguirre Sparma Wickersham	Fox Gladding Sherry Pena Nischwitz	Dressen
1966 3rd	Freehan McFarlane	Cash	Lumpe Wood Tracewski	Wert	McAuliffe Oyler	Horton G. Brown	Kaline Stanley Demeter*	Northrup		McLain Lolich Wilson Wickersham Monbouquette	Sherry Pena Podres Gladding Aguirre	Dressen Swift Skaff

*traded during the season

Players By Position (continued)

YEAR/FINISH	C	1B	2B	3B	SS	LF	CF	RF	DH/UT	SP	RP	MGR.
1967 2nd	Freehan Price	Cash	McAuliffe Lumpe	Wert Mathews	Oyler Tracewski	Horton G. Brown	Northrup	Kaline Green	Stanley	Wilson McLain Sparma Lolich Podres	Gladding Marshall Lasher Hiller Wickersham	Smith
1968 1st	Freehan Price	Cash	McAuliffe	Wert Mathews	Oyler Matchick Tracewski	Horton G. Brown	Stanley	Northrup Comer	Kaline	McLain Lolich Wilson Sparma Hiller	Dobson Lasher Patterson Warden Wyatt	Smith
1969 2nd	Freehan Price	Cash Campbell	McAuliffe Matchick I. Brown	Wert	Tresh Tracewski	Horton G. Brown	Northrup	Kaline	Stanley	McLain Lolich Wilson Kilkenny Sparma	Dobson McMahon* Hiller Timmerman Lasher	Smith
1970 4th	Freehan Price	Cash	McAuliffe D. Jones I. Brown	Wert	Gutierrez Szotkiewicz	Northrup Horton	Stanley	Kaline G. Brown	E. Maddox	Lolich J. Niekro Cain Kilkenny McLain	Timmerman Hiller Patterson Scherman B. Reed	Smith
1971 2nd	Freehan Price	Cash I. Brown	McAuliffe Taylor	Rodriguez	Brinkman Gutierrez	Horton D. Jones	Stanley Northrup	Kaline G. Brown		Lolich Coleman Cain J. Niekro Chance	Scherman Timmerman Kilkenny Denehy Zepp	Martin
1972 1st	Freehan Haller Sims	Cash Jata	McAuliffe Taylor	Rodriguez	Brinkman	Horton G. Brown I. Brown	Stanley	Northrup Kaline		Lolich Coleman Fryman Timmerman Slayback	Seelbach Scherman Zachary Hiller LaGrow	Martin

*traded during the season

204

Year												
1973 3rd	Freehan Sims*	Cash I. Brown Reese*	McAuliffe Taylor	Rodriguez	Brinkman	Horton	Stanley Sharon	Northrup Kaline	G. Brown Howard	Coleman Lolich J. Perry Fryman Strahler	Hiller Farmer Scherman LaGrow B. Miller	Martin Schultz
1974 6th	Moses Lamont	Freehan Cash	Sutherland Knox	Rodriguez	Brinkman	Horton Oglivie Lane	Stanley LeFlore	Northrup* Sharon Nettles	Kaline G. Brown	Lolich Coleman LaGrow Fryman Holdsworth	Hiller L. Walker Ray Lemanczyk	Houk
1975 6th	Freehan Wockenfuss Humphrey	Pierce	Sutherland Knox	Rodriguez	Veryzer Michael	Oglivie Meyer	LeFlore Stanley	Roberts Baldwin	Horton	Lolich Ruhle Coleman Bare LaGrow	Hiller T. Walker Lemanczyk Arroyo	Houk
1976 5th	Freehan Kimm Wockenfuss	Thompson	Garcia Scrivener	Rodriguez	Veryzer Wagner	Johnson Meyer	LeFlore Stanley	Staub Oglivie	Horton	Fidrych D. Roberts Ruhle Bare	Hiller Crawford Laxton Lemanczyk Grilli	Houk
1977 4th	M. May	Thompson	Fuentes Scrivener	Rodriguez Mankowski	Veryzer Wagner	Kemp Corcoran	LeFlore	Oglivie Stanley	Staub	Rozema Arroyo Wilcox Sykes Fidrych	Foucault Hiller Crawford Grilli Taylor	Houk
1978 5th	M. May Parrish	Thompson	Whitaker Dillard	Rodriguez Mankowski	Trammell Wagner	Kemp Wockenfuss	LeFlore	Corcoran Stanley	Staub	Slaton Billingham Wilcox Rozema Young	Hiller Morris Crawford Sykes Baker	Houk
1979 5th	Parrish	Thompson	Whitaker	Rodriguez Brookens Mankowski	Trammell Wagner	Kemp Greene	LeFlore Jones	Morales	Summers Wockenfuss	Morris Wilcox Billingham P. Underwood Petry	Lopez Hiller Tobik Baker Rozema	Moss Tracewski Anderson

*traded during the season

Players By Position (continued)

YEAR/FINISH	C	1B	2B	3B	SS	LF	CF	RF	DH/UT	SP	RP	MGR.
1980 4th (tie)	Parrish Dyer	Hebner Thompson* Corcoran	Whitaker Papi	Brookens	Trammell Wagner	Kemp Lentine	Peters Gibson Stegman	Cowens	Summers Wockenfuss	Morris Wilcox Schatzeder Petry Fidrych	Lopez Underwood Rozema Weaver Tobik	Anderson

*traded during the season

28.   MEMORABLE BOX SCORES

Tigers Tie Their First Series Game
After Schmidt's Error Lets Cubs Tie the Score

October 8, 1907   Game 1: October 8 at Chicago

Detroit	Pos	AB	R	H	RBI	PO	A	E
Jones	lf	5	1	3	0	3	1	0
Schaefer	2b	6	1	1	0	7	4	0
Crawford	cf	5	1	3	2	1	0	0
Cobb	rf	5	0	0	0	0	0	0
Rossman	1b	4	0	0	1	9	3	0
Coughlin	3b	5	0	0	0	1	0	1
Schmidt	c	5	0	2	0	13	2	2
O'Leary	ss	4	0	0	0	0	3	0
Donovan	p	5	0	0	0	2	2	0
Totals		44	3	9	3	36	15	3

Chicago	Pos	AB	R	H	RBI	PO	A	E
Slagle	cf	6	0	2	0	2	0	0
Sheckard	lf	5	0	1	0	2	0	0
Chance	1b	4	2	1	0	15	0	0
Steinfeldt	3b	3	1	1	0	1	2	1
Kling	c	4	0	2	1	7	4	1
Evers	2b-ss	4	0	2	0	4	2	2
Schulte	rf	5	0	1	1	2	0	0
Tinker	ss	3	0	0	0	3	5	1
a Howard		1	0	0	0	0	0	0
Zimmerman	2b	1	0	0	0	0	2	0
Overall	p	3	0	0	0	0	2	0
b Moran		0	0	0	0	0	0	0
Reulbach	p	2	0	0	0	0	0	0
Totals		41	3	10	2	36	17	5

Det.   0 0 0   0 0 0   0 3 0   0 0 0* — 3
Chi.   0 0 0   1 0 0   0 0 2   0 0 0 — 3

Pitching	IP	H	R	ER	BB	SO
Detroit						
Donovan	12	10	3	1	3	12
Chicago						
Overall	9	9	3	1	2	5
Reulbach	3	0	0	0	0	2

* Game called on account of darkness.
a Struck out for Tinker in 9th but safe on dropped third strike.
b Announced for Overall in 9th.

Stolen Bases—Chance, Evers, Howard, Jones 2, Sheckard, Slagle 2, Steinfeldt. Sacrifice Hits—Evers, O'Leary, Steinfeldt. Double Plays—Evers to Tinker, Schaefer to Rossman. Left on Bases—Detroit 8, Chicago 8. Hit by Pitcher—Scheckard and Steinfeldt (by Donovan). Umpires—O'Day (N), Sheridan (A). Attendance—24,377. Time of Game—2:40.

Mullin Pitches Tigers to Their First Series
Win Ever Against the '08 Cubs

October 12, 1908

Game 3: October 12 at Chicago

Detroit	Pos	AB	R	H	RBI	PO	A	E
McIntyre	lf	4	1	1	0	1	0	0
O'Leary	ss	4	2	0	0	1	3	1
Crawford	cf	5	1	2	1	3	0	0
Cobb	rf	5	1	4	2	0	0	0
Rossman	1b	4	2	2	2	9	0	2
Schaefer	2b	4	0	0	0	4	4	0
Thomas	c	3	0	1	1	9	2	0
Coughlin	3b	3	0	0	1	0	1	1
Mullin	p	3	1	1	1	0	1	0
Totals		35	8	11	8	27	11	4

Chicago	Pos	AB	R	H	RBI	PO	A	E
Sheckard	lf	4	0	0	0	1	0	0
Evers	2b	3	1	0	0	1	6	0
Schulte	rf	4	0	1	0	1	0	0
Chance	1b	4	1	2	1	14	0	0
Steinfeldt	3b	4	1	1	0	1	4	1
Hofman	cf	4	0	2	1	3	1	0
Tinker	ss	3	0	1	0	3	1	0
Kling	c	3	0	0	0	3	2	0
Pfiester	p	2	0	0	0	0	0	0
a Howard		1	0	0	0	0	0	0
Reulbach	p	0	0	0	0	0	1	0
Totals		32	3	7	2	27	15	1

```
Det.    1 0 0   0 0 5   0 2 0—8
Chi.    0 0 0   3 0 0   0 0 0—3
```

Pitching	IP	H	R	ER	BB	SO
Detroit						
Mullin (W)	9	7	3	0	1	8
Chicago						
Pfiester (L)	8	10	8	7	3	1
Reulbach	1	1	0	0	1	0

a Grounded out for Pfiester in 8th.

Doubles—Cobb, Thomas. Triple—Hofman. Stolen Bases—Chance 2, Cobb 2, Rossman, Steinfeldt. Sacrifice Hits—Coughlin, O'Leary. Double Plays—Schaefer to Rossman, Schaefer to O'Leary to Rossman, Evers to Chance, Hofman to Kling. Left on Bases—Detroit 6, Chicago 3. Umpires—O'Day, Sheridan. Attendance—14,543. Time of Game—2:10.

Schmidt's Four RBIs Pace '09 Series Win

October 9, 1909

Game 2 October 9 at Pittsburgh

Detroit	Pos	AB	R	H	RBI	PO	A	E
D. Jones	lf	5	1	1	0	1	0	0
Bush	ss	3	1	1	0	0	2	0
Cobb	rf	3	1	1	0	0	0	0
Crawford	cf	4	1	1	0	3	0	0
Delahanty	2b	3	1	1	2	3	1	1
Moriarty	3b	3	1	1	0	3	1	0
T. Jones	1b	3	1	1	0	8	1	0
Schmidt	c	4	0	2	4	9	1	1
Donovan	p	4	0	0	0	0	4	1
Totals		32	7	9	6	27	10	3

Pittsburgh	Pos	AB	R	H	RBI	PO	A	E
Byrne	3b	3	1	0	0	4	2	0
Leach	cf	4	1	2	1	2	1	0
Clarke	lf	3	0	0	0	3	0	0
Wagner	ss	4	0	1	0	1	2	0
Miller	2b	4	0	1	1	0	5	0
Abstein	1b	4	0	1	0	12	1	1
Wilson	rf	4	0	0	0	0	0	0
Gibson	c	2	0	0	0	4	2	0
Camnitz	p	1	0	0	0	0	1	0
Willis	p	2	0	0	0	1	2	0
Totals		31	2	5	2	27	16	1

Det.   0 2 3   0 2 0   0 0 0 — 7
Pit.   2 0 0   0 0 0   0 0 0 — 2

Pitching	IP	H	R	ER	BB	SO
Detroit						
Donovan (W)	9	5	2	2	2	7
Pittsburgh	2 2/3	6	4	3	1	2
Willis	6 1/3	3	3	3	4	2

Doubles—Crawford, Leach 2, Miller, Schmidt. Stolen Bases—Cobb, Gibson, Wagner. Sacrifice Hits — Bush, Clarke. Double Plays — Bush to T. Jones to Moriarty, Miller to Abstein to Bryne. Left on Bases — Detroit 4, Pittsburgh 5. Umpires — Evans (A), Klem (N). Attendance—30,915. Time of Game—1:45.

George Mullin Pitches the First No-Hitter by a Tiger

July 4, 1912   St. Louis at Detroit

ST. LOUIS

	AB	R	B	P	A	E
Shotten, cf	1	0	0	4	1	0
Jantzen, rf	3	0	0	1	0	0
Kutina, 1b	4	0	0	7	1	0
Pratt, ss	4	0	0	3	4	1
Laporte, 2b	3	0	0	2	1	0
Austin, 3b	1	0	0	3	1	0
Hogan, lf	2	0	0	1	0	0
Compton, lf	1	0	0	0	0	0
Stephens, c	3	0	0	3	4	2
Adams, p	1	0	0	0	1	0
Hamilton, p	1	0	0	0	0	0
Mitchell, p	0	0	0	0	0	0
*Stovail	1	0	0	0	0	0
Totals	25	0	0	24	13	3

DETROIT

	AB	R	B	P	A	E
Vitt, 3b	5	1	0	0	0	0
Bush, ss	3	1	1	4	1	0
Cobb, cf	4	1	3	6	0	0
Crawford, rf	3	1	1	2	0	0
Delahanty, lf	3	1	1	0	0	0
Moriarty, 1b	4	0	1	6	1	0
Louden, 2b	3	2	3	1	3	1
Stanage, c	4	0	1	7	1	0
Mullin, p	4	0	3	1	3	0
Totals	33	7	14	27	9	1

* Batted for Hamilton in eighth inning.

```
St. Louis        0 0 0   0 0 0   0 0 0 — 0
Detroit          1 1 1   0 0 0   0 4 x — 7
```

Two-base hits—Delahanty, Mullin. Stolen bases—Vitt, Louden, Shotten, Austin. Sacrifice hit—Jantzen. Sacrifice fly—Delahanty. Struck out—By Mullin 5, Adams 1. First on balls—Off Mullin 5, Adams 1, Hamilton 1. Double plays—Mullin, Moriarty, Bush; Shotten, Pratt, Stephens; Stephens, Kutina. Stephens; Pratt, Laporte. First on errors—Detroit 2, St. Louis 1, Left on bases—Detroit 6, St. Louis 4. Hits—Off Adams 6 in 4 innings, Hamilton 2 in 3 innings, Mitchell 6 in 1 inning. Hit by pitcher—By Adams 1. Time—2:05. Umpires—Dineen and Sheridan.

Charley Robertson's Perfect Game Against Detroit

April 30, 1922 Chicago at Detroit

CHICAGO

	A	R	H	O	A
Mulligan, s	4	0	1	0	0
McClellan, 3	3	0	1	1	3
Collins, 2	3	0	1	4	3
Hooper, rf	3	1	0	3	0
Mostil, lf	4	1	1	3	0
Strunk, cf	3	0	0	0	0
Sheely, 1	4	0	2	9	0
Schalk, c	4	0	1	7	1
Robertson, p	4	0	0	0	1
Totals	32	2	7	27	8

DETROIT

	A	R	H	O	A
Blue, 1	3	0	0	11	3
Cutshaw, 2	3	0	0	2	3
Cobb, c	3	0	0	1	0
Veach, lf	3	0	0	2	0
Heilmann, rf	3	0	0	1	0
Jones, 3	3	0	0	1	5
Rigney, s	2	0	0	2	1
Manion, c	3	0	0	7	1
Pillette, p	2	0	0	0	3
*Clark	1	0	0	0	0
†Bassler	1	0	0	0	0
Totals	27	0	0	27	16

* Batted for Rigney in the ninth.
† Batted for Pillette in the ninth.

Chicago	0 2 0 0 0 0 0 0 0—2
Detroit	0 0 0 0 0 0 0 0 0—0

Error—Blue. Two-base hits—Mulligan, Sheely. Sacrifice hits—McClellan, Collins, Strunk. Left on bases—Chicago 8. Bases on balls—Off Pillette 2. Struck out—By Pillette 5, by Robertson 6. Umpires—Nallin and Evans. Time—1:55. Attendance 25,000.

211

Memorable Box Scores (continued)

Rowe Goes Twelve Innings to Beat the Cardinals

October 4, 1934

Game 2 October 4 at Detroit

St. Louis	Pos	AB	R	H	RBI	PO	A	E
Martin	3b	5	1	2	0	1	1	1
Rothrock	rf	4	0	0	0	4	0	0
Frisch	2b	5	0	1	0	3	6	1
Medwick	lf	5	0	1	1	0	0	0
Collins	1b	5	0	1	0	12	2	0
DeLancey	c	5	1	1	0	10	0	0
Orsatti	cf	4	0	1	1	2	0	0
Durocher	ss	4	0	0	0	1	3	0
Hallahan	p	3	0	0	0	1	3	1
B. Walker	p	1	0	0	0	0	1	0
Totals		41	2	7	2	x34	16	3

Detroit	Pos	AB	R	H	RBI	PO	A	E
White	cf	4	0	0	0	4	0	0
a G. Walker		1	0	1	1	0	0	0
Doljack	cf	1	0	0	0	1	0	0
Cochrane	c	4	0	0	0	8	0	0
Gehringer	2b	4	1	1	0	3	6	0
Greenberg	1b	4	0	0	0	13	1	0
Goslin	lf	6	0	2	1	3	1	0
Rogell	ss	4	1	1	0	1	2	0
Owen	3b	5	0	0	0	0	1	0
Fox	rf	5	1	2	1	2	0	0
Rowe	p	4	0	0	0	1	1	0
Totals		42	3	7	3	36	12	0

St. L.   0 1 1   0 0 0   0 0 0   0 0 0 — 2
Det.   0 0 0   1 0 0   0 0 1   0 0 1 — 3

Pitching	IP	H	R	ER	BB	SO
St. Louis						
Hallahan	8 1/3	6	2	2	4	6
B. Walker (L)	3	1	1	1	3	2
Detroit						
Rowe (W)	12	7	2	2	0	7

a Singled for White in 9th.
x One out when winning run scored.

Doubles—Fox, Martin, Rogell. Triple—Orsatti. Stolen Base—Gehringer. Sacrifice Hits—Rothrock, Rowe. Left on Bases—St. Louis 4, Detroit 13. Umpires—Klem, Geisel, Reardon, Owens. Attendance—43,451. Time of Game—2:49.

Tommy Bridges Outduels Dizzy Dean for Series Win

October 7, 1934

Game 5 October 7 at St. Louis

Detroit	Pos	AB	R	H	RBI	PO	A	E
White	cf	2	0	0	0	2	0	0
Cochrane	c	4	0	1	0	10	0	0
Gehringer	2b	4	1	1	1	4	1	0
Goslin	lf	4	0	1	0	1	0	0
Rogell	ss	4	1	2	0	0	2	0
Greenberg	1b	3	1	0	1	6	0	0
Owen	3b	4	0	0	0	1	0	0
Fox	rf	4	0	1	1	3	0	0
Bridges	p	4	0	1	0	0	2	0
Totals		33	3	7	3	27	5	0

St. Louis	Pos	AB	R	H	RBI	PO	A	E
Martin	3b	4	0	2	0	0	1	0
Rothrock	rf	4	0	0	0	2	0	0
Frisch	2b	4	0	1	0	2	3	0
Medwick	lf	4	0	0	0	3	0	0
Collins	1b	4	0	1	0	5	1	0
DeLancey	c	4	1	1	1	6	0	0
Fulis	cf	3	0	0	0	5	0	1
d Orsatti		1	0	0	0	0	0	0
Durocher	ss	2	0	1	0	3	2	0
a Davis		1	0	1	0	0	0	0
b Whitehead	ss	0	0	0	0	1	0	0
D. Dean	p	2	0	0	0	0	0	0
c Crawford		1	0	0	0	0	0	0
Carlton	p	0	0	0	0	0	0	0
Totals		34	1	7	1	27	7	1

Det.	0 1 0 0 0 2 0 0 0—3
St. L.	0 0 0 0 0 0 1 0 0—1

Pitching	IP	H	R	ER	BB	SO
Detroit						
Bridges (W)	9	7	1	1	0	7
St. Louis						
D. Dean (L)	8	6	3	2	3	6
Carleton	1	1	0	0	0	0

a Singled for Durocher in 8th.
b Ran for Davis in 8th.
c Fouled out for D. Dean in 8th.
d Hit into force out for Fullis in 9th.

Doubles—Fox, Goslin, Martin. Home Runs—DeLancey, Gehringer. Stolen Base—Rogell. Double Play—Collins to Durocher to Collins. Hit by Pitcher—White (by D. Dean). Wild Pitch—Bridges. Left on Bases—Detroit 7, St. Louis 6. Umpires—Owens, Klem, Geisel, Reardon. Attendance—38,536. Time of Game—1:58.

Greenberg's Homer Paces Game Two Win

October 3, 1935

Game 2 October 3 at Detroit

Chicago	Pos	AB	R	H	RBI	PO	A	E
Galan	lf	4	0	0	0	3	1	0
Herman	2b	4	0	1	1	2	6	0
Lindstrom	cf	3	0	0	0	1	0	0
Hartnett	c	4	0	1	0	4	2	0
Demaree	rf	4	0	1	0	0	1	0
Cavarretta	1b	4	1	0	0	9	0	0
Hack	3b	3	0	1	0	2	1	0
Jurges	ss	3	1	1	1	3	1	0
Root	p	0	0	0	0	0	0	0
Henshaw	p	1	0	0	0	0	1	0
Kowalik	p	2	1	1	0	0	2	1
a Klein		1	0	0	0	0	0	0
Totals		33	3	6	2	24	15	1

Detroit	Pos	AB	R	H	RBI	PO	A	E
White	cf	3	2	1	0	3	0	0
Cochrane	c	2	1	1	1	2	0	0
Gehringer	2b	3	2	2	3	2	5	0
Greenberg	1b	3	1	1	2	8	2	2
Goslin	lf	3	0	0	0	2	0	0
Fox	rf	4	0	1	1	4	0	0
Rogell	ss	4	0	2	0	3	2	0
Owen	3b	2	1	0	0	2	0	0
Bridges	p	4	1	1	0	1	2	0
Totals		28	8	9	7	27	11	2

```
Chi.        0 0 0   0 1 0   2 0 0 — 3
Det.        4 0 0   3 0 0   1 0 x — 8
```

Pitching	IP	H	R	ER	BB	SO
Chicago						
Root (L)	*0	4	4	4	0	0
Henshaw	3 2/3	2	3	3	5	2
Kowalik	4 1/3	3	1	1	1	1
Detroit						
Bridges (W)	9	6	3	2	4	2

aFlied out for Kowalik in 9th.
*Pitched to four batters in 1st.

Doubles—Cochrane, Demaree, Rogell. Home Run—Greenberg. Sacrifice Hit—Owen. Double Plays—Bridges to Rogell to Greenberg, Rogell to Gehringer to Greenberg, Herman to Cavarretta, Jurges to Herman to Cavarretta. Hit Batsman—Owen (by Henshaw), Greenberg (by Kowalik). Wild Pitch—Henshaw. Left on Bases—Chicago 7, Detroit 5. Umpires—Quigley, McGowan, Stark, Moriarty. Attendance—46,742. Time of Game—1:59.

Crowder's Five-Hitter Wins Game Four of '35 Series

October 5, 1935

Game 4 October 5 at Chicago

Detroit	Pos	AB	R	H	RBI	PO	A	E
White	cf	3	0	1	0	0	0	0
Cochrane	c	4	0	1	0	6	0	0
Gehringer	2b	4	0	2	1	3	3	0
Goslin	lf	3	0	1	0	1	0	0
Fox	rf	5	0	1	0	0	0	0
Rogell	ss	3	0	0	0	2	2	0
Owen	1b	4	0	0	0	13	1	0
Clifton	3b	4	1	0	0	0	4	0
Crowder	p	3	1	1	0	2	2	0
Totals		33	2	7	1	27	12	0

Chicago	Pos	AB	R	H	RBI	PO	A	E
Galan	lf	4	0	0	0	2	0	1
Herman	2b	4	0	1	0	4	1	0
Lindstrom	cf	4	0	0	0	3	0	0
Hartnett	c	4	1	1	1	7	0	0
Demaree	rf	4	0	1	0	4	0	0
Cavarretta	1b	4	0	2	0	3	1	0
Hack	3b	4	0	0	0	0	0	0
Jurges	ss	1	0	0	0	4	2	1
Carleton	p	1	0	0	0	0	2	0
a Klein		1	0	0	0	0	0	0
Root	p	0	0	0	0	0	1	0
Totals		31	1	5	1	27	7	2

Det.	0 0 1 0 0 1 0 0 0 — 2
Chi.	0 1 0 0 0 0 0 0 0 — 1

Pitching	IP	H	R	ER	BB	SO
Detroit						
Crowder (W)	9	5	1	1	3	5
Chicago						
Carleton (L)	7	6	2	1	7	4
Root	2	1	0	0	1	2

a Grounded out for Carleton in 7th.

Doubles—Fox, Gehringer, Herman. Home Run—Hartnett. Sacrifice Hit—Gehringer. Stolen Base—Gehringer. Double Plays—Jurges to Herman, Rogell to Gehringer to Owen. Balk—Carleton. Left on Bases—Detroit 13, Chicago 6. Umpires—Stark, Moriarty, Quigley, McGowan. Attendance—49,350. Time of Game—2:28.

Goslin Drives in Winning Run as
Tigers Win Their First Championship

October 7, 1935

Game 6 October 7 at Detroit

Chicago	Pos	AB	R	H	RBI	PO	A	E
Galan	lf	5	0	1	0	2	0	0
Herman	2b	4	1	3	3	3	4	0
Klein	rf	4	0	1	0	0	0	0
Hartnett	c	4	0	2	0	9	1	0
Demaree	cf	4	0	0	0	0	0	0
Cavarretta	1b	4	0	1	0	8	0	0
Hack	3b	4	0	2	0	0	4	0
Jurges	ss	4	1	1	0	3	2	0
French	p	4	1	1	0	1	2	0
Totals		37	3	12	3	*26	13	0

Detroit	Pos	AB	R	H	RBI	PO	A	E
Clifton	3b	5	0	0	0	2	0	0
Cochrane	c	5	2	3	0	7	0	0
Gehringer	2b	5	0	2	0	0	4	0
Goslin	lf	5	0	1	1	2	0	0
Fox	rf	4	0	2	1	3	1	1
Walker	cf	2	1	1	0	0	0	0
Rogell	ss	4	1	2	0	2	3	0
Owen	1b	3	0	1	1	11	0	0
Bridges	p	4	0	0	1	0	3	0
Totals		37	4	12	4	27	11	1

Chi.   0 0 1   0 2 0   0 0 0 — 3
Det.   1 0 0   1 0 1   0 0 1 — 4

Pitching	IP	H	R	ER	BB	SO
Chicago						
French (L)	8 2/3	12	4	4	2	7
Detroit						
Bridges (W)	9	12	3	3	0	7

* Two outs when winning run was scored.

Doubles—Fox, Gehringer, Hack, Rogell. Triple—Hack. Home Run—Herman. Sacrifice Hit—Walker. Double Play—Gehringer to Rogell to Owen. Left on Bases—Chicago 7, Detroit 10. Umpires—Quigley, McGowan, Stark, Moriarty. Attendance—48,420. Time of Game—1:57.

Bobo Newsom Wins Game One of the 1940 Series

October 2, 1940

Game 1 October 2 at Cincinnati

Detroit	Pos	AB	R	H	RBI	PO	A	E
Bartell	ss	4	0	2	2	2	0	1
McCosky	cf	5	0	2	1	2	0	0
Gehringer	2b	4	0	0	0	4	3	0
Greenberg	lf	5	1	1	0	4	0	0
York	1b	4	2	2	0	7	1	0
Campbell	rf	3	1	2	2	3	0	0
Higgins	3b	4	1	1	2	0	5	0
Sullivan	c	3	1	0	0	4	2	0
Newsom	p	4	1	0	0	1	0	0
Totals		36	7	10	7	27	11	1

Cincinnati	Pos	AB	R	H	RBI	PO	A	E
Werber	3b	4	1	1	0	1	2	1
M. McCormick	cf	4	0	1	0	2	0	0
Goodman	rf	4	1	2	1	1	0	0
F. McCormick	1b	3	0	0	0	6	1	0
Ripple	lf	4	0	1	1	2	0	0
Wilson	c	2	0	0	0	9	1	0
a Riggs		1	0	0	0	0	0	0
Baker	c	1	0	1	0	3	0	1
Joost	2b	4	0	2	0	3	1	0
Myers	ss	4	0	0	0	0	1	1
Derringer	p	0	0	0	0	0	1	0
Moore	p	2	0	0	0	0	1	0
b Craft		1	0	0	0	0	0	0
Riddle	p	0	0	0	0	0	0	0
Totals		34	2	8	2	27	8	3

```
Det.        0 5 0  0 2 0  0 0 0 — 7
Cin.        0 0 0  1 0 0  0 1 0 — 2
```

Pitching	IP	H	R	ER	BB	SO
Detroit						
Newsom (W)	9	8	2	2	1	4
Cincinnati						
Derringer (L)	1 1/3	5	5	5	1	1
Moore	6 2/3	5	2	2	4	7
Riddle	1	0	0	0	0	2

a Struck out for Wilson in 7th.
b Fouled out for Moore in 8th.

Doubles—Goodman, M. McCormick, Werber. Triple—York. Home Run—Campbell. Sacrifice Hit—Campbell. Double Plays—Higgins to Gehringer to York, Wilson to Joost. Left on Bases—Detroit 8, Cincinnati 6. Umpires—Klem (N), Ormsby (A), Ballanfant (N), Basil (A). Attendance—31,793. Time of Game—2:09.

Newsom Throws a Three-Hit Series Shutout

October 6, 1940

Game 5 October 6 at Detroit

Cincinnati	Pos	AB	R	H	RBI	PO	A	E
Werber	3b	4	0	1	0	0	0	0
M. McCormick	cf	4	0	1	0	5	1	0
Goodman	rf	4	0	0	0	1	0	0
F. McCormick	1b	4	0	1	0	5	0	0
Ripple	lf	2	0	0	0	4	0	0
Wilson	c	1	0	0	0	3	1	0
a Baker	c	2	0	0	0	2	0	0
Joost	2b	3	0	0	0	2	1	0
Myers	ss	2	0	0	0	2	0	0
Thompson	p	1	0	0	0	0	1	0
Moore	p	0	0	0	0	0	0	0
b Frey		1	0	0	0	0	0	0
Vander Meer	p	0	0	0	0	0	0	0
c Riggs		1	0	0	0	0	0	0
Hutchings	p	0	0	0	0	0	1	0
Totals		29	0	3	0	24	5	0

Detroit	Pos	AB	R	H	RBI	PO	A	E
Bartell	ss	4	1	2	1	0	1	0
McCosky	cf	3	2	2	0	3	0	0
Gehringer	2b	4	2	2	0	2	4	0
Greenberg	lf	5	2	3	4	1	0	0
York	1b	4	0	0	0	7	0	0
Campbell	rf	4	0	3	2	2	0	0
Higgins	3b	2	0	0	0	1	3	0
Sullivan	c	4	1	1	0	11	0	0
Newsom	p	4	0	0	0	0	0	0
Totals		34	8	13	7	27	8	0

```
Cin.    0 0 0   0 0 0   0 0 0 — 0
Det.    0 0 3   4 0 0   0 1 x — 8
```

Pitching	IP	H	R	ER	BB	SO
Cincinnati						
Thompson (L)	3 1/3	8	6	6	4	2
Moore	2/3	1	1	1	2	0
Vander Meer	3	2	0	0	3	2
Hutchings	1	2	1	1	1	0
Detroit						
Newsom (W)	9	3	0	0	2	7

a Struck out for Wilson in 5th.
b Grounded out for Moore in 5th.
c Struck out for Vander Meer in 8th.

Double—Bartell. Home Run—Greenberg. Sacrifice Hit—Newsom. Double Play—Bartell to Gehringer to York. Passed Ball—Wilson. Wild Pitch—Hutchings. Left on Bases—Cincinnati 4, Detroit 13. Umpires—Klem, Ormsby, Ballanfant, Basil. Attendance—55,189. Time of Game—2:26.

Greenberg's Homer Paces Game Two Win in '45

October 4, 1945

Game 2 October 4 at Detroit

Chicago	Pos	AB	R	H	RBI	PO	A	E
Hack	3b	3	0	3	0	0	2	0
Johnson	2b	3	0	0	0	2	4	0
Lowrey	lf	4	0	2	0	3	0	0
Cavarretta	1b	4	1	1	0	8	0	0
Pafko	cf	4	0	0	0	4	0	0
Nicholson	rf	3	0	1	1	2	0	0
Gillespie	c	4	0	0	0	3	0	0
Hughes	ss	3	0	0	0	2	2	0
Wyse	p	2	0	0	0	0	0	0
a Secory		1	0	0	0	0	0	0
Erickson	p	0	0	0	0	0	0	0
b Becker		1	0	0	0	0	0	0
Totals		32	1	7	1	24	8	0

Detroit	Pos	AB	R	H	RBI	PO	A	E
Webb	ss	4	1	2	0	0	4	0
Mayo	2b	3	1	0	0	3	3	0
Cramer	cf	4	1	3	1	2	0	0
Greenberg	lf	3	1	1	3	2	1	0
Cullenbine	rf	2	0	0	0	2	0	0
York	1b	4	0	0	0	11	1	0
Outlaw	3b	4	0	1	0	1	0	0
Richards	c	4	0	0	0	5	0	0
Trucks	p	3	0	0	0	1	1	0
Totals		31	4	7	4	27	10	0

Chi.		0 0 0	1 0 0	0 0 0—1	
Det.		0 0 0	0 4 0	0 0 x—4	

Pitching	IP	H	R	ER	BB	SO
Chicago						
Wyse (L)	6	5	4	4	3	1
Erickson	2	2	0	0	1	1
Detroit						
Trucks (W)	8	7	1	1	3	4

a Flied out for Wyse in 7th.
b Struck out for Erickson in 9th.

Doubles—Cavarretta, Hack. Home Run—Greenberg. Sacrifice Hit—Johnson. Left on Bases—Chicago 8, Detroit 7. Umpires—Jorda, Passarella, Conlan, Summers. Attendance—53,636. Time of Game—1:47.

Greenberg's Three Doubles Pace Game Five Win

October 7, 1945

Game 5 October 7 at Chicago

Detroit	Pos	AB	R	H	RBI	PO	A	E
Webb	ss	4	1	1	1	2	4	0
Mayo	2b	4	0	2	0	2	1	0
Cramer	cf	4	2	1	1	1	0	0
Greenberg	lf	5	3	3	1	0	0	0
Cullenbine	rf	4	1	2	2	1	0	0
York	1b	5	1	1	1	9	2	0
Outlaw	3b	4	0	0	1	0	3	0
Richards	c	4	0	1	0	11	1	0
Newhouser	p	3	0	0	1	1	3	0
Totals		37	8	11	8	27	14	0

Chicago	Pos	AB	R	H	RBI	PO	A	E
Hack	3b	3	0	1	1	2	2	1
Johnson	2b	3	0	0	0	1	3	0
Lowrey	lf	4	1	1	0	1	0	0
Cavaretta	1b	3	1	1	0	10	0	0
Pafko	cf	4	1	0	0	5	0	1
Nicholson	rf	4	0	1	2	1	0	0
Livingston	c	4	0	1	1	4	0	0
Merullo	ss	2	0	0	0	2	1	0
b Williams		1	0	0	0	0	0	0
Schuster	ss	1	0	0	0	1	2	0
Borowy	p	1	1	1	0	0	1	0
Vandenberg	p	0	0	0	0	0	1	0
Chipman	p	0	0	0	0	0	0	0
a Sauer		1	0	0	0	0	0	0
Derringer	p	0	0	0	0	0	0	0
c Secory		1	0	1	0	0	0	0
Erickson	p	0	0	0	0	0	1	0
Totals		32	4	7	4	27	11	2

```
Det.          0 0 1   0 0 4   1 0 2 — 8
Chi.          0 0 1   0 0 0   2 0 1 — 4
```

Pitching	IP	H	R	ER	BB	SO
Detroit						
Newhouser (W)	9	7	4	4	2	9
Chicago						
Borowy (L)	*5	8	5	5	1	4
Vandenberg	2/3	0	0	0	2	0
Chipman	1/3	0	0	0	1	0
Derringer	2	1	1	1	0	0
Erickson	1	2	2	2	0	0

*Faced 4 batters in 6th.

a Struck out for Chipman in 6th.
b Struck out for Merullo in 7th.
c Singled for Derringer in 8th.

Doubles—Borowy, Cavarretta, Cullenbine, Greenberg 3, Livingston. Sacrifice Hits—Cullenbine, Johnson, Outlaw. Double Plays—Mayo to York to Webb to Mayo, Johnson to Merullo to Cavarretta. Hit by Pitcher—Cramer (by Erickson). Left on Bases—Detroit 9, Chicago 4. Umpires—Summers, Jorda, Passarella, Conlan. Attendance—43,463. Time of Game—2:18.

Tigers Win the '45 Series Behind Newhouser

October 10, 1945

Game 7 October 10 at Chicago

Detroit	Pos	AB	R	H	RBI	PO	A	E
Webb	ss	4	2	1	0	0	5	0
Mayo	2b	5	2	2	1	2	1	0
Cramer	cf	5	2	3	1	2	0	0
Greenberg	lf	2	0	0	1	0	0	0
Mierkowicz	lf	0	0	0	0	0	0	0
Cullenbine	rf	2	2	0	0	2	0	0
York	1b	4	0	0	1	8	1	0
Outlaw	3b	4	1	1	1	1	2	0
Richards	c	4	0	2	4	9	0	0
Swift	c	1	0	0	0	2	0	0
Newhouser	p	4	0	0	0	1	2	1
Totals		35	9	9	9	27	11	1

Chicago	Pos	AB	R	H	RBI	PO	A	E
Hack	3b	5	0	0	0	1	3	0
Johnson	2b	5	1	1	0	1	3	0
Lowrey	lf	4	1	2	0	3	0	0
Cavarretta	1b	4	1	3	1	10	0	0
Pafko	cf	4	0	1	1	6	0	0
Nicholson	rf	4	0	1	1	1	0	0
Livingston	c	4	0	1	0	4	1	0
Hughes	ss	3	0	1	0	1	1	0
Borowy	p	0	0	0	0	0	0	0
Derringer	p	0	0	0	0	0	0	0
Vandenberg	p	1	0	0	0	0	1	0
a Sauer		1	0	0	0	0	0	0
Erickson	p	0	0	0	0	0	0	0
b Secory		1	0	0	0	0	0	0
Passeau	p	0	0	0	0	0	0	0
Wyse	p	0	0	0	0	0	0	0
c McCullough		1	0	0	0	0	0	0
Totals		37	3	10	3	27	9	0

Det.   5 1 0 0 0 0 1 2 0—9
Chi.   1 0 0 1 0 0 0 1 0—3

Pitching	IP	H	R	ER	BB	SO
Detroit						
Newhouser (W)	9	10	3	3	1	10
Chicago						
Borowy (L)	*0	3	3	3	0	0
Derringer	1 2/3	2	3	3	5	0
Vandenberg	3 1/3	1	0	0	1	3
Erickson	2	2	1	1	1	2
Passeau	1	1	2	2	1	0
Wyse	1	0	0	0	0	0

*Pitched to 3 batters in first.

a Struck out for Vandenberg in 5th.
b Struck out for Erickson in 7th.
c Struck out for Wyse in 9th.

Doubles—Johnson, Mayo, Nicholson, Richards 2. Triple—Pafko. Stolen Bases—Cramer, Outlaw. Sacrifice Hit— Greenberg. Double Play— Webb to Mayo to York. Wild Pitch— Newhouser. Umpires— Passarella. Conlan, Summers, Jorda. Attendance— 41,590. Time of Game— 2:31.

Virgil Trucks's Double No-Hitters in 1952

May 15, 1952   Washington at Detroit

WASHINGTON

	AB	R	H	TB	O	A	E
Yost, 3b	3	0	0	0	2	1	0
Busby, cf	3	0	0	0	3	0	0
Jensen, rf	4	0	0	0	2	0	0
Vernon, 1b	4	0	0	0	9	0	0
Runnels, ss	3	0	0	0	3	3	0
Coan, lf	3	0	0	0	2	0	0
Marsh, 2b	3	0	0	0	1	2	0
Kluttz, c	2	0	0	0	4	2	0
Porterfield, p	3	0	0	0	0	0	0
Totals	28	0	0	0	*26	8	0

DETROIT

	AB	R	H	TB	O	A	E
Lipon, ss	4	0	0	0	1	4	0
Kell, 3b	3	0	1	1	1	2	0
Mullin, lf	4	0	0	0	3	0	0
Wertz, rf	3	1	2	6	1	0	0
Souchock, 1b	3	0	0	0	9	0	0
Ginsberg, c	3	0	0	0	7	0	0
Groth, cf	3	0	0	0	5	0	0
Priddy, 2b	3	0	0	0	0	1	3
Trucks, p	3	0	1	1	0	0	0
Totals	29	1	4	8	27	7	3

* Two out when winning run scored.

| Washington | 0 0 0 0 0 0 0 0 0 — 0 |
| Detroit | 0 0 0 0 0 0 0 0 1 — 1 |

Run batted in—Wertz. Two-base hit—Wertz. Home run—Wertz. Left on bases—
Washington 4, Detroit 4. Base on balls—Off Trucks 1 (Kluttz), off Porterfield 2 (Kell,
Wertz). Struck out—By Trucks 7 (Yost 2, Busby, Vernon, Runnels, Coan, Kluttz), by
Porterfield 5 (Souchock, Ginsberg, Groth, Priddy, Trucks). Hit by pitcher—By Trucks
2 (Yost, Busby). Earned run—Off Porterfield 1. Winning pitcher—Trucks (1-2). Losing
pitcher—Porterfield (3-4). Umpires—Honochick, Duffy, Summers and McKinley.
Time of game—1:32. Attendance—2,215. Official scorer—Leo Macdonell.

August 25, 1952   Detroit at New York

DETROIT

	AB	R	H	TB	O	A	E
Groth, cf	4	0	0	0	2	0	0
Pesky, ss	4	0	0	0	3	2	1
Hatfield, 3b	3	0	1	1	2	0	0
Dropo, 1b	4	1	2	3	5	3	0
Souchock, rf	4	0	1	1	3	0	0
Delsing, lf	4	0	0	0	2	1	0
Batts, c	2	0	1	1	6	2	1
Federoff, 2b	3	0	0	0	0	1	0
Trucks, p	2	0	0	0	4	2	0
Totals	30	1	5	6	27	11	2

NEW YORK

	AB	R	H	TB	O	A	E
Mantle, cf	3	0	0	0	3	0	0
Collins, 1b	4	0	0	0	10	1	0
Bauer, rf	4	0	0	0	0	1	0
Berra, c	3	0	0	0	7	0	0
Woodling, lf	3	0	0	0	3	0	0
Babe, 3b	3	0	0	0	3	2	0
Martin, 2b	3	0	0	0	1	4	0
Rizzuto, ss	2	0	0	0	0	5	0
*Mize	1	0	0	0	0	0	0
Brideweser, ss	0	0	0	0	0	0	0
Miller, p	1	0	0	0	0	1	0
†Noren	1	0	0	0	0	0	0
Scarborough, p	0	0	0	0	0	0	0
Totals	28	0	0	0	27	14	0

*Fouled out for Rizzuto in eighth.
†Flied out for Miller in eighth.

| Detroit | 0 0 0 0 0 0 1 0 0 — 1 |
| New York | 0 0 0 0 0 0 0 0 0 — 0 |

Run batted in—Souchock. Two-base hit—Dropo. Sacrifice—Miller. Double play—
Babe, Martin and Collins. Left on bases—Detroit 6, New York 3. Bases on balls—Off

Trucks 1 (Mantle), off Miller 2 (Hatfield, Trucks). Struck out—By Trucks 8 (Mantle 2, Collins, Bauer 2, Woodling, Babe, Martin), by Miller 7 (Groth, Pesky 3, Hatfield 2, Delsing). Hit by pitcher—By Miller 1 (Batts). Pitching records—Off Miller 4 hits, 1 run, 1 earned in 8 innings; off Scarborough 1 hit, 0 runs in 1 inning. Winning pitcher—Trucks (5-15). Losing pitcher—Miller (3-5). Umpires—Robb, Grieve, Honochick and Passarella. Time of game—2:03. Attendance—13,442. Official scorer—John Drebinger.

Jim Bunning's 1958 No-Hitter

July 20, 1958   Detroit at Boston

DETROIT

	AB	R	H	TB	O	A	E
Kuenn, cf	4	0	2	3	3	0	0
Martin, ss	4	0	1	1	1	1	0
Kaline, rf	4	0	0	0	4	0	0
Harris, 1b	4	1	1	3	5	0	0
Zernial, lf	4	1	2	3	0	0	0
‡Groth, lf	0	0	0	0	0	0	0
F. Bolling, 2b	4	0	0	0	1	0	0
Virgil, 3b	4	0	1	1	0	3	0
Wilson, c	4	1	1	1	13	0	0
Bunning, p	3	0	1	1	0	0	0
Totals	35	3	9	13	27	4	0

BOSTON

	AB	R	H	TB	O	A	E
Stephens, cf	2	0	0	0	0	0	1
Runnels, 2b	1	0	0	0	1	2	0
Lepcio, 2b	3	0	0	0	2	3	0
Williams, lf	4	0	0	0	1	0	0
Malzone, 3b	3	0	0	0	2	1	0
Jensen, rf	2	0	0	0	3	0	0
Gernert, 1b	3	0	0	0	9	0	0
Berberet, c	3	0	0	0	7	0	0
Consolo, ss	3	0	0	0	2	4	0
Sullivan, p	1	0	0	0	0	1	0
*Keough	1	0	0	0	0	0	0
Byerly, p	0	0	0	0	0	0	0
†Klaus	1	0	0	0	0	0	0
Bowsfield, p	0	0	0	0	0	0	0
Totals	27	0	0	0	27	11	1

*Struck out for Sullivan in sixth.
†Struck out for Byerly in eighth.
‡Ran for Zernial in ninth.

Detroit	0 0 0 0 3 0 0 0 0—3
Boston	0 0 0 0 0 0 0 0 0—0

Runs batted in—Kuenn, Zernial, Wilson. Two-base hits—Zernial, Kuenn. Three-base hit—Harris. Double play—Consolo, Runnels and Gernert. Left on bases—Detroit 5, Boston 3. Bases on balls—Off Bunning 2 (Stephens 2). Struck out—By Bunning 12 (Lepcio 3, Berberet 3, Consolo 2, Stephens, Malzone, Keough, Klaus), by Sullivan 4 (Wilson, Martin, Kaline, Virgil), by Byerly 2 (Bolling, Kaline). Hits—Off Sullivan 6 in 6 innings, off Byerly 2 in 2 innings, off Bowsfield 1 in 1 inning. Runs and earned runs—Sullivan 3-3, Byerly 0-0, Bowsfield 0-0. Hit by pitcher—By Bunning 1 (Jensen). Winning pitcher—Bunning (8-6). Losing pitcher—Sullivan (8-3). Umpires—Umont, Summers, Honochick and Soar. Time of game—2:02. Attendance—29,529.

Longest Game (7 Hours) in Baseball History; Tigers Lose 9-7 on Jack Reed's Home Run

June 24, 1962

NEW YORK	AB	R	H	RBI	DETROIT	AB	R	H	RBI
Tresh, ss	9	0	2	0	Boros, 3b-2b	10	1	1	0
Richardson, 2b	11	2	3	0	Bruton, cf	9	2	2	0
Maris, cf	9	2	2	2	Goldy, rf	10	1	1	3
Mantle, rf	3	1	1	0	Colavito, lf	10	1	7	1
Pepitone, rf	1	0	0	0	Cash, 1b	8	1	2	0
fLinz	0	0	0	0	McAuliffe, 2b	5	0	1	0
Reed, rf	4	1	1	2	gMorton	1	0	0	0
Blanchard, lf	10	1	1	0	Osborne, 3b	1	0	0	0
Berra, c	10	0	3	1	Fernandez, ss	10	1	1	1
Skowron, 1b	10	1	2	1	Roarke, c	5	0	2	2
Boyer, 3b	9	1	3	3	eWood	0	0	0	0
Turley, p	1	0	0	0	Brown, c	4	0	1	0
Coates, p	0	0	0	0	Lary, p	0	0	0	0
bLopez	1	0	1	0	aMaxwell	1	0	1	0
Stafford, p	0	0	0	0	Casale, p	1	0	0	0
Bridges, p	0	0	0	0	cWertz	1	0	0	0
dHoward	1	0	0	0	Nischwitz, p	0	0	0	0
Clevenger, p	2	0	0	0	Kline, p	1	0	0	0
hCerv	1	0	0	0	Aguirre, p	2	0	0	0
Daley, p	1	0	0	0	Fox, p	2	0	0	0
Bouton, p	2	0	1	0	iMossi	1	0	0	0
Totals	85	9	20	9	Regan, p	0	0	0	0
					Totals	82	7	19	7

```
New York   6 1 0   0 0 0   0 0 0   0 0 0   0 0 0   0 0 0   0 0 0   2—9
Detroit    3 0 3   0 0 1   0 0 0   0 0 0   0 0 0   0 0 0   0 0 0   0—7
```

Pitchers	IP	H	R	ER	BB	SO
Turley	1/3	1	3	3	3	0
Coates	2 2/3	4	3	3	1	6
Stafford	2 2/3	4	1	1	1	3
Bridges	1/3	0	0	0	0	0
Clevenger	6 1/3	5	0	0	3	1
Daley	2 2/3	2	0	0	0	2
Bouton (W. 2-1)	7	3	0	0	2	6
Lary	2	7	7	7	1	1

Casale	3	1	0	0	2	0
Nischwitz	1 2/3	2	0	0	2	0
Kline	1	0	0	0	2	0
Aguirre	5 1/3*	2	0	0	1	8
Fox	8	7	0	0	0	1
Regan (L. 4-7)	1	1	2	2	1	2

*Pitched to one batter in fourteenth.

aSingled for Lary in second. bSingled for Coates in fourth. cStruck out for Casale in fifth. dGrounded out for Bridges in seventh. eRau for Roarke in tenth. fWalked intentionally for Pepitone in thirteenth. gFlied out for McAuliffe in fifteenth. hHit into force play for Daley in sixteenth. iCalled out on strikes for Fox in twenty-first. 2B—Richardson, Roarke. 3B—Colavito. HR—Boyer, Reed, Goldy. SB—Tresh, Bruton. SH—Tresh, Fox, Brown. SF—Berra. E—Berra, Boyer, Daley, Tresh, Goldy, Fernandez, McAuliffe. Po-A—New York 66-20, Detroit 66-27. DP—Clevenger and Skowron; Berra and Boyer; Tresh, Richardson and Skowron; Boyer, Richardson and Skowron. LOB—New York 21, Detroit 22. HP—Daley (Goldy). WP—Kline, Fox. U—McKinley, Napp, Umont and Drummond. T—7:00. Attendance—35,638.

Tigers Win Despite Oriole No-Hitter

April 30, 1967   Detroit at Baltimore

DETROIT	AB	R	H	RBI	BALTIMORE	AB	R	H	RBI
McAuliffe, 2b	3	0	0	0	Aparicio, ss	3	0	0	1
Horton, ph	1	0	0	0	Snyder, cf	4	0	0	0
Lumpe, 2b	0	0	0	0	F. Robinson, rf	4	0	1	0
Stanley, cf	2	0	0	0	B. Robinson, 3b	3	0	0	0
Wert, 2b	3	0	0	0	Epstein, 1b	4	0	0	0
Kaline, rf	4	0	0	0	Blefary, lf	2	1	0	0
Northrup, lf	4	0	0	0	Held, 2b	2	0	0	0
Freehan, c	1	0	0	0	Haney, c	0	0	0	0
Cash, 1b	1	0	0	0	Etcheba'n, c	2	0	1	0
Tracewski, ph-ss	0	1	0	0	Lau, ph	0	0	0	0
Oyler, ss	2	0	0	0	Belanger, 2b	0	0	0	0
Wood, ph-1b	0	1	0	0	Barber, p	1	0	0	0
Wilson, p	3	0	0	0	S. Miller, p	0	0	0	0
Gladding, p	0	0	0	0	Totals	25	1	2	1
Totals	24	2	0	0					

Detroit   0 0 0   0 0 0   0 0 2 — 2
Baltimore   0 0 0   0 0 0   0 1 0 — 1

DETROIT

	IP	H	R	ER	BB	SO
Wilson (W. 2–2)	8	2	1	1	4	4
Gladding (Save 2)	1	0	0	0	0	1

226

BALTIMORE

	IP	H	R	ER	BB	SO
Barber (L. 2–1)	8 2/3	0	2	1	10	3
S. Miller	1/3	0	0	0	0	0

E—Kaline, Belanger, Barber. DP—Detroit 1, Baltimore 1. LOB—Detroit 11, Baltimore 4. SB—Freehan, F. Robinson. SH—Cash, Oyler, Wilson, Barber, Held. SF—Aparicio. HBP—By Barber (McAuliffe, Freehan). WP—Barber. U—Stevens, Stewart, Valentine and Springstead. T—2:38. A—26,884.

Denny McLain Wins His Thirtieth Game

September 14, 1968

Oakland	AB	R	H	Detroit	AB	R	H
Campaneris, ss	4	0	1	McAuliffe, 2b	5	0	1
Monday, cf	4	0	1	Stanley, cf	5	1	2
Cater, 1b	4	1	2	Northrup, rf	4	1	0
Bando, 3b	3	0	0	Horton, lf	5	1	2
Jackson, rf	4	2	2	Cash, 1b	4	1	2
Green, 2b	4	0	0	Freehan, c	3	0	1
Keough, lf	3	0	0	Matchick, ss	4	0	1
Gosger, lf	0	0	0	Wert, 3b	2	0	0
Duncan, c	2	1	0	Brown, ph	1	0	0
Dobson, p	1	0	0	Tracewski, 3b	0	0	0
Aker, p	0	0	0	McLain, p	1	0	0
Lindblad, p	0	0	0	Kaline, ph	0	1	0
Donaldson, ph	0	0	0	Total	34	5	9
Segui, p	1	0	0				
Total	30	4	6				

Oakland	000 210 001—4
Detroit	000 300 002—5

Errors — Bando, Cater, Matchick, Runs batted in — Campaneris, Jackson 3, Northrup, Horton, Cash 3. Home runs — Jackson 2, Cash. Sacrifices — Bando, Donaldson, McLain. Bases on balls—Dobson 2, Aker 1, Segui 2, McLain 1. Struck out—Dobson 4, Linblad 1, Segui 1, McLain 10. Hits off—Dobson, 4 in 3 2/3; Aker, 0 in 0 (pitched to one batter in fourth); Linblad, 0 in 1/3; Segui, 5 in 4 1/3; McLain, 6 in 9. Left on base—Oakland 2, Detroit 10. Wild pitch—Aker. Loser—Segui. Umpires—Napp, Umont, Haller and Neudecker. Time—3:00. Attendance—33,688.

Memorable Box Scores (continued)

Mickey Lolich's Six-Hitter Wins Game Two of the Series

October 3, 1968

Game 2: October 3 at St. Louis

Detroit	Pos	AB	R	H	RBI	PO	A	E
McAuliffe	2b	5	0	2	2	1	5	0
Stanley	ss-cf	5	0	1	0	0	3	1
Kaline	rf	5	2	2	0	2	0	0
Cash	1b	5	2	3	1	11	0	0
Horton	lf	3	2	2	1	0	0	0
Oyler	ss	0	0	0	0	0	0	0
Northrup	cf-lf	5	1	1	0	4	0	0
Freehan	c	4	0	0	0	9	1	0
Wert	3b	2	0	0	1	0	2	0
Lolich	p	4	1	2	2	0	0	0
Totals		38	8	13	7	27	11	1

St. Louis	Pos	AB	R	H	RBI	PO	A	E
Brock	lf	3	1	1	0	0	0	0
Javier	2b	4	0	2	0	3	2	0
Flood	cf	3	0	1	0	2	0	0
Cepeda	1b	4	0	2	1	6	0	0
Shannon	3b	4	0	0	0	1	3	1
McCarver	c	4	0	0	0	7	0	0
Davis	rf	4	0	0	0	4	0	0
Maxvill	ss	3	0	0	0	4	3	0
Briles	p	2	0	0	0	0	0	0
Carlton	p	0	0	0	0	0	0	0
Willis	p	0	0	0	0	0	0	0
a Gagliano		1	0	0	0	0	0	0
Hoerner	p	0	0	0	0	0	0	0
Totals		32	1	6	1	27	8	1

```
Det.    0 1 1   0 0 3   1 0 2 — 8
St. L.  0 0 0   0 0 1   0 0 0 — 1
```

Pitching	IP	H	R	ER	BB	SO
Detroit						
Lolich (W)	9	6	1	1	2	9
St. Louis						
Briles (L)	*5	7	4	4	1	2
Carlton	**1	4	2	2	1	1
Willis	2	1	0	0	2	2
Hoerner	1	1	2	0	3	1

*Pitched to 2 batters in 6th.
**Pitched to 2 batters in 7th.

228

a Grounded out for Willis in 8th.

Home Runs—Cash, Horton, Lolich. Stolen Bases—Brock 2. Sacrifice Hit—Oyler. Double Plays—Stanley to McAuliffe to Cash, Maxvill to Cepeda, Javier to Maxvill to Cepeda. Left on Bases—Detroit 11, St. Louis 6. Umpires—Honochick, Landes, Kinnamon, Harvey, Haller, Gorman. Attendance—54,692. Time of Game—2:41.

Mickey Lolich Wins His Second Series Game

October 7, 1968

Game 5: October 7 at Detroit

St. Louis	Pos	AB	R	H	RBI	PO	A	E
Brock	lf	5	1	3	0	2	0	0
Javier	2b	4	0	2	0	2	1	0
Flood	cf	4	1	1	1	3	0	0
Cepeda	1b	4	1	1	2	7	0	0
Shannon	3b	4	0	0	0	1	2	0
McCarver	c	3	0	1	0	6	0	0
Davis	rf	3	0	0	0	1	0	0
a Gagliano		1	0	0	0	0	0	0
Maxvill	ss	3	0	0	0	1	2	0
b Spiezio		1	0	1	0	0	0	0
c Schofield		0	0	0	0	0	0	0
Briles	p	2	0	0	0	0	2	0
Hoerner	p	0	0	0	0	0	0	0
Willis	p	0	0	0	0	1	0	0
d Maris		1	0	0	0	0	0	0
Totals		35	3	9	3	24	7	0

Detroit	Pos	AB	R	H	RBI	PO	A	E
McAuliffe	2b	4	1	1	0	1	2	0
Stanley	ss-cf	3	2	1	0	2	3	0
Kaline	rf	4	0	2	2	3	0	0
Cash	1b	2	0	2	2	7	1	1
Horton	lf	4	1	1	0	1	1	0
Oyler	ss	0	0	0	0	1	0	0
Northrup	cf-lf	3	0	1	1	2	0	0
Freehan	c	4	0	0	0	9	1	0
Wert	3b	3	0	0	0	0	1	0
Lolich	p	4	1	1	0	1	2	0
Totals		31	5	9	5	27	11	1

St. L.   300 000 000—3
Det.   000 200 30x—5

Memorable Box Scores (continued)

Pitching	IP	H	R	ER	BB	SO
St. Louis						
Briles	6 1/3	6	3	3	3	5
Hoerner (L)	*0	3	2	2	1	0
Willis	1 2/3	0	0	0	0	1
Detroit						
Lolich (W)	9	9	3	3	1	8

*Pitched to 4 batters in 7th.

a Flied out for Davis in 9th.
b Singled for Maxvill in 9th.
c Ran for Spiezio in 9th.
d Struck out for Willis in 9th.

Doubles—Brock 2. Triples—Horton, Stanley. Home Run—Cepeda. Stolen Base—Flood. Sacrifice Fly—Cash. Double Play—Shannon to Javier to Cepeda. Hit by Pitcher—Briles (by Lolich). Left on Bases—St. Louis 7, Detroit 7. Umpires—Harvey, Haller, Gorman, Honochick, Landes, Kinnamon. Attendance—53,634. Time of Game—2:43.

Denny McLain Wins Game Six of the '68 Series

October 9, 1968

Game 6 October 9 at St. Louis

Detroit	Pos	AB	R	H	RBI	PO	A	E
McAuliffe	ab	2	2	0	0	3	1	0
Stanley	ss-cf	5	2	1	0	2	1	1
Kaline	rf	4	3	3	4	7	0	0
Cash	1b	4	2	3	2	5	0	0
Horton	lf	3	2	2	2	0	0	0
Oyler	ss	0	0	0	0	0	0	0
Northrup	cf-lf	5	1	2	4	1	0	0
Freehan	c	4	0	1	1	7	0	0
Wert	3b	3	1	0	0	2	2	0
McLain	p	4	0	0	0	0	1	0
Totals		34	13	12	13	27	5	1

St. Louis	Pos	AB	R	H	RBI	PO	A	E
Brock	lf	4	0	1	0	1	0	1
Flood	cf	4	0	0	0	0	0	0
Maris	rf	4	1	2	0	2	0	0
Cepeda	1b	4	0	2	0	7	2	0
McCarver	c	4	0	1	0	8	0	0
Shannon	3b	4	0	1	0	1	2	0
Javier	2b	4	0	1	1	3	2	0
Maxvill	ss	4	0	0	0	4	5	0
Washburn	p	0	0	0	0	0	0	0

Jaster	p	0	0	0	0	0	0	0
Willis	p	0	0	0	0	0	0	0
Hughes	p	0	0	0	0	0	0	0
a Ricketts		1	0	1	0	0	0	0
Carlton	p	0	0	0	0	1	1	0
Tolan		1	0	0	0	0	0	0
Granger	p	0	0	0	0	0	1	0
c Edwards		1	0	0	0	0	0	0
Nelson	p	0	0	0	0	0	0	0
Totals		35	1	9	1	27	13	1

```
Det.     0 2 10   0 1 0   0 0 0 — 13
St. L.   0 0  0   0 0 0   0 0 1 —  1
```

Pitching	IP	H	R	ER	BB	SO
Detroit						
McLain (W)	9	9	1	1	0	7
St. Louis						
Washburn (L)	*2	4	5	5	3	3
Jaster	**0	2	3	3	1	0
Willis	2/3	1	4	4	2	0
Hughes	1/3	2	0	0	0	0
Carlton	3	3	1	1	0	2
Granger	2	0	0	0	1	1
Nelson	1	0	0	0	0	1

*Pitched to 3 batters in 3rd.
**Pitched to 3 batters in 3rd.

a Singled for Hughes in 3rd.
b Struck out for Carlton in 6th.
c Struck out for Granger in 8th.

Double—Horton. Home Runs—Kaline, Northrup. Sacrifice Hit—McLain. Double Plays—Maxvill to Javier to Cepeda 2. Stanley to McAuliffe to Cash, Granger to Maxvill to Cepeda. Hit by Pitchers—Wert (by Willis), Kaline and Horton (by Granger). Left on Bases—Detroit 5, St. Louis 7. Umpires—Haller, Gorman, Honochick, Landes, Kinnamon, Harvey. Attendance—54,692. Time of Game—2:26.

Memorable Box Scores (continued)

Mickey Lolich Becomes the First Left-Hander to Pitch Three Complete-Game Victories in a World Series as the Tigers Win the World's Championship

October 10, 1968

Detroit (AL)

	AB	R	H	PO	A
McAuliffe, 2b	4	0	0	1	3
Stanley, ss-cf	4	0	1	5	2
Kaline, rf	4	0	0	2	0
Cash, 1b	4	1	1	11	2
Horton, lf	4	1	2	0	0
b Tracewski	0	1	0	0	0
Oyler, ss	0	0	0	1	0
Northrup, cf-lf	4	1	2	1	0
Freehan, c	4	0	1	6	0
Wert, 3b	3	0	1	0	6
Lolich, p	4	0	0	0	2
Total	35	4	8	27	15

St. Louis (NL)

	AB	R	H	PO	A
Brock, lf	3	0	1	1	0
Javier, 2b	4	0	0	3	2
Flood, cf	4	0	2	3	0
Cepeda, 1b	3	0	0	7	0
Shannon, 3b	4	1	1	1	2
McCarver, c	3	0	1	8	0
Maris, rf	3	0	0	3	0
Maxvill, ss	2	0	0	0	1
a Gagliano	1	0	0	0	0
Schofield, ss	0	0	0	0	0
Gibson, p	3	0	0	1	0
Total	30	1	5	27	5

a — Grounded out for Maxvill in eighth.
b — Ran for Horton in ninth.

Detroit	0 0 0 0 0 0 3 0 1 — 4
St. Louis	0 0 0 0 0 0 0 0 1 — 1

Error—Northrup. Runs batted in—Northrup 2, Freehan, Wert, Shannon. Two-base hit—Freehan. Three-base hit—Northrup. Home run—Shannon. Stolen base—Flood. Double play—Detroit 1. Left on base—Detroit 5, St. Louis 5. Bases on balls—Lolich 3, Gibson 1. Struck out—Lolich 4, Gibson 8. Umpires—Gorman (NL), Honochick (AL). Landes (NL), Kinnamon (AL), Harvey (NL), and Haller (AL). Time—2:07. Attendance—54,692.

Cesar Gutierrez Goes Seven for Seven

June 21, 1970

Detroit	AB	R	H		Cleveland	AB	R	H
Stanley, cf	6	1	2		Heidemann, ss	5	1	1
Gutierrez, ss	7	3	7		Leon, 2b	5	1	1
Kaline, 1b	6	1	1		Uhlaender, cf	6	2	3
W. Horton, lf	6	1	3		Fosse, c	6	1	2
Northrup, rf	5	2	2		T. Horton, 1b	5	1	4
Maddox, 3b	6	0	0		Foster, lf	4	0	0
I. Brown, 2b	3	0	0		Lasher, p	0	0	0
G. Brown, ph	1	1	1		Rollins, ph	1	0	0
Freehan, c	1	0	0		Ellsworth, p	0	0	0
Price, c	1	0	0		Klimchock, ph	1	0	0
Cash, ph	1	0	0		Hennigan, p	0	0	0
Hiller, p	0	0	0		Hinton, rf-lf	6	1	3
Wert, ph	1	0	1		Nettles, 3b	3	1	3
Timmerman, p	1	0	0		Austin, p	1	0	0
Kilkenny, p	0	0	0		Higgins, p	1	0	0
Patterson, p	2	0	0		Pinson, rf	3	0	0
Nagelson, ph	1	0	0		Total	47	8	17
Scherman, p	0	0	0					
McAuliffe, 2b	3	0	0					
Total	51	9	17					

Detroit	1 0 4 0 0 0 2 1 0 0 0 1 — 9
Cleveland	5 1 0 0 1 1 0 0 0 0 0 0 — 8

Error—T. Horton. Runs batted in—Stanley, Gutierrez, Kaline 2, Northrup 5, Heidemann, Uhlaender, T. Horton 5, Hinton. Two-base hits—T. Horton, Fosse, Gutierrez, G. Brown. Home runs—T. Horton, Hinton, Uhlaender, Kaline, Northrup 2, Stanley. Sacrifice—Higgins. Sacrifice flies—T. Horton, Heidemann. Double plays—Detroit 1, Cleveland 1. Left on base—Detroit 13, Cleveland 11. Bases on balls—Kilkenny 1, Patterson 1, Hiller 1, Timmerman 2, Austin 2, Higgins 2, Lasher 1, Ellsworth 1, Hennigan 1. Struck out — Kilkenny, 2, Patterson 3, Hiller 1, Timmerman 1, Austin 3, Higgins 5, Lasher 1. Hits off — Kilkenny, 5 in 2/3; Patterson, 4 in 4 1/3; Scherman, 2 in 2; Hiller, 2 in 2; Timmerman, 4 in 3; Austin, 5 in 2 1/3; Higgins, 4 in 4 2/3; Lasher, 3 in 2; Ellsworth, 3 in 2; Hennigan, 2 in 1. Wild pitch — Scherman. Passed ball — Price. Winner — Timmerman. Loser — Hennigan. Umpires — Napp, Rice, Springstead and Barnett. Time — 4:00. Attendance — 23,904.

Joe Coleman Strikes Out Fourteen A's in 1972 Playoff Game at Home

October 10, 1972

GAME OF TUESDAY, OCTOBER 10, AT DETROIT

OAKLAND	AB	R	H	RBI	PO	A
Alou, rf	5	0	3	0	1	0
Maxvill, ss	2	0	0	0	1	2
Duncan, ph-c	1	0	0	0	1	0
Rudi, lf	4	0	3	0	2	0
Jackson, cf	4	0	0	0	4	0
Epstein, 1b	4	0	0	0	9	0
Bando, 3b	4	0	1	0	0	3
Tenace, c-2b	2	0	0	0	3	3
Green, 2b	1	0	0	0	1	0
Mincher, ph	1	0	0	0	0	0
Kubiak, 2b	0	0	0	0	2	2
Marquez, ph	1	0	0	0	0	0
Cullen, ss	1	0	0	0	0	0
Holtzman, p	1	0	0	0	0	1
Mangual, ph	1	0	0	0	0	0
Fingers, p	0	0	0	0	0	0
Blue, p	0	0	0	0	0	0
Hegan, ph	1	0	0	0	0	0
Locker, p	0	0	0	0	0	0
Hendrick, ph	1	0	0	0	0	0
Totals	34	0	7	0	24	11

DETROIT	AB	R	H	RBI	PO	A
Taylor, 2b	4	0	0	0	2	3
Rodriguez, 3b	4	0	0	0	0	0
Kaline, rf	3	1	2	0	0	0
Freehan, c	3	2	2	1	14	1
Horton, lf	2	0	0	0	0	0
Northrup, lf	1	0	0	0	1	0
Stanley, cf	3	0	1	0	3	0
I. Brown, 1b	2	0	1	2	2	0
Cash, ph-1b	1	0	0	0	0	1
McAuliffe, ss	3	0	1	0	5	2
Coleman, p	2	0	1	0	0	0
Totals	28	3	8	3	27	7

```
Oakland       0 0 0   0 0 0   0 0 0 — 0
Detroit       0 0 0   2 0 0   0 1 x — 3
```

OAKLAND	IP	H	R	ER	BB	SO
Holtzman (Loser)	4	4	2	2	2	2
Fingers	1 2/3	2	0	0	1	1
Blue	1/3	0	0	0	0	0
Locker	2	2	1	1	0	1

DETROIT	IP	H	R	ER	BB	SO
Coleman (Winner)	9	7	0	0	3	14

Error—McAuliffe. Double plays—Oakland 3, Detroit 1. Left on base—Oakland 10, Detroit 5. Two-base hits—Alou 2, Freehan. Home run—Freehan. Stolen bases—Alou, Maxvill. Sacrifice hit—Freehan. Umpires—Rice, Denkinger, Chylak, Frantz, Flaherty and Barnett. Time—2:27. Attendance—41,156.

Ted Williams' Homer Wins Detroit's First All-Star Game

July 8, 1941   At Briggs Stadium, Detroit

NATIONALS	AB	R	H	PO	A	E
Hack (Cubs), 3b	2	0	1	3	0	0
(f)Lavagetto (Dodgers), 3b	1	0	0	0	0	0
T. Moore (Cardinals), lf	5	0	0	0	0	0
Reiser (Dodgers), cf	4	0	0	6	0	2
Mize (Cardinals), 1b	4	1	1	5	0	0
F. McCormick (Reds), 1b	0	0	0	0	0	0
Nicholson (Cubs), rf	1	0	0	1	0	0
Elliot (Pirates), rf	1	0	0	0	0	0
Slaughter (Cardinals), rf	2	1	1	0	0	0
Vaughan (Pirates), ss	4	2	3	1	2	0
Miller (Braves), ss	0	0	0	0	1	0
Frey (Reds), 2b	1	0	1	1	3	0
(c)Herman (Dodgers), 2b	3	0	2	3	0	0
Owen (Dodgers), c	1	0	0	0	0	0
Lopez (Pirates), c	1	0	0	3	0	0
Danning (Giants), c	1	0	0	3	0	0
Wyatt (Dodgers), p	0	0	0	0	0	0
(a)Ott (Giants)	1	0	0	0	0	0
Derringer (Reds), p	0	0	0	0	1	0
Walters (Reds), p	1	1	1	0	0	0
(d)Medwick (Dodgers)	1	0	0	0	0	0
Passeau (Cubs), p	1	0	0	0	0	0
Totals	35	5	10	26	7	2

AMERICANS	AB	R	H	PO	A	E
Doerr (Red Sox), 2b	3	0	0	0	0	0
Gordon (Yankees), 2b	2	1	1	2	0	0
Travis (Senators), 3b	4	1	1	1	2	0
J. DiMaggio (Yanks), cf	4	3	1	1	0	0
Williams (Red Sox), lf	4	1	2	3	0	1
Heath (Indians), rf	2	0	0	1	0	1
D. DiMaggio (R. Sox), rf	1	0	1	1	0	0
Cronin (Red Sox), ss	2	0	0	3	0	0
Boudreau (Indians), ss	2	0	2	0	1	0
York (Tigers), 1b	3	0	1	6	2	0
Foxx (Red Sox), 1b	1	0	0	2	2	0
Dickey (Yankees), c	3	0	1	4	2	0
Hayes (Athletics), c	1	0	0	2	0	0
Feller (Indians), p	0	0	0	0	1	0
(b)Cullenbine (Browns)	1	0	0	0	0	0
Lee (White Sox), p	1	0	0	0	1	0
Hudson (Senators), p	0	0	0	0	0	0
(e)Keller (Yankees)	1	0	0	0	0	0
Smith (White Sox), p	0	0	0	1	0	1
(g)Keltner (Indians)	1	1	1	0	0	0
Totals	36	7	11	27	11	3

National League	0 0 0	0 0 1	2 2 0 — 5
American League	0 0 0	1 0 1	0 1 4 — 7

Two out when winning run scored.

Pitching Summary

NATIONAL LEAGUE	IP	H	R	ER	BB	SO
Wyatt	2	0	0	0	1	0
Derringer	2	2	1	0	0	1
Walters	2	3	1	1	2	2
Passeau (L)	2 2/3	6	5	4	1	3

AMERICAN LEAGUE	IP	H	R	ER	BB	SO
Feller	3	1	0	0	0	4
Lee	3	4	1	1	0	0
Hudson	1	3	2	2	1	1
Smith (W)	2	2	2	2	0	2

(a)Struck out for Wyatt in third. (b)Grounded out for Feller in third. (c)Singled for Frey in fifth. (d)Grounded out for Walters in seventh. (e) Struck out for Hudson in seventh. (f)Grounded out for Hack in ninth. (g)Singled for Smith in ninth. Runs batted in—Williams 4, Moore, Boudreau, Vaughan 4, D. DiMaggio, J. DiMaggio. Two-base hits—Travis, Williams, Walters, Herman, Mize, J. DiMaggio. Home runs—Vaughan 2, Williams. Sacrifice hits—Hack, Lopez. Double plays—Frey, Vaughan, and Mize; York and Cronin. Left on bases—Americans 7, Nationals 6. Managers: Del Baker, Detroit (AL); Bill McKechnie, Cincinnati (NL). Umpires—Summers and Grieve (AL), Jorda and Pinelli (NL). Time—2:23. Attendance—54,674.

Wertz and Kell Hit Home Runs in a Losing Cause in Detroit's Second Mid-Year Classic

July 10, 1951   At Briggs Stadium, Detroit

NATIONALS	AB	R	H	PO	A	E
Ashburn (Phillies), cf	4	2	2	4	1	0
Snider (Dodgers), cf	0	0	0	0	0	0
Dark (Giants), ss	5	0	1	0	3	0
Reese (Dodgers), ss	0	0	0	0	1	0
Musial (Cards), lf-rf-lf	4	1	2	0	0	0
Westlake (Cardinals), lf	0	0	0	0	0	0
J. Robinson (Dodgers), 2b	4	1	2	3	1	1
Schoendienst (Cards), 2b	0	0	0	0	0	0
Hodges (Dodgers), 1b	5	2	2	6	0	0
Elliot (Braves), 3b	2	1	1	1	1	0
Jones (Phillies), 3b	2	0	0	3	0	0
Ennis (Phillies), rf	2	0	0	0	0	0
Kiner (Pirates), lf	2	1	1	1	0	0
Wyrostek (Reds), lf	1	0	0	0	0	0
Campanella (Dodgers), c	4	0	0	9	1	0
Roberts (Phillies), p	0	0	0	0	0	0
(a)Slaughter (Cardinals)	1	0	0	0	0	0

Maglie (Giants), p	1	0	0	0	0	0
Newcombe (Dodgers), p	2	0	1	0	1	0
Blackwell (Reds), p	0	0	0	0	0	0
Totals	39	8	12	27	9	1

AMERICANS	AB	R	H	PO	A	E
D. DiMaggio (Red Sox), cf	5	0	1	1	0	0
Fox (White Sox), 2b	3	0	1	3	1	1
(e)Doerr (Red Sox), 2b	1	0	1	1	0	0
Kell (Tigers), 3b	3	1	1	4	2	0
Williams (Red Sox), lf	3	0	1	3	0	0
Busby (White Sox), lf	0	0	0	0	0	0
Berra (Yankees), c	4	1	1	4	2	1
Wertz (Tigers), rf	3	1	1	2	0	0
Rizzuto (Yankees), ss	1	0	0	1	2	0
Fain (Athletics), 1b	3	0	1	5	0	0
(f)E. Robinson						
(White Sox), 1b	1	0	0	0	1	0
Carrasquel (White Sox), ss	2	0	1	0	3	0
(c)Minoso (White Sox), rf	2	0	0	2	0	0
Garver (Browns), p	1	0	0	0	0	0
Lopat (Yankees), p	0	0	0	0	0	0
(b)Doby (Indians)	1	0	0	0	0	0
Hutchinson (Tigers), p	0	0	0	0	0	0
(d)Stephens (Red Sox)	1	0	0	0	0	0
Parnell (Red Sox), p	0	0	0	0	0	0
Lemon (Indians), p	0	0	0	1	0	0
(g)Hegan (Indians)	1	0	1	0	0	0
Totals	35	3	10	27	11	2

National League   1 0 0 3 0 2 1 1 0 — 8
American League   0 1 0 1 1 0 0 0 0 — 3

Pitching Summary

NATIONAL LEAGUE	IP	H	R	ER	BB	SO
Roberts	2	4	1	1	1	1
Maglie (W)	3	3	2	2	1	1
Newcombe	3	2	0	0	0	3
Blackwell	1	1	0	0	1	2

AMERICAN LEAGUE	IP	H	R	ER	BB	SO
Garver	3	1	1	0	1	1
Lopat (L)	1	3	3	3	0	0
Hutchinson	3	3	3	3	2	0
Parnell	1	3	1	1	1	1
Lemon	1	2	0	0	1	1

(a)Lined out for Roberts in third. (b)Popped out for Lopat in fourth. (c)Grounded out for Carrasquel in sixth. (d)Struck out for Hutchinson in seventh. (e)Singled for Fox in seventh. (f)Grounded out for Fain in eighth. (g)Doubled for Lemon in ninth. Runs batted in—Fain, Musial, Elliot 2, Wertz, Kell, Hodges 2, J. Robinson, Kiner. Two-base hits—Ashburn, Hegan. Three-base hits—Fain, Williams. Home runs—Musial, Elliot, Wertz, Kell, Hodges, Kiner. Sacrifice hit — Kell. Double play — Berra and Kell. Passed ball — Campanella. Left on bases — Nationals 8, Americans 9. Managers: Casey Stengel, New York (AL); Edwin Sawyer, Philadelphia (NL). Umpires — Passarella, Hurley, and Honochick (AL); Robb, Jorda, and Dascoli (NL). Time — 2:41. Attendance — 52,075.

Detroit's Third All-Star Game Features Jackson's Titanic Blast

July 13, 1971   At Tiger Stadium, Detroit (Night)

NATIONALS	AB	R	H	PO	A	E
Mays (Giants), cf	2	0	0	0	0	0
Clemente (Pirates), rf	2	1	1	1	0	0
Millan (Braves), 2b	0	0	0	1	1	0
Aaron (Braves), rf	2	1	1	0	0	0
May (Reds), 1b	1	0	0	6	0	0
Torre (Cardinals), 3b	3	0	0	1	0	0
(f)Santo (Cubs), 3b	1	0	0	0	1	0
Stargell (Pirates), lf	2	1	0	2	0	0
(g)Brock (Cardinals)	1	0	0	0	0	0
McCovey (Giants), 1b	2	0	0	4	0	0
Marichal (Giants), p	0	0	0	0	1	0
Kessinger (Cubs), ss	2	0	0	1	1	0
Bench (Reds), c	4	1	2	5	0	0
Beckert (Cubs), 2b	3	0	0	0	5	0
Rose (Reds), rf	0	0	0	0	0	0
Harrelson (Mets), ss	2	0	0	1	2	0
Jenkins (Cubs), p	0	0	0	0	0	0
(c)Colbert (Padres)	1	0	0	0	0	0
Wilson (Astros), p	0	0	0	0	0	0
Ellis (Pirates), p	1	0	0	0	0	0
Davis (Dodgers), cf	1	0	1	2	0	0
(e)Bonds (Giants), cf	1	0	0	0	0	0
Totals	31	4	5	24	11	0

AMERICANS	AB	R	H	PO	A	E
Carew (Twins), 2b	1	1	0	1	2	0
Rojas (Royals), 2b	1	0	0	1	1	0
Murcer (Yankees), cf	3	0	1	1	0	0
Cuellar (Orioles), p	0	0	0	0	0	0
(d)Buford (Orioles)	1	0	0	0	0	0
Lolich (Tigers), p	0	0	0	0	3	0
Yastrzemski (Red Sox), lf	3	0	0	0	0	0
F. Robinson (Orioles), rf	2	1	1	2	0	0
Kaline (Tigers), rf	2	1	1	2	0	0
Cash (Tigers), 1b	2	0	0	7	0	0
Killebrew (Twins), 1b	2	1	1	4	0	0
B. Robinson (Orioles), 3b	3	0	1	1	3	0
Freehan (Tigers), c	3	0	0	6	1	0
Munson (Yankees), cf	0	0	0	1	0	0
Aparicio (Red Sox), ss	3	1	1	1	2	0
Blue (Athletics), p	0	0	0	0	0	0
(a)Jackson (Athletics)	1	1	1	0	0	0

Palmer (Orioles), p	0	0	0	0	0	0
(b)Howard (Senators)	1	0	0	0	0	0
Otis (Royals), cf	1	0	0	0	0	0
Totals	29	6	7	27	12	0

National League   0 2 1   0 0 0   0 1 0 — 4
American League   0 0 4   0 0 2   0 0 x — 6

Pitching Summary

NATIONAL LEAGUE	IP	H	R	ER	BB	SO
Ellis (L)	3	4	4	4	1	2
Marichal	2	0	0	0	1	1
Jenkins	1	3	2	2	0	0
Wilson	2	0	0	0	1	2

AMERICAN LEAGUE	IP	H	R	ER	BB	SO
Blue (W)	3	2	3	3	0	3
Palmer	2	1	0	0	0	2
Cuellar	2	1	0	0	1	2
Lolich	2	1	1	1	0	1

(a)Homered for Blue in third. (b)Grounded out for Palmer in fifth. (c)Struck out for Jenkins in seventh. (d)Struck out for Cuellar in seventh. (e)Struck out for Davis in eighth. (f)Grounded out for Torre in eighth. (g)Bunted for Stargell in ninth and was thrown out. Runs batted in—Bench 2, Jackson 2, F. Robinson 2, Aaron, Killebrew 2, Clemente. Home runs—Bench, Aaron, Jackson, F. Robinson, Killebrew, Clemente. Double plays—B. Robinson, Rojas, and Killebrew; Beckert, Kessinger, and May; Santo, Millan, and May. Hit by pitcher—By Blue (Stargell). Left on bases—Nationals 2, Americans 2. Managers: Earl Weaver, Baltimore (AL); George "Sparky" Anderson, Cincinnati (NL). Umpires—Umont (AL), plate; Pryor (NL), first base; O'Donnell (AL), second base; Harvey (NL), third base; Denkinger (AL), right field; Colosi (NL), left field. Time—2:05. Attendance—53,559.